ON OUR
OWN SOIL

ON OUR OWN SOIL

WILLIAM LOWTHER JACKSON AND THE CIVIL WAR IN WEST VIRGINIA'S MOUNTAINS

Ronald V. Hardway

QUARRIER PRESS
CHARLESTON, WV

Quarrier Press
Charleston, WV 25301

Library of Congress Card Catalog Number: 2003091253
ISBN: 1-891852-27-2

10 9 8 7 6 5 4 3 2 1
Printed in the United States of America

Cover and book design: Mark S. Phillips / Marketing+Design Group

Distributed by:
Pictorial Histories Distribution
1416 Quarrier Street
Charleston, WV 25301

wvbooks@ntelos.net

DEDICATION

On Our Own Soil is dedicated to the men
from central West Virginia who fought
first for their families and farms,
and secondly for Virginia.

Ense et aratro.

TABLE OF CONTENTS

ACKNOWLEDGMENTS

Most of this biography of William Lowther Jackson was prepared during 1998 when I was the resident Blake Scholar in Confederate History at Marshall University, Huntington, WV. Among the many people at Marshall who helped guide this project to completion, a few stand out. Among them are Marshall University history professors Robert Maddox, Robert Sawrey, Paul Lutz, and David Woodward. This quartet of professional historians, all of them authors in their areas of expertise, were generous with their advice and helpful with their criticism. Leonard Deuitsch, of the Marshall University Graduate School, quietly added encouragement, inspiration, and, on two occasions, opened the door to financial assistance that allowed the manuscript to be completed.

Much of my time during the fifteen months I worked on the manuscript was spent in the labyrinths of various libraries. The staffs at the James E. Morrow Library at Marshall, the Wood County Public Library in Parkersburg, and the Search Room of the West Virginia Department of Archives and History in Charleston showed extreme patience and cheerful cooperation on numerous occasions.

Joe Ferrell of St. Albans and Joe Geiger of Huntington provided helpful materials and insight that smoothed some rough edges and filled some noteworthy gaps in the narrative.

Special thanks are due Ken Slack, librarian emeritus at Marshall, whose stewardship of the phenomenal Roseanna Blake Collection of Confederate History, was exceptional. Slack's encyclopedic knowledge of the content and location of every scrap of Confederate history located amid the crowded shelves and stuffed filing cabinets allowed work on this manuscript to proceed expeditiously, and probably reduced the time to complete the manuscript by at least half.

Finally, special recognition is due Victoria Cowger who devoted countless hours poring over microfilms and dusty books, and who resolved one computer crisis after another without complaint.

The publisher would like to thank, among many others, Terry Lowry and Tim McKinney for their valuable assistance with this publication.

INTRODUCTION

On the eve of the American Civil War, Judge William Lowther Jackson of Parkersburg, Wood County, was one of the most prominent politicians and businessmen in western Virginia. Jackson, a native of Harrison County and a member of one of the wealthiest and most politically powerful clans in northwestern Virginia, represented his region in the Virginia Assembly for three consecutive terms in the 1850s. He served as Second Auditor for the State of Virginia, directed the Virginia Literary Fund for public education, and was lieutenant governor of the state during the administration of Governor Henry A. Wise. Jackson served two terms as prosecuting attorney for Pleasants County, and was the recognized leader of the Democratic Party in Wood, Pleasants, and Ritchie counties during the 1850s. In 1860 voters elected him judge of the nineteenth circuit of the Superior Court of Virginia, a circuit that covered the central section of western Virginia from Lewis County to the Ohio River. Jackson played a leading role in extending the Baltimore and Ohio Railroad from Grafton to Parkersburg. He invested heavily in real estate in Wood and Pleasants counties, and owned at least three slaves. Jackson acquired a share of the Burning Springs oil field in Wirt County and operated his own oil wells. His pre-war political and business associates included Johnson N. Camden, Arthur I. Boreman, John J. and Jacob Jackson, Jacob B. Blair, John C. Rathbone, William J. Bland, Matthew Edmiston, and William E. Stevenson. All of these men became prominent figures in the formation of West Virginia and post-war political and economic development of the new state.

When the Civil War began in 1861 Judge Jackson did not hesitate to offer his services to the state of Virginia which he had served faithfully since his admission to the Virginia bar in 1847. He organized the first Confederate regiment in northwestern Virginia and was elected colonel of the regiment. He led the regiment safely through the first hectic six months of the war and directed defense of the Confederacy's western front with only a few companies of inexperienced volunteers. William Jackson served as aide-de-camp on Stonewall Jackson's staff during the latter days of Jackson's famous Shenandoah Valley Campaign. He accompanied General Jackson on the campaign to defend Richmond in 1862 and was commended by him for his efficiency during the second Battle of Manassas and Sharpsburg. In 1863 William Jackson organized two cavalry regiments for Virginia service. The regiments were created to regain control of western Virginia's breakaway northern counties, but during the last year of the war Jackson's troops defended the Shenandoah Valley. By the end of the war Jackson held the rank of brigadier general in the Confederate States Army commanding three regiments and two battalions.

Following the Civil War, many former Confederate army officers and state officials from western Virginia counties returned to their homes and resumed lives and careers. After a brief period of adjustment many former Confederates regained their pre-war political and business eminence under the aegis of the new state, West Virginia. Among them were numerous wartime associates of William Jackson. Jacob B. Jackson, William Jackson's cousin, spent time in Atheneum Prison in Wheeling for his secessionist views, but was elected governor of the new state. Jonathan M. Bennett, a Jackson in-law and legislative colleague, served as Virginia State Auditor throughout the war. Bennett was elected to the West Virginia legislature and helped rewrite the state's constitution in 1870. Charles J. Faulkner, who served on Stonewall Jackson's staff with William Jackson, also moved on to the West Virginia legislature and played an important role in restoring political rights to former Confederate soldiers in West Virginia. William E. Lively, who tried to form a western Virginia infantry regiment in 1861 with William Jackson as its colonel, reopened his law practice in Weston, was elected prosecuting attorney of Gilmer County, and was appointed director of the West Virginia State Hospital for the Insane at Weston. William P. Thompson, colonel of the Twentieth Virginia Cavalry in Jackson's brigade, returned to Parkersburg and became wealthy in the oil business. William J. Bland, Jackson's brigade surgeon, returned to Lewis County to practice medicine and succeeded William Lively as director of the state Hospital for the Insane. William Jackson's brother, George Jackson, returned to Parkersburg after serving as a cavalry colonel in North Carolina for three years. He became successful in the oil industry. John McCausland, a brigade commander with William Jackson in Robert Ransom's and Lundsford Lomax's divisions, returned to his life as a gentleman farmer in Mason County. As late as 1922 McCausland still was referred to as the "Hun of Chambersburg" in northern newspapers, and when he died in 1927 his funeral procession down the Kanawha River on a barge resembled that of a far eastern potentate.

Like his Confederate colleagues, William L. Jackson should have returned to Parkersburg after the war and played an important part in charting the future of the new state of West Virginia. Jackson's pre-war political prominence and popularity equaled or exceeded that of any returning Confederates. His military service record compared favorably to any surviving West Virginia Confederate veteran. However, not only was Jackson not permitted to enter West Virginia politics and recover his prewar business investments, he was encouraged strongly to leave West Virginia altogether. He was ostracized by Parkersburg business and social communities and vilified by the local press. His physical presence in one community resulted in a riot which forced him to leave town. The United States Army needed four years and two months to force William Jackson into exile. His pre-war Wood County associates needed only three months to accomplish the same object. William Jackson moved down the Ohio River to Louisville, Kentucky, in December 1865. He opened a law office, became involved in Kentucky state politics, and in 1872 was elected judge of the Jefferson County, Kentucky, circuit court, a position he held until his death in 1890. The only recorded instance of his presence in West Virginia after 1865 occurred in 1883 when he came to Parkersburg to visit his dying brother.

From the beginning of his exile to Kentucky, William L. Jackson became a non-person in West Virginia. Authors of general histories of West Virginia and textbook histories of the state did not mention his name. Histories of Wood County and Parkersburg published after the war did not include Jackson among the luminaries of the city. Civil War historians of West Virginia mentioned Jackson only in passing and included few if any details about his military exploits. Few West Virginia and Virginia county histories published in the first two decades of the twentieth century mentioned Jackson.

West Virginia historians not only erased William L. Jackson from state annals, they also omitted the military record of the two regiments he formed, the Nineteenth and Twentieth Virginia cavalries. When these units were mentioned in historical accounts of the Civil War in West Virginia, they were denigrated as a collection of inept misfits, outlaws, bushwhackers and horse thieves. Yet, when Civil War records were examined, the Nineteenth and Twentieth Virginia cavalry regiments were found to have performed efficiently in every campaign in which they participated. During the last year of the war as Confederate manpower, horses, and supplies dwindled, the Nineteenth and Twentieth cavalries fielded the largest contingent of troops in the Virginia Valley. Elements of both regiments were still in the field skirmishing with federal troops in the Allegheny Mountains nearly two weeks after Lee's surrender at Appomattox.

The exclusion of William L. Jackson and his Confederate cavalry regiments from West Virginia history begs an explanation. Early state historians, who wrote in an era when Civil War veterans were plentiful, failed to utilize these invaluable primary sources. Jackson wrote no memoirs of his war service and he contributed no personal archives to any collection or library. Veterans of Jackson's regiments had little to say following the war. Only four post-war memoirs by Jackson's cavalrymen were published, and only one of those memoirs focused exclusively on wartime activities of Jackson's regiments. Modern historians either forgot that Jackson and his regiments existed, or they considered them inconsequential. The omission of William L. Jackson and the Nineteenth and Twentieth Virginia cavalry regiments from West Virginia's Civil War history created a gap in the state's historical narrative. The pages that follow close that gap.

I

IRELAND

The ancestry of William Lowther Jackson, Jr. began with landed Irish aristocrats, who crossed the Irish Sea to London criminal courts, then made the long voyage across the Atlantic Ocean to colonial Maryland. In Maryland, Jackson's ancestors began their colonial experience as indentured servants. Attracted by the availability of inexpensive land and a nearly complete absence of governmental authority, they moved first into the valley of the South Branch of the Potomac River of Virginia. The lure of land led them to move again beyond the Allegheny Mountains into the unsettled wilderness of the West Fork River of northwestern Virginia. From their first isolated settlements on the Allegheny frontier, the Jacksons created a wilderness empire. The Jacksons fought the British for the right to control their own destiny, and they struggled with the Ohio Indians for control of the western Allegheny region. They contributed to the political and economic growth of the young American republic. Imitating their Irish ancestors of the early eighteenth century, the Jacksons in the West Fork valley became aristocratic landlords, but with a uniquely American twist. They became self-reliant, ambitious, wealthy and influential leaders in their region, and they achieved their status through their own efforts, each generation adding to the power and prestige earned by the preceding generation.

The Jackson family in northern Ireland exercised political and economic power before members of the clan began migrating to the American colonies. In the early 1700s one William Jackson and three of his uncles secured a lease on much of the valley of the River Bann in Derry. They leased the land through the Irish Society, a group of London land speculators who controlled much of the county. Control of land in Ireland meant political power as well as economic strength. The Jacksons' lease on the Bann valley from Coleraine to Kilrea gave them the opportunity to set rates and collect rents from tenants. They also distributed political patronage among relatives and friends. The only threat to their continued prestige and power came from the Irish Society, whose proprietors demanded greater profits. To satisfy the expectations of their London investors, the Jacksons raised rents on their financially exhausted tenants.[1]

Raising rents created complaints against the Jacksons, and in 1713 a discontented group of local politicians from Derry demanded that the mayor of Coleraine investigate the Jacksons for abuse of power. The Jacksons had succeeded in stacking the Common Council—a governing body for Derry composed of aldermen and burgesses—with friends and relatives. With the Council firmly in hand, William Jackson had managed to raise rents on his tenants to a level deemed excessive by the farmers and tradesmen who had to pay them. The mayor of Coleraine, a Jackson relative who owed his position to William Jackson's patronage, refused to launch an investigation, despite local laws which required him to honor the complaint.[2]

Resentment against the Jacksons and other landlords continued to build over the next decade. Rents continued to escalate while the tenants' ability to pay them declined, largely due to outbreaks of deadly infections among their sheep herds, severe frosts which greatly reduced food supplies, and smallpox and fever epidemics. Dublin Archbishop William King complained about the situation in a letter to an Irish official in London in 1716:

> *I do not see how Ireland can pay greater taxes than it does without starving the inhabitants and leaving them entirely without meat or clothes. They have already given their bread, their flesh, their butter, their shoes, their stockings, their beds, their house furniture and houses to pay their landlords and taxes. I cannot see how any more can be got from them, except we take away their potatoes and butter milk, or flay them and sell their skins.*[3]

By 1730 tenants in the Bann valley had begun a massive exodus from Ireland, all bound for the uncertain freedom of the American colonies. Archbishop Hugh Boulter warned London officials in 1727 that excessive rents and taxes and repressive agricultural policies were forcing Irish tenants "to go into foreign service at the hazard of their lives . . . And if some stop be not put to this evil, we must daily decrease in the numbers of our people."[4] Boulter's warning did not begin to accurately anticipate the extent of Irish migration to America. Between 1728 and 1750 Ulster alone lost more than twenty-five percent of its population to American immigration. By 1770 more than 200,000 Ulstermen had resettled in America.[5]

Around 1730 several families in the Bann valley gave up trying to satisfy the insatiable demands of their landlords. They migrated, not to America, but to London, where most of them found employment as servants and menial laborers. One of the families which joined this early exodus was a Jackson clan, relatives of the landlords, but landless themselves. Among the members of this Jackson family was John Jackson, then around ten years old.[6] For nearly twenty years John Jackson lived in London and worked first as a carpenter then as a servant to a more prosperous cousin, Henry Jackson of St. Giles. In late December 1748, John Jackson— overwhelmed by frustration with his lack of economic success and low social status— stole one hundred and seventy pounds in cash and some pieces of gold lace from his cousin's cupboard and started for America. He only got as far as a neighboring town where his victimized cousin and the authorities caught up with him. Jackson confessed to the crime of larceny, and at the January 1749 session of Old Bailey he was sentenced to transportation to America to serve a seven-year indenture.[7]

In April 1749, the same session of Old Bailey which had convicted John Jackson of larceny also convicted an Irish-born woman named Elizabeth Cummins of the same crime. Cummins had stolen nineteen pieces of silver, some jewelry, and fine lace from her employer, one Thomas Holland of St. Catherine Coleman parish. The court sentenced her to transportation and a seven-year indenture in the colonies.[8]

MARYLAND AND VIRGINIA

Jackson and Cummins were transported to America in May 1749 aboard the prison ship Litchfield. One hundred and fifty fellow convicts accompanied them, only a few of whom were Irish. The Litchfield docked at Baltimore in July. Cummins was put to work as a domestic servant in Baltimore. Jackson was sent to a Cecil County tobacco plantation. At some point the seven-year sentences for both Cummins and Jackson were reduced. In July 1755, only six years after their involuntary arrival in Maryland colony, John Jackson and Elizabeth Cummins were married.[9]

John and Elizabeth Jackson began their married life at a propitious time for Irish settlers in America. In the late 1740s Virginia's Shenandoah Valley had been opened to settlement through land grants to real estate entrepreneurs such as William Beverley, John Lewis, James Patton, Benjamin Borden, and Lord Fairfax. Most of these grants required their proprietors to settle a specified number of families on their lands as a condition for keeping the grant. For the thousands of Irish pouring into the colonies, the Shenandoah Valley was an ideal destination. Land was inexpensive, available, and productive.[10]

The Jacksons settled first in the South Branch Valley of the Potomac River, an area popular with German immigrants. According to Jackson family tradition, John and Elizabeth Jackson moved to the South Branch in 1758 shortly after the Virginia House of Burgesses had created Hampshire County. Their first homestead in western Virginia was located on the Fairfax grant near Moorefield in present-day Hardy County.[11] The Jackson presence in old Hampshire County cannot be documented through Hampshire records.

Although numerous early Hampshire records did not survive, an explanation for Jackson's absence in Hampshire land books may reflect Jackson's realization that he had escaped a land rental system in Ireland only to encounter the same system in the South Branch Valley. In 1745 British courts had confirmed Lord Fairfax's claim to more than five million acres of land between the Rappahannock and Potomac rivers. Fairfax agreed to recognize Virginia land grants already issued on his property as a condition for the British court's confirmation of his title. For the remainder of the original grant, which still totaled more than five million acres, Fairfax immediately launched an ambitious program of land leasing to new German and Irish settlers while battling already settled Virginians through lawsuits designed to remove them from his lands or force them to pay rent.[12] When John Jackson arrived on the South Branch in 1758, he did not find any land available to purchase. Instead he found a land lease policy eerily similar to the situation in Ireland from which thousands of Irishmen, including John Jackson's father, had fled. Jackson had no desire to live on land under such conditions, but the French and Indian War precluded further westward movement in 1758. The war ended in 1762, but the British government blocked frontier settlers from moving west of the Allegheny Mountains with the Proclamation of 1763. The Proclamation banned white settlement west of the Alleghenies in an attempt to create a buffer zone between Indian settlements in Ohio and English settlements in the Shenandoah Valley, western Maryland, and western Pennsylvania. The treaties of Fort Stanwix and Hard Labour, negotiated by the British government with the Iroquois and Cherokees in 1768, removed Indian claims to territory west of the Allegheny Mountains.[13] The British opened the western region to new settlers, and the Jacksons were among the first adventurers to seek new home sites in the Trans-Allegheny region. In 1768 John Jackson staked a claim to several hundred acres where Turkey Creek emptied into the Buckhannon River, and around 1770 he moved to his new land.[14]

THE TRANS-ALLEGHENY

The Buckhannon River valley in 1770 was on the leading edge of the western Virginia frontier. Relations between Indians living on the west side of the Ohio River and white settlers establishing settlements on the western side of the Allegheny mountains had been quiet since the close of the French and Indian War in 1763. However, despite Indian land cessions of 1768, the threat of renewed hostilities between Indians and whites remained. One of the first orders of business for new settlers on western lands was to establish forts and blockhouses for protection of the community when hostile Shawnees and Delawares were in the vicinity. John Jackson, assisted by some of his new

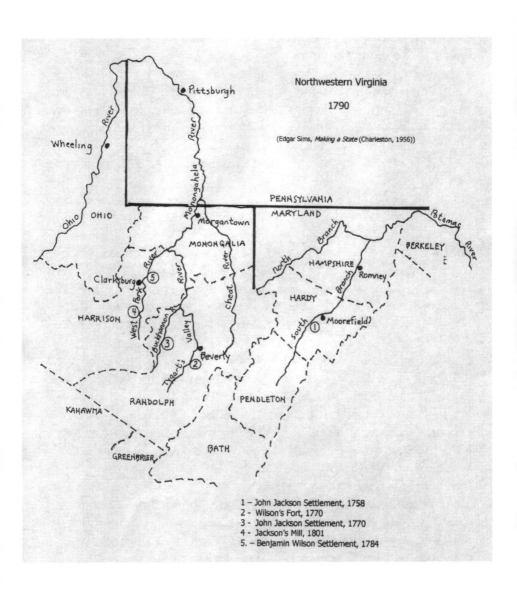

Northwestern Virginia

1790

(Edgar Sims, *Making a State* (Charleston, 1956))

1 – John Jackson Settlement, 1758
2 - Wilson's Fort, 1770
3 - John Jackson Settlement, 1770
4 - Jackson's Mill, 1801
5. – Benjamin Wilson Settlement, 1784

neighbors, built Jackson's Fort on the site of present-day Buckhannon. Between 1777 and 1782 Indian raiding parties often appeared in the area of Jackson's settlement and settlers took refuge in Jackson's Fort and Bush's Fort located a few miles up the Buckhannon River. Jackson's Fort was never attacked directly by Indians, but in March 1782 Shawnee raids along the West Fork River convinced residents on the Buckhannon to retire to Clarksburg for greater security. The Shawnee raiders discovered an abandoned Fort Jackson and burned it to the ground.[15]

John Jackson and his two oldest sons, George and Edward, played active roles in the defense of the frontier during the Revolutionary War. They served as scouts and furnished supplies to local military units. George Jackson recruited a company and joined George Rogers Clark on Clark's failed attempt to capture Detroit in 1781. Jackson served as captain of the company he raised, and in 1787 he was appointed Lieutenant Colonel of the Harrison County Regiment of Virginia Militia.[16]

In the period immediately following the Revolutionary War, the Jackson family emerged as economic and political leaders in Harrison County. From the time of John Jackson's first settlement on the Buckhannon River in 1768 until the close of the Revolutionary War, Jackson had acquired numerous tracts of wilderness land. His five sons, George, Edward, John, Jr., Henry and Samuel, came of age during and immediately after the Revolution. They continued their father's practice of securing title to unimproved land in Harrison and Randolph counties through the Virginia Land Office. Between 1784 and 1804 the five sons of John Jackson individually amassed nearly 60,000 acres of land evenly divided between Harrison and Randolph counties. In 1796 they jointly received two grants totaling 106,000 acres along Tygart's Valley River. After the formation of Lewis County in 1816, several of John Jackson's grandsons acquired an additional 4,000 acres in that county. Even the matriarch of the Jackson clan entered the land buying frenzy. In 1806 Elizabeth Jackson, John Jackson's widow, received a grant from the Virginia Land Office for 3,000 acres located near the headwaters of the Buckhannon River in Randolph County.[17]

Ownership of land in such vast quantities obligated the Jacksons to assume a position of political leadership in Harrison and Randolph counties. John Jackson was appointed commissioner of revenue at the first meeting of the Randolph county court in 1787. He later served the county as a county justice and a lieutenant and captain of militia. Randolph County called on Edward Jackson to serve the new county as its first county surveyor. He was also appointed to the first Randolph county court. During the 1790s Edward held commissions as captain and colonel of the Randolph militia, commissioner of revenue, and served a term as sheriff of Randolph County. Around 1801 Edward Jackson moved from Buckhannon to the West Fork

River in Harrison County. On this site he established the best known of the Jackson plantations in central West Virginia, Jackson's Mill. He served as a county justice in Harrison County, and when Lewis County was formed from Harrison in 1816 he represented Lewis in the Virginia Assembly for one term. Henry Jackson succeeded his brother as surveyor of Randolph County. A Jackson daughter, Mary, married Phillip Reger, who became the first sheriff of Lewis County.[18]

GEORGE JACKSON

The most prosperous and politically powerful branch of the Jackson family was George Jackson and his descendants. George Jackson was born in Cecil County, Maryland on 9 January 1757, the oldest son of John and Elizabeth Cummins Jackson. He served the Buckhannon community as an Indian scout while he was still in his teens. In 1781 he led a company of Buckhannon valley men to serve with George Rogers Clark during Clark's second campaign to capture Detroit.[19]

In March 1782, George Jackson and all of the settlers along the Buckhannon River took refuge at Nutter's Fort in Clarksburg during a Shawnee incursion into the West Fork valley. The flood of refugees at Nutter's Fort strained the food supplies, and Jackson volunteered to lead a group of men back to the Buckhannon settlements to collect grain which was stored there. When the foraging party arrived at the site of Jackson's Fort they discovered that the Shawnees had burned the abandoned fort to the ground. Despite indications that Indians were still in the vicinity, the men went from farm to farm and gathered grain supplies. They returned to the burned out fort in the evening and spent the night in an outbuilding, which the Indians had not destroyed. Before the foraging party could start for Clarksburg the following morning, Indians were observed crossing the Buckhannon River. Securing themselves in the outbuilding, the settlers and the Shawnees poked and prodded at each other throughout the day. When night fell, George Jackson, recognized leader of the settlers, decided that if the Shawnees attacked the building there were insufficient men and ammunition to hold them off. There was also the danger that the Indians might succeed in setting fire to the building. Jackson volunteered to attempt to slip through the Indian lines and get reinforcements from Nutter's Fort. No one questioned Jackson's decision, and he succeeded in getting past the Indians and reached Clarksburg without misadventure. He immediately organized a relief force and arrived back at Buckhannon just after daylight. The Shawnees recognized that they were outgunned, and they lifted their siege without exchanging shots with the settlers.[20]

George Jackson manipulated his leadership abilities demonstrated during the Revolutionary War and subsequent Indian wars into a political career between 1784 and 1800. The first session of the Harrison County court was held at Jackson's home on the Buckhannon River on 29 June 1784. Jackson was one of Harrison County's first justices and colonel of the Harrison militia. In 1785 he was elected to represent Harrison County in the Virginia Assembly and was reelected in 1788. He attended the Virginia convention, which ratified the United States Constitution in June 1788. In the 1790s Jackson was elected to three terms in the United States House of Representatives.[21]

George Jackson had married Elizabeth Brake, a daughter of Jacob Brake, at the Brake home in Moorefield, Hampshire County, on 13 November 1776.[22] They built a cabin on the Buckhannon River near the John Jackson homestead and lived there for thirty years. They were the parents of eleven children, several of whom were politically and socially prominent in northwestern Virginia. John George Jackson (1777-1825), their oldest son, represented Harrison County in the Virginia Assembly, succeeded his father as United States Congressman in 1803, served as Brigadier General of the 20th Brigade, Virginia Militia, and was appointed federal judge of the newly created Western District of Virginia in 1819 by James Monroe. He married Mary Payne, sister of Dolly Payne Madison, and was an intimate friend of James Madison, Monroe, and Thomas Jefferson. After the death of his first wife he married Sophia Meigs, daughter of Ohio governor Return Jonathan Meigs. Locally John G. Jackson dominated Harrison County business interests. He operated a furnace, sawmill, and gristmill near Clarksburg, and received a charter from the Virginia Assembly to construct a series of canals and locks to divert the flow of the Buckhannon River into the West Fork River. If successful this project would have made the West Fork River navigable to its junction with the Monongahela River at Fairmont, and Pittsburgh and Weston would have been linked by a commercial waterway. Although some work was completed on this ambitious project, a flood in 1827 destroyed several completed dams and the scheme was abandoned.[23]

Edward Brake Jackson (1793-1826), third son of George Jackson and Elizabeth Brake, attended the Randolph Academy in Clarksburg, founded by his father. After completing his academic studies at the academy, Edward studied medicine. He served as surgeon's mate for the Third Virginia Militia at Fort Meigs, Ohio, during the War of 1812. He opened a medical practice in Clarksburg in 1815, and that same year he was elected to represent the county in the Virginia Assembly. When his older brother John George Jackson received the appointment as judge of the United States District Court for Western Virginia, Edward served as his clerk. When Congressman James Pindall unexpectedly resigned his office in 1819, Edward Brake Jackson was elected to fill Pindall's vacancy. In 1820 he was elected in his own right to a term in Congress, but declined to run again in 1822. He resumed his medical practice in Clarksburg only to die prematurely in 1826 at the height of his political influence and power.[24]

In the mid-1790s George Jackson began looking beyond the limits of Harrison County and Virginia for economic opportunity. He discovered an opportunity in the neighboring Ohio Territory, which promised excellent returns for a small investment. The United States Congress passed an act in 1796 designed to facilitate bounty land grants promised to Continental Army officers and soldiers. The land designated to satisfy bounty claims lay in the Northwest Territory between the headwaters of the Muskingum River and the Scioto River. More than two million acres were set aside for Revolutionary War veterans in what was known as the "United States Military Tract.[25] George Jackson secured an appointment for his son, John George, to help survey the United States Military Tract. While working for the government as a surveyor, John George selected four thousand-acre tracts for himself and his father, which they bought in 1800. George and his oldest son then developed a plan, which secured the political future of John George and economic security for George. George intended to complete the term of Congress he was then serving, and use his considerable influence to secure the 1802 election to Congress for John George. With John George safely elected to Congress, George planned to move to Ohio and manage the lands purchased by him and John George. George Jackson's plan worked to perfection. In 1802 he announced that he would not be a candidate for reelection to Congress, John George was elected in his place, and George moved to Zanesville, Ohio in 1806.[26]

WILLIAM LOWTHER JACKSON, SR.

The youngest surviving child of George and Elizabeth Brake Jackson was William Lowther Jackson, born 11 August 1798.[27] William was only eight years old when his parents abandoned the comparatively civilized environment of Clarksburg and relocated to Zanesville, then a crude frontier settlement on the Muskingum River. George Jackson intended to devote his time to managing the large land holdings around Zanesville owned by him and his son, John George, but he found Ohio politics irresistible. In 1808 he successfully campaigned for election to the Ohio House of Representatives, and in 1817 he moved up to the state senate.[28]

William Lowther Jackson grew up in a household filled with lively political debate and frantic financial adventurism. His father joined forces with Return Jonathan Meigs, leader of the Jeffersonian element in Ohio and father-in-law of John George Jackson.[29] George Jackson helped Meigs win the governorship of Ohio in 1810 and continued to play an active role in

Republican politics in Ohio until he retired voluntarily in 1819. In the midst of feverish political activity George Jackson, assisted by his sons Jacob and George, continued to buy and sell land in the United States Military Grant

William Jackson, too young to participate in the political and economic life of his father and older brothers, probably planned to live in Ohio and eventually play an active role in Jackson family ventures. A death in his family changed his plans. In March 1812 William's mother, Elizabeth Brake Jackson, died. Shortly after her death George Jackson developed a relationship with a Zanesville widow, Nancy Adams Richardson, whom he married in November 1814. Six months later she produced William's new half-brother, Andrew R. Jackson.[30] Around the time of Andrew's birth William Jackson left his father's home and returned to Harrison County. Back in Clarksburg, William Jackson worked for his brother, John George Jackson, who had numerous commercial operations in Harrison County.

William Jackson lacked the financial resources of his father and older brothers and never played a prominent part in Jackson businesses or political endeavors. The only public office he held was that of aide-de-camp to Isaac Booth, Brigadier General of the Twentieth Brigade of Virginia Militia.[31] However, William was often called upon to act in family business dealings where trustworthiness was paramount. In 1820 William Jackson became part of a complicated plot among the Jackson family to safeguard the Jackson homestead at Jackson's Mill, Lewis County. The Jackson's Mill property had been included as security for a bond due John White, Edward Jackson's son-in-law. Edward Jackson, owner of Jackson's Mill, was one of the sureties for the bond. As the due date for White's bond neared, William L. Jackson filed a suit in Harrison County chancery court against Edward Jackson, David Sleeth, and George White for repayment of a bond due him. To satisfy William's claim and to forestall the possible loss of Jackson's Mill to Edward White, title to the Jackson's Mill property was transferred from Edward Jackson to his nephew, William L. Jackson. When the bond due John White was retired a few months later, William deeded Jackson's Mill back to Edward Jackson.[32] William Jackson's brother, Edward Brake Jackson, a former Virginia legislator, veteran of the War of 1812, and a member of Congress from Virginia, died in 1826. In his will, written only a few days prior to his death, Edward appointed William as executor of his estate. By the terms of the will William received title to a Harrison County farm known as "Monticello" and a one-third share of Edward Jackson's library.[33] George Jackson, the family patriarch, died in Zanesville, Ohio in 1831. Around 1833 William Jackson moved back to Ohio and spent two years helping his brother George W. Jackson settle their father's complex estate. William returned to Clarksburg in 1835 and entered his father's will in the records of Harrison County.[34]

THE WILSON FAMILY

In 1820 William L. Jackson married Harriet B. Wilson, daughter of Benjamin Wilson, Jr. and Patsey Davisson.[35] Jackson's wife was a granddaughter of Colonel Benjamin Wilson, a pioneer western Virginian of even greater wealth and influence than the Jacksons. Benjamin Wilson, born in Augusta County in 1747, settled with his parents in Hampshire County in the 1750s. In 1774 he served on the staff of Earl, Lord Dunmore, in the campaign against the Shawnees. Wilson was present during the Camp Charlotte negotiations between Dunmore and Hokolesqua, better known as Cornstalk. On his way home from the Dunmore campaign, Wilson traveled through Tygart's Valley and admired the country to the extent that he purchased two tracts of land from settlers. Wilson moved his family to a site near Beverly a few months later and built Wilson's Fort. Wilson was captain of Tygart's Valley militia forces, then under the jurisdiction of Augusta County. During the Revolutionary War he was appointed colonel of the Monongalia County militia. When Harrison County was established in 1784, Wilson was appointed clerk of the county court, a position he would hold for thirty years. In 1788 Wilson represented newly formed Randolph County at Virginia's ratification convention for the United States Constitution. Wilson moved to a new farm near Bridgeport that same year to remain eligible to hold the clerk's position in Harrison County. He represented Harrison County in the Virginia Assembly on several occasions.[36] Wilson married twice and was the father of thirty children, twenty-two of whom married and raised families in Harrison and surrounding counties.[37]

Benjamin Wilson took his responsibilities as militia captain in Tygart's Valley seriously. Wilson organized a company to pursue Indians responsible for murdering the Connolly and Stewart families on Tygart's Valley River in December 1777. He led a party of thirty men through heavy snow for five days in pursuit of the Indians but failed to overtake them. The men were short of provisions, and frequent crossing of streams had soaked everyone's clothing. Despite their discomfort, Wilson persuaded the men to continue the pursuit for one more day. When they still failed to overtake the rapidly moving Indians after the sixth day, Wilson reluctantly gave up the chase.[38] Wilson's devotion to duty inspired one historian to write that "he took an active part in the pursuit of Indian marauders and was always prompt to relieve the suffering inhabitants and conducted his military operations with marked ability and prudence." Although Wilson retired from active military duty after the close of the Ohio Valley Indian wars in 1794, he retained an interest in the Harrison County militia. County authorities consulted Wilson when militia appointments needed to be filled, and his opinion often was decisive in choosing militia officers.[39]

Benjamin Wilson, Jr., born 13 June 1778, was the fourth child of Colonel Benjamin Wilson and his first wife, Ann Ruddell. He inherited his father's capabilities and sense of public responsibility. He succeeded his father as clerk of the circuit court for Harrison County and held the position from 1809 to 1830. Wilson also was an officer in the Harrison County militia. William L. Jackson's appointment as aide-de-camp to Brigadier General Isaac Booth in 1824 probably resulted from his father-in-law's influence. Wilson's main interest was business, not politics. He managed most of his father's diverse business interests and acquired a personal fortune in Harrison County land.[40] His marriage to Patsey Davisson in 1802 linked him to another aristocratic Harrison County family nearly as wealthy and influential as the Wilsons and Jacksons.[41]

William Jackson's choice of Harriet Wilson as a wife had political implications. No love letters between William and Harriet have survived, and no family traditions concerning their relationship were preserved. However, the Wilson and Jackson families had been bitter political and economic rivals since the 1790s. Differences between the families erupted most seriously in 1804 when Benjamin Wilson, Sr., county clerk of Harrison County, filed a suit against John George Jackson, then representing Virginia in the United States House of Representatives, for stating publicly that Wilson had stolen two hundred dollars of county tax money. By the time the furor over the issue died down, various lawsuits had been filed by Wilson and several of his friends against Jackson, and Jackson had countersued. George Jackson attempted to resolve the dispute between the two hot-tempered public figures by suggesting an amicable discussion and arbitration of the problem. Wilson replied to Jackson's offer by charging that the elder Jackson had no authority to enter the dispute. Wilson's disputatious reply enraged George Jackson to the point where he refused to speak to any member of the Wilson family. More trouble developed between the families in 1810 when Benjamin Wilson, Jr. and John George Jackson offered lots in Clarksburg for the use of the county to construct a new courthouse. When the Harrison County court selected Wilson's site for the courthouse, Jackson and his friends appealed to the Virginia General Assembly to review the decision making process by the court in selecting Wilson's site and rejecting Jackson's offer. Through the influence of Wilson's friend and business associate Isaac Coplin, Harrison County's delegate to the Assembly, the Assembly upheld the court's choice of Wilson's lot. In his argument before the Assembly, Coplin stated that John George Jackson frequently had "charged the Court of Harrison with corruption in many cases" and on several occasions had physically threatened Coplin with physical harm from his numerous "uncles (,) cousins (,) etc."[42] In this atmosphere of family rivalry and contentiousness, the marriage between John George Jackson's brother and Benjamin Wilson, Jr.'s daughter must have provoked much comment among the Wilsons and Jacksons as well as the Clarksburg community.

WILLIAM AND HARRIET

William and Harriet Jackson lived in Harrison County surrounded by politically influential and economically prosperous relatives. The fact that those relatives were hostile to each other appeared not to affect the young couple. They named their first son, born 3 February 1825,[43] William Lowther Jackson, Jr., in honor of his father. Harriet's father received his due when a second son, Benjamin Wilson Jackson, was born in 1827. William's father was honored when their third son, George Jackson, was born six years later. Independence from family loyalties was evident in the naming of William and Harriet's last child, a daughter. She was named Josephine, a name not used previously by either the Jackson or Wilson clans.

William Jackson farmed for a living, but he profited from many of the varied Jackson and Wilson financial ventures. His oldest brother, John George Jackson, established an industrial community in the east end of Clarksburg, which included a flour mill, carding machines, furnaces, foundries, and a tanning yard. A few miles from Clarksburg, John Jackson operated an iron foundry. On Elk Creek he established a salt works, and on Davisson's Run he built the largest sawmill in Harrison County. Jackson also controlled a fleet of flatboats, which carried local products down the West Fork to the Monongahela River and on to Pittsburgh. Among the items shipped to Pittsburgh were flax, tobacco, ginseng, woolen cloth, salt, maple sugar, leather, iron, nails, horseshoes, pots, skillets, and lumber. William Jackson's father-in-law, Benjamin Wilson, produced many of the products carried by John Jackson's flatboats. At nearby Bridgeport, Wilson had established flour and saw mills and a large trade in raw wool.[44] Although William Jackson had little financial investment in any of these family businesses, he participated in their enterprises by producing raw materials on his farm for the mills and the Pittsburgh trade. William was a member of the board of trustees of the Monongalia Navigation Company, an ill-fated scheme conceived by John George Jackson to divert the flow of the Buckhannon River into the West Fork River creating a navigable stream from Weston to Pittsburgh. He did not invest any money in the venture.[45]

In the mid-1830s the young Jackson family with four thriving children appeared well entrenched in Harrison County surrounded by relatives and friends. By Jackson and Wilson standards, William was not wealthy, but his farm produced enough to make him one of the more prosperous residents of Harrison County. Then, around 1836, William Jackson died suddenly.[46]

On Our Own Soil

2

THOMAS STINCHCOMB

The death of William Lowther Jackson left his widow and four children in uncertain financial conditions. Unlike his brothers, William Jackson had not invested money in the numerous Jackson family enterprises in Harrison and Lewis counties. His only involvement in Jackson businesses included a term as trustee of John George Jackson's ill-fated Monongalia Navigation Company. In 1825 he severed his ties to the unsuccessful attempt to improve navigation on the West Fork River when he declined reelection to the board of directors.[1] William Jackson's only assets at the time of his death consisted of his farm, his dwelling house, and his farm implements and livestock.[2]

William Jackson's farm became the responsibility of his widow and two oldest sons. The tightly knit Jackson network of uncles and cousins throughout Lewis County guaranteed that William's family would not starve and that adequate help would be available at harvest time. However, the brunt of daily chores essential to the maintenance and prosperity of the farm fell on the shoulders of eleven year old William Jackson, Jr. and his nine year old brother Benjamin. The family did not prosper, but it survived until 1838 when Harriet Jackson remarried.

The new head of the Jackson household was Thomas Stinchcomb, a Methodist Episcopal minister originally from Maryland.[3] Thomas Stinchcomb left few records behind him, but around 1840-41 he moved his new family from their old farm in Lewis County to Harrisville, a small town on the eastern edge of Wood County. Although a Methodist minister, Stinchcomb did not move to Harrisville to pastor a church. During the Methodist Schism of 1844 Stinchcomb allied himself with the southern, or slave holding church.[4] However, he did not own slaves. Methodist Church records indicate that Thomas Stinchcomb never pastored a Methodist Church in Virginia. In Harrisville, Stinchcomb bought a farm near the small town and involved himself in local politics. Stinchcomb and Harriet became parents of three children, two daughters and one son.[5]

The environment at Harrisville may have stimulated Thomas Stinchcomb's interest in local politics. He settled in Harrisville at a time when political agitation to form a new county in the region had reached a fevered pitch. The formation of Lewis County in 1816 fragmented geographical unity of settlers living along the north and south forks of Hughes River. Upper reaches of both streams fell within the jurisdiction of Lewis County while lower sections of the rivers came under the authority of Wood County. Settlers faced lengthy and arduous journeys to courthouses at either Weston or Parkersburg to transact legal business. During the 1830s increases in population in the valleys of the two forks of Hughes River generated popular support for a new county with a courthouse more conveniently located to area inhabitants. Thomas Stinchcomb arrived in Harrisville with his new wife, one daughter, and four stepchildren as the drive to form a new county around the two forks of Hughes River gained new momentum. Stinchcomb subscribed to the new county movement, and when the Virginia Assembly created Ritchie County in February 1843, Stinchcomb received an appointment as Ritchie County's first clerk of the circuit court.[6]

Thomas Stinchcomb's duties as Ritchie County circuit clerk placed him in frequent contact with attorneys, nearly all of whom held leadership roles in local political organizations. As clerk of the circuit court, Stinchcomb worked closely with the prosecuting attorney for Ritchie County, John Jay Jackson, Sr., of Parkersburg, the most prominent Democrat in Wood County. John Jay Jackson was a nephew of William Jackson Lowther, Sr., but he knew William's branch of the Jackson family mostly by reputation. John Jay had left Harrison County for Parkersburg around the time William Jackson returned to Harrison County from Ohio. Their paths probably had never crossed. Jackson developed a particular interest in the oldest son of his uncle's family, William Lowther Jackson, Jr. William, a strapping eighteen-year old farm laborer, admired the dignity and professionalism of his much older first cousin, and he noticed the respect afforded him by the community. John Jay Jackson set a good example for a young man with ambitions. In the early 1840's, Jackson served as prosecuting attorney for Wood and Ritchie counties and represented the district in the Virginia House of Delegates. For nearly twenty years he had been a political leader among Wood County Democrats.[7] In 1845, William Lowther Jackson, Jr., then twenty years old, left the family farm in Harrisville and moved to Parkersburg, perhaps at the suggestion of the elder Jackson. Once settled in the bustling Ohio River city, William Jackson began to study law under the tutelage of the most accomplished attorney in northwestern Virginia, his cousin John Jay Jackson, Sr.

JOHN JAY JACKSON

The personal history of John Jay Jackson, Sr., patriarch of the Jackson family in Wood County, made him unusual even by Jackson family standards. Born in Parkersburg 13 February 1800, Jackson was an illegitimate son of John George Jackson of Clarksburg, William Lowther Jackson, Sr.'s oldest brother. His mother was Frances Emelia Triplett, daughter of Francis Triplett, a wealthy Wood County landowner and one of Parkersburg's first settlers. When Jackson's father married Mary Payne in 1801, Emelia Triplett sued him for breach of promise and won a judgment against him. Although John George Jackson never denied responsibility for his son, his first wife forbid him from having an active role in the child's upbringing. For the first ten years of his life the boy lived with his grandfather Francis Triplett, and was known as "Jack Triplett." When John George Jackson married Sophia Meigs in 1810, she insisted that Jackson bring his young son to Clarksburg and give him the Jackson name. Jack Triplett moved to Clarksburg in 1810 and thereafter was known as John Jay Jackson. Jackson spent less than a year as a member of the Jackson household in Clarksburg. In 1811 he was sent to boarding school at Washington College in Pennsylvania. When John Jay was fifteen years old his father secured an appointment to West Point for his precocious son. John Jay graduated with the Class of 1818 in time to serve as an aide to General Andrew Jackson during the Seminole War in Florida. He resigned from the army in 1822 and returned to Clarksburg to study law under the direction of his father. He passed the Virginia bar exam in 1823 and returned to Parkersburg to open a law office. After his father's unexpected death in 1825, John Jay Jackson had little contact with his Jackson relatives in Harrison County.[8]

Not long after his return to Parkersburg, John Jay Jackson married Emma Beeson, daughter of Jacob Beeson, one of the original settlers of the small Ohio River town.[9] Jackson immediately set to work creating a political base from which he dominated Democratic Party politics in Wood County between 1825 and 1850. He represented Wood County in the Virginia Assembly between 1825 and 1844 and served as Wood County prosecuting attorney during the same period. A Democrat in the Jeffersonian tradition, Jackson's loyalty to the State of Virginia and his relentless efforts to bring economic prosperity to the northwestern Virginia region made him a nearly unanimous choice to represent Wood County's interests for over twenty years.[10]

In 1842, John Jay Jackson began tutoring his sons and other relatives in his Parkersburg law office. His first two students were his oldest son, John Jay Jackson, Jr., and his nephew Jacob Beeson Blair. These young men passed the Virginia bar exam in 1844.[11] John J. Jackson, Jr. joined a partnership in Parkersburg with his father. Jacob Blair moved to Harrisville, Ritchie County, where he opened a law office and accepted referrals from the Jacksons.[12] In 1845 Jackson accepted two new students; his second son, James Monroe Jackson, and his first cousin, William Lowther Jackson, Jr. James M. Jackson

and William L. Jackson received their Virginia law licenses in 1847.[13] James
M. Jackson remained in Parkersburg and entered a partnership with his father and older brother. William L. Jackson went home to Harrisville.

HARRISVILLE

Harrisville in 1847 had two resident attorneys, Jacob B. Blair and Thomas R. Jones. Jones had multiple business interests outside his law practice,
and he offered to take in William L. Jackson as a partner primarily to handle
legal business. The firm of Jones and Jackson opened for business in November 1847. The two attorneys pledged to prospective clients that they would
"give their joint attention to any business in the line of their profession entrusted to either."[14] To supplement his income and to become acquainted
with as many people as possible, William L. Jackson also accepted the position of United States postmaster at Harrisville.[15]

As a new attorney in Harrisville, Jackson was introduced to local politicians by his stepfather, Thomas Stinchcomb. Educated professionals among
a society of less educated farmers often were expected to assume leadership
roles in their community. Jackson's keen mind and quick wit made him popular with Ritchie Countians. Common knowledge of Jackson's farming background also helped Jackson win friends, business, and political support. In-
doctrinated with Democratic Party philosophy through his association with
John Jay Jackson, William Jackson quickly moved into a leadership position
among Ritchie County Democrats. In February 1848, only three months
after Jackson had returned to Harrisville, Ritchie and Doddridge County
Democrats met in Harrisville to discuss local strategy for upcoming state
and national elections. At the meeting, William L. Jackson introduced a
motion that the gathering appoint a committee to draft a document for
publication expressing local Democratic positions on national issues. The
group chose Jackson and his law partner Thomas Jones to serve on the committee. The committee reported twelve resolutions to the convention for
their approval. The first resolution announced unqualified support for the
Democratic Party and endorsed President James K. Polk for a second term.
Another resolution supported the annexation of Texas, an act of Congress
already achieved three years earlier but bitterly opposed by Whigs because of
the extension of slavery into the West. A third resolution charged Mexico
with having started the recently concluded Mexican War. Yet another resolution condemned the Wilmot Proviso, an 1846 amendment attached to a
military appropriations bill in Congress which called for a ban on slavery in
any territory captured from Mexico. After accepting the committee's report
the Ritchie and Doddridge Democrats elected William L. Jackson and Thomas Jones as two members of a three-man delegation to represent the district
at the Virginia Democratic Convention in Richmond on 28 February 1848.

The third delegate selected to go to Richmond was Benjamin W. Jackson, William Jackson's younger brother.[16] The trip to Richmond to attend the state Democratic Convention introduced William L. Jackson to politics at the state level. During the next twelve years he spent much of his time in Virginia's capital city in various political capacities.

During the summer of 1848 Jackson's law partner and Democratic Party crony Thomas Jones decided to move to the Midwest. Jackson and Jones dissolved their partnership in September 1848. By December Jackson had found a new partner. Jackson's brother, Benjamin Wilson Jackson, had passed the Virginia bar exam in 1848. He had opened a practice in West Union, the seat of government for Doddridge County. With the departure of Thomas Jones from the area and William Jackson's increasing development as a politician, William needed a partner to maintain his legal practice. He invited Benjamin to join him in a new partnership, and the firm of Jackson and Jackson announced its formation in December 1848. Benjamin continued to live in West Union and work from his office there. William kept his office open in Harrisville.[17]

The Democratic defeat in the national Election of 1848 had little effect in the Fourteenth Delegate District of Virginia. Although the Whig Party had an organization in Wood and Ritchie counties, the Jackson family and traditional Southern Democrats continued to control local offices. Democrats of the Fourteenth District met in Parkersburg in January 1849 to analyze the party's failure on the national level in 1848, and to insure its continued success in Wood and Ritchie counties in the 1850 elections. At this convention William L. Jackson emerged as a new leader of Fourteenth District Democrats.

The Fourteenth Virginia Delegate District in 1849 included Wood and Ritchie counties and parts of adjacent Wirt and Doddridge counties. When delegates from each county gathered in Parkersburg in January, a dispute broke out over representation on the party's policy committee. Since the Fourteenth District took in all of Wood and Ritchie counties but only parts of Wirt and Doddridge, Wood and Ritchie delegates demanded greater representation on policy committees. Delegates from Wirt and Doddridge insisted on equal representation. As the debate over representation grew more acrimonious, William L. Jackson stepped forward with a solution. He proposed that the delegates elect one member from each county represented at the convention to form a credentials committee. The credentials committee would then determine the number of votes to which each county would be entitled. The convention approved Jackson's plan and elected him to serve as chairman of the four-man committee. Under Jackson's direction the credentials committee worked out an apportionment plan satisfactory to the convention at large.[18]

Local party leaders took note of Jackson's efficient arbitration of the representation controversy, and throughout 1849 he appeared at many Democratic gatherings throughout the district. In February he discussed the Wilmot Proviso with Doddridge County Democrats and assisted them in resolving a representational dispute similar to the dispute at Parkersburg in January.[19] He addressed a Democratic meeting in Tyler County in April and denounced the proposal to admit California to the Union as a free state.[20]

Even dispassionate observers of local party politics recognized that William L. Jackson had surged to the front of Democratic Party leadership in the region. In February 1850 Jackson finally realized his ambition to serve as a political leader in his district. Ritchie County Democrats met at Harrisville on 16 February and endorsed Jackson as the party's candidate to represent the Fourteenth District in the upcoming state election.[21] Party organizations in Wood, Doddridge and Tyler counties quickly agreed with Ritchie County's endorsement. On 25 April 1850, voters in the Fourteenth District gave Jackson a solid majority over his two opponents, Daniel Haymond, an independent candidate from Ritchie County, and the previously invincible John Jay Jackson, Sr. The elder Jackson, disappointed by the Democrats who had chosen his young cousin as their nominee, had been a reluctant standard bearer for the Whig Party.[22]

PLEASANTS COUNTY

Much of Jackson's support in the 1850 election came from the northwestern corner of Ritchie County, northern Wood County, and southern Tyler County. In every session of the Assembly since 1842 residents had petitioned the Virginia Assembly to create a new county encompassing those areas.[23] The Assembly, controlled by eastern Virginians increasingly alarmed at the growing population of western Virginia and the potential for western domination of the Assembly, routinely rejected the new county proposal between 1843 and 1849.[24] William Jackson promised voters in the area in question that he would work hard for their proposed new county. Jackson took the oath of office as a Virginia state delegate in November 1850. He introduced the petition to form the new county a few weeks later. To the delight of his new constituents, the Assembly approved the formation of Pleasants County on 29 March 1851.[25]

Jackson had a personal interest in the formation of Pleasants County. At some point in 1848 or 1849 he met Alexander H. Creel, a resident of St. Mary's and one of the leaders in the movement to form Pleasants County. Creel had an attractive teenage daughter with whom the rising young star of the Democratic party fell in love. In late 1849 or early 1850 William Jackson and Sarah Creel were married.[26] The young couple returned to Harrisville in

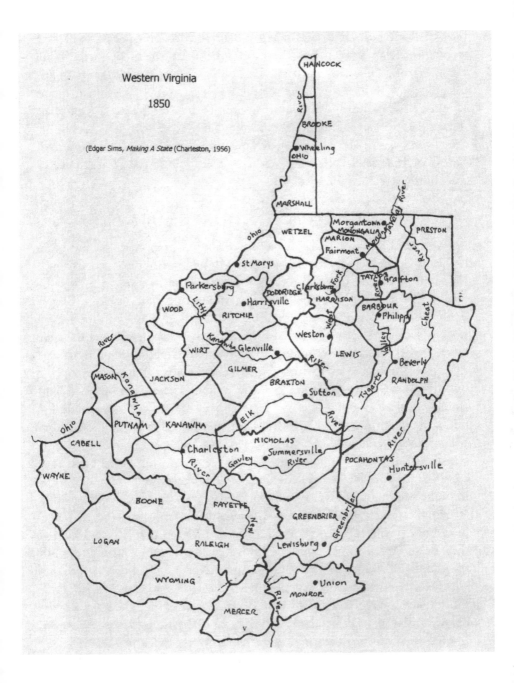

Western Virginia

1850

(Edgar Sims, *Making A State* (Charleston, 1956))

time to help celebrate a second marriage in the Jackson family. On 21 November 1850 Jacob Blair, Harrisville's other resident attorney and nephew of John Jay Jackson, married Josephine Jackson, William Jackson's younger sister.[27] Politically the marriage of Jacob Blair and Josephine Jackson created strange bedfellows. Blair was the leader of the Fourteenth District Whig Party, a strong Unionist, and an abolitionist.[28] He represented every political position abhorred by his new brother-in-law, yet the two men maintained a close friendship through the 1850s. When Josephine Jackson Blair died in 1856, Blair and their two daughters moved in with his in-laws, the Stinchcombs.[29] In 1857 William Jackson and Jacob Blair opened the firm of Jackson and Blair in Parkersburg, a partnership that lasted until the beginning of the Civil War in 1861.[30]

DELEGATE TO THE ASSEMBLY

William L. Jackson had ambitions as a Virginia politician. His success in mediating local Democratic Party disputes in Wood, Ritchie, and surrounding counties served to reinforce his self-confidence as a leader. When he arrived in Richmond to begin his first term as a delegate, he immediately made himself known to established Democratic leaders in the Virginia Assembly. Jackson did not ingratiate himself with other legislators to curry favor. He believed in the Democratic Party and the right of states to manage their own internal affairs without interference from Washington or other outside forces. He was a Virginian during a time of rising national sectionalism, but within Virginia Jackson was a regionalist. The world that interested him lay between the Allegheny Mountains and the Ohio River. Jackson was willing to cooperate and compromise with the Tidewater planters and eastern aristocrats who dominated the Virginia legislature, but he expected concessions in return. He demanded that his colleagues regard him as their equal from the beginning of his first term in the Assembly. He quickly realized that favors he extended to a fellow legislator would be returned later. However, he did not shrink from controversy when he believed that he was acting in the best interest of Virginia and the Trans Allegheny region. Within a month after taking office, Jackson's political insight faced a critical test.

Elected to the Virginia Assembly as a dedicated Democrat, William Jackson adhered to the party line without deviation. He earned the respect of his fellow legislators in December 1850 with an eloquent defense of James M. Mason when Mason's campaign for re-election to the United States Senate ran into opposition in the Assembly. Virginia Whigs united in opposition to Mason's re-election because he had written the text of the controversial Fugitive Slave Act, one of the acts which made up the Compromise of 1850. After several Whigs denounced Mason on the floor of the Assembly, James

H. Ferguson of Logan County placed Mason's name in nomination. William L. Jackson rose to second the nomination. Jackson's speech to the Assembly supporting James Mason contained the essence of Democratic ideology in Virginia in the 1850s. After praising the personal qualities of James Mason, Jackson said:

> *(Mr. Mason) represents a constituency as loyal and as true to Virginia as the people of any other portion of the State. . . . He is identified with the fugitive slave law, and with the true policy of Virginia. . . . The South has conceded all that she can with honor concede. At this critical juncture, when danger menaces the stability of our institutions, I, for one, feel unwilling to desert a son of Virginia. . . . He (Mason) is in favor of the Union as long as the principles laid down by our patriotic ancestors in its formation are kept in view. . . . When the Union ceases to be a blessing and becomes an instrument of oppression and injustice, when the North, after a fair trial, refuses to enforce the provisions of the fugitive slave law and the requirements of the Constitution, then we will have reached a point in this march of aggression beyond which forbearance ceases to be a virtue. I trust that God will avert so dire a calamity to our country and liberty, but, if come it must, every true son of the South will know his place.[31]*

Mason won re-election to the United States Senate, and Democratic leaders in the Assembly took note of the persuasive oratory powers of the new delegate from Pleasants County.

In January 1851 William Jackson endorsed another Democratic candidate for high state office, but this time his political opponents at home took partisan exception to his position. Assembly Democrats nominated John M. Daniel, the caustic and radical states' rights editor of the *Richmond Examiner*, for the position of Virginia Executive Councilor, or State Attorney General. Daniel antagonized politicians and citizens alike in western Virginia with relentless opposition to every proposal in the Assembly designed to benefit western counties. Two issues, which irritated Daniel, were western efforts to gain more seats in the Assembly and the extension of banking facilities to western areas. His vitriolic condemnation of the west on these issues made him a figure of notoriety among westerners. When William Jackson announced his support for Daniel as Executive Councilor, Andrew Sterrett, publisher of the *Parkersburg Gazette and Courier*, took him to task. Sterrett charged that Jackson was an ultra Democrat who allowed his party bias to override his better judgment and the wishes of his constituency. Jackson, Sterrett claimed, did not represent the ideals of the voters in Wood, Pleasants and Ritchie counties who had sent him to Richmond to represent them. Sterrett noted that he could find little to admire or commend in Jackson's conduct in the Assembly.[32] In an almost unprecedented turn of events, two weeks later the conservative Democratic editor retracted his remarks about Jackson. In his retraction, Sterrett equivocated by stating that while he did not agree with Jackson's "ways and means," he acknowledged that recent announcements in the *Examiner* demonstrated that the new Executive Councilor was not as anti-western as Sterrett supposed him to be. As for Jackson, Sterrett conceded that "his acts and the legislative proceedings show that he has been constant and energetic in discharge of the trusts confided to him."[33]

The issue which forced Andrew Sterrett to amend his condemnation of William L. Jackson was the Northwest Virginia Railroad bill. Despite strong opposition from the city of Wheeling and Baltimore and Ohio Railroad officials, Jackson persuaded committee members in the Assembly to report favorably on the bill to establish a new rail line from Grafton to Parkersburg. Jackson's lobbying efforts on behalf of the railroad had occurred in closed meetings during January 1851. The legislative committee's endorsement of the railroad bill caught many of the new rail line's opponents by surprise. Wheeling businessmen had no desire to share the prosperity brought to them by the Baltimore and Ohio Railroad, and Norfolk shippers had fought hard to prevent northwestern Virginia commerce from connecting with coastal trading centers outside Norfolk's sphere of influence. However, a few days after approval of his selection as Executive Councilor, John Daniel wrote an editorial in the *Richmond Examiner* endorsing the Northwest Virginia Railroad project. Assembly passage of the charter occurred shortly afterwards. Parkersburg businessmen had lobbied for the northwestern extension of the Baltimore and Ohio for several years without success. John Jay Jackson in particular had spent much time and energy in futile attempts to persuade the Assembly to charter the railroad. Sterrett, sufficiently sophisticated to understand William Jackson's previously inexplicable support of a proclaimed enemy of western Virginia, had no choice but to concede that he had been in error for criticizing Jackson's support for Daniel.[34]

THOMAS J. JACKSON

During December 1850 William Jackson received an unexpected visit from one of his Lewis County cousins. United States Army Lieutenant Thomas J. Jackson, on his way to a new posting at Fort Meade, Florida, stopped by Jackson's quarters in Richmond to introduce himself to the new political star of the Jackson family. Although the cousins were contemporaries – Thomas Jackson was one year older than William – and both had been born in Clarksburg, they most likely had never met before Thomas Jackson's surprise visit to Richmond. While Thomas Jackson had been a child at Jackson's Mill, William Jackson's family had moved to Ohio to settle George Jackson's estate. About the time William Jackson returned to Harrison County, Thomas Jackson left for West Point. Shortly afterwards William Jackson's stepfather had moved his family to Harrisville, and William lost contact with his Harrison and Lewis county relatives. Throughout his life Thomas Jackson had a strong sense of family. On several occasions he made long trips to central western Virginia to visit his relatives, and he seldom missed an opportunity to meet a distant cousin if the opportunity arose.[35] Neither Thomas nor William Jackson made notes on their visit, but Thomas Jackson was impressed with his legislator cousin. In a letter to his sister, Laura Arnold, who lived at Beverly, Randolph County, Jackson remarked, "I am much pleased at seeing Cousin Wm. L. Jackson," Thomas Jackson wrote. "Indeed I have some hopes that our ancient reputation may be revived."[36] He did not explain what he meant by reviving the Jackson's "ancient reputation," but he may have been referring to George Jackson and John George Jackson, both of whom had served in the United States Congress in the 1790s and early 1800s.

DEMOCRATIC POLITICIAN

When the spring session of the Assembly adjourned in March 1851 Jackson rushed home to Harrisville. He closed his law office, collected his wife and their few belongings, and moved to the home of Sarah Jackson's parents in St. Mary's in time to be present for the organizational meeting of the Pleasants County court. The first session of the Pleasants court met 15 May 1851 in St. Mary's at the home of Alexander Creel, William Jackson's father-in-law. Governor John B. Floyd appointed Creel to the first county court for Pleasants County. The court appointed Rodney Hickman, a next door neighbor of Alexander Creel, as clerk of the court. Eleven attorneys received the court's approval to practice law in the new county. Among them were William L. Jackson, Benjamin W. Jackson, John J. Jackson, Jr., James M. Jackson, and Jacob B. Blair. Near the end of the long and busy day organizing Pleasants County, the county court elected William L. Jackson as the county's first prosecuting attorney.[37]

In December 1851 Jackson left his legal affairs in the capable hands of his brother and made the long trip to Richmond for the opening of the January session of the Assembly. He had barely unpacked his bags when he became involved in another political dispute within the Assembly. Robert M. T. Hunter, a Tidewater planter from Essex County, had been a Virginia politician since 1830. He had served several terms in the United States House of Representatives and had been elected Speaker of the House during one of his terms. In 1846 the Assembly had elected him to the United States Senate where he became an outspoken supporter of the states-rights extremism of John C. Calhoun.[38] His senatorial term expired in 1852 and Hunter wished to return to Washington. Hunter's political power in Virginia discouraged other politicians from challenging his candidacy, and his re-election was a foregone conclusion. However, eastern planters realized that Hunter was not popular with western Virginians. His extremist states' rights views and un-abashed support for the southern slave system offended many westerners, and Hunter consistently opposed reforms in the Virginia state government designed to increase western political strength. Hunter also argued against the establishment of banks in western Virginia and fought allocation of funds for internal improvements in western counties. Virginia's new constitution ratified in 1851 had based representation in the Assembly on white popula-tion, a reform demanded by western politicians since the mid-1820s. The new basis for representation had given Trans Allegheny counties, whose white population outnumbered the rest of Virginia combined, a majority in the House of Delegates. Eastern counties, however, had retained control of the state senate which had veto power over bills passed by the House of Del-egates.[39] Aware that westerners were dissatisfied over not having control of both houses of the Virginia Assembly, Tidewater strategists determined that if a western delegate nominated Hunter for re-election to the Senate, an impression would be left with Virginia voters that Hunter had western sup-port. Hunter's Tidewater cronies, recalling the effectiveness with which Wil-liam L. Jackson had spoken on previous controversial appointments, asked Jackson to nominate Hunter. On 22 January 1852 Jackson placed Hunter's name in nomination for the United States Senate from Virginia. In his nomi-nation speech Jackson focused on Hunter's dedication to the Democratic Party and his devotion to the State of Virginia. He did not refer to Hunter's sectional tendencies. Jonathan M. Bennett, John J. Jackson, Jr., and six other western delegates symbolically registered their protest to Hunter's election by voting for Henry A. Wise of Accomac County for senator. Wise was not a candidate.[40]

William Jackson had no qualms about nominating Robert Hunter to represent Virginia in the United States Senate despite objections from other western delegates. Philosophically Jackson agreed with Hunter's southern nationalism, and he had campaigned successfully on many of the issues sup-ported by Hunter: territorial expansion of slavery, reduction of tariffs, and non-interference in state institutions.[41] Jackson calculated that Hunter, a national figure deeply involved in the growing sectional crisis in Congress, would have little time or interest for local issues. Western Virginia's eco-nomic growth and political progress between 1852 and 1860 validated Jackson's theory.[42]

There may have been a more practical motive behind Jackson's nomination of Hunter. In December 1852 the Virginia Assembly elected William Jackson to the executive position of Second Auditor for the State of Virginia.[43] Although his duties as Second Auditor hardly challenged Jackson's abilities, the honor and trust associated with the position more than compensated for the lack of political power. At least one historian suggested that Jackson's election to the auditor's position was a political payoff for nominating Hunter in the face of opposition from other western delegates.[44] If Jackson did receive a favor from Robert Hunter it more likely was received in the spring of 1852 when Hunter nominated Jackson's younger brother George for appointment to the United States Military Academy at West Point. George Jackson graduated from West Point in 1856 and served in the United States Army with the rank of lieutenant until 1861 when he resigned his commission and entered the Confederate Army.[45]

FAMILY INTERLUDE

During the early 1850s William Jackson earned admiration and respect from his constituents commensurate with the high regard in which his political colleagues held him. In 1852 John H. Hays, a former neighbor of the Jacksons in Lewis County, wrote a letter of advice to his son David. Hayes urged his son to emulate leading men of the Lewis County area. He listed several prominent Lewis Countians whom Hays claimed were men whose "names might shown (sic) bright on pages of history." William L. Jackson's name appeared on Hays' list.[46]

Between 1851 and 1855 William Jackson and Sarah Creel became parents of three children, Lucy, Alexander, and William Lowther, III.[47] Growing family responsibilities and his neglected law practice persuaded Jackson he needed to spend some time at home. He did not run for re-election to the House of Delegates in 1855. His wife's uncle, Henry Clay Creel, replaced him as Pleasants County's delegate.[48] However, Jackson could not stay away from politics. He ran for prosecuting attorney of Pleasants County, a position he had held in 1851-52, and he defeated his cousin Jacob B. Jackson for the job.[49] Jackson also assumed the duties of tax commissioner for delinquent lands in Pleasants County, and he used his office to purchase a home in St. Mary's from his father-in-law, Alexander Creel. Jackson sold Lot Number Twenty-Two in St. Mary's to Creel for one dollar, then purchased the lot and the house on it from Creel for one hundred and forty-two dollars.[50] Jackson also opened a new law office in Parkersburg with his brother-in-law, Jacob B. Blair, the former Whig leader in Ritchie County. The firm of Jackson and Blair was located in "Butcher's brick building near the courthouse" in Parkersburg.[51]

By 1856 William Jackson planned to retire from the frantic pace of Virginia state politics. He intended to live in the moderately prosperous river town of St. Mary's, serving the public in a variety of capacities and practicing law. In the meantime his children could grow up in a stable, small town environment where their parents formed part of the local aristocracy. Jackson had reached a point in his life where he could live the life of a country squire much in the fashion of his mentor, John Jay Jackson. Although William Jackson apparently was through with state politics, politicians in Richmond had other plans for him.

RETURN TO RICHMOND

Henry Wise of Accomac County, a radical Democrat in the style of Robert Hunter and John Daniel, won election as governor of Virginia in 1856. Elisha McComas of Kanawha County ran for lieutenant governor on the ticket with Wise. Wise preferred Jonathan M. Bennett of Lewis County as his running mate, but political exigencies threw the nomination to McComas. McComas received the nomination for lieutenant governor to placate voters in southwestern Virginia who had failed repeatedly in the 1850s to elect an area resident to high state office. In July, Virginia state auditor George W. Clutter from Preston County died. Wise immediately offered the job to Bennett, who accepted the position on 29 July 1857.[52] Then, three months later, McComas unexpectedly resigned as lieutenant governor. Wise owed his election to voters from western Virginia, and he took every opportunity to bring western Virginians into state government. After consultation with a small group of close advisors, one of whom was Jonathan M. Bennett, Wise offered the vacant lieutenant governor's position to William L. Jackson. The lieutenant governorship of Virginia often served as a stepping stone to the governor's office, and Jackson did not hesitate to accept the appointment. He relinquished his law practice to the care of his brother-in-law, and by November Jackson was back in Richmond. This time he brought his wife and children with him.[53]

William L. Jackson was in Richmond at the center of power when the secession issue became a serious option for southern rights advocates. Southern states had threatened to secede from the Union for a decade. Northern abolitionists in Congress had threatened the southern institution of slavery even longer. Until 16 October 1859 all of the threats had been rhetorical exercises, but events at the little town of Harper's Ferry, Virginia elevated the rhetoric to a dangerous level. John Brown was an eccentric abolitionist who had murdered pro-slavery settlers in Kansas in 1856. He and a small group of supporters seized control of the United States arsenal at Harper's Ferry. Brown's attempt to arm slaves and lead a slave revolt in Virginia momentarily threw Virginians into a state of shock. Brown's subsequent execution and the revelation that northern abolitionists had supplied Brown with money and weapons unified many Virginians, east and west, perhaps for the only time in the state's history. William Jackson's 1850 warning that when the North refused to enforce the requirements of the Constitution "every true son of the South will know his place" seemed alarmingly prophetic and timely. However, the initial outburst of southern outrage and patriotism quickly waned in western counties. Calls for southern rights conventions met with little enthusiasm in western Virginia.[54]

A few months before John Brown's ill-advised adventure at Harper's Ferry, William Jackson already had decided that he wanted out of Richmond. The Virginia Democratic Convention in January 1859 had nominated John Letcher for governor, a moderate Democrat from Rockbridge County. Letcher supported states rights, but he believed that Virginia should remain in the Union. His defense of slavery was lukewarm, an attitude that found much favor among western Virginians.[55] If John Letcher's philosophy accurately reflected the feelings of Virginia's electorate, Jackson realized that his radical viewpoints made it impossible for him to rise any higher in Virginia politics than the position he then held as lieutenant governor.

JUDGE JACKSON

Jackson decided to abandon the legislative and executive branches of Virginia state government and try the judiciary branch. During the Democratic nominating conventions in January 1860 Jackson announced his candidacy for judge of the Nineteenth Judicial District which included Wood, Ritchie and Lewis counties among others. The Jackson family and in-laws rallied to William Jackson's support. In April, Jonathan M. Bennett, recently re-elected for a second term as state auditor, received a letter from Thomas J. Jackson, his wife's cousin who was a professor of philosophy at the Virginia Military Institute. Jackson wrote:

> *I am anxious to see us possess that influence in our section of the State that will enable us to secure any office there, . . . and now in my opinion is the time to test our strength by electing Wm. L. Jackson to the judge-ship. . . . I have been told by a member of the old Whig party that Wm. L. J. is one of the shrewdest political managers of his party in the State, and I am in hopes that with his influence united to that of his friends we may be able to set up for ourselves. All of us who may be looking forward to advancement may expect to have our prospects brightened by Jackson's election, and diminished by his defeat. . . . I hope that you will if possible give Lewis and Braxton to him.[56]*

Thomas Jackson's letter to Jonathan Bennett suggested that a cooperative effort among Jackson relatives, in-laws and friends would return the Jackson family in central western Virginia to the position of power and dominance the family had enjoyed in the early 1800s. Thomas Jackson's letter implied that he may have harbored political ambitions of his own. In January 1860, Thomas Jackson visited William Jackson in Richmond. Their conversation probably focused on the approaching election.

Whether the Jackson family, relatives and friends managed to influence the May 1860 election or not, William L. Jackson recorded a convincing victory for judge of the Nineteenth Virginia Circuit.. He received a majority of more than thirteen hundred votes over his opponent, Weston attorney Matthew Edmiston.[57] Between the time of the state election in May and the national election in November 1860, the Jackson family returned to western Virginia. They moved into a home on the corner of Ann Street and Isabel Street in Parkersburg only four blocks from the Wood County courthouse and the new judge's courtroom.[58]

On 1 December 1860 Thomas J. Jackson wrote to his sister, "I hope that William will exchange with Judge Thompson and would be glad if he would do so next term which commences the 12th of next September. I hope if he comes he will bring his wife with him."[59] Jackson could hardly foresee that on 12 September 1861 he would be in command of a victorious Confederate army in the field near Manassas Junction, Virginia. At the same time his cousin would be leading a ragtag regiment up the steep slopes of Cheat Mountain in Randolph County to attack a United States fort at the top of the mountain.

3

THE JACKSONS
AND WOOD COUNTY

Results of the 1860 presidential election in Wood County foreshadowed partisan politics that divided the county during the first six months of 1861 and would continue to cause discord long after 1865. Of the four major candidates for president of a United States teetering on the brink of disintegration, the two front runners, Abraham Lincoln and Stephen Douglas, gathered just slightly more than one hundred votes between them in Wood County. John Bell, candidate for the middle-of-the-road Constitutional Union Party collected 832 votes. John Breckinridge, the Democratic secessionist candidate, also collected 832 votes.[1] Bell's vote came almost entirely from unionists in Wood County, most of whom were Parkersburg residents. Breckinridge's support was universally secessionist and reflected support from throughout Wood County. The 1860 presidential vote accurately reflected divided loyalties in Wood County.[2] The Jackson family, which controlled all of the important judicial and military offices in Wood County in 1861, divided along lines that paralleled the confusion and uncertainty felt by Wood Countians in general.

John Jay Jackson was the military leader of Wood County in 1860. As Brigadier General of the Twenty-third Brigade, Virginia Militia, he controlled militia musters, distribution of state armaments, and militia assignments.[3] Three of John Jay Jackson's sons held important political and military offices in Wood County and surrounding areas. James Monroe Jackson, a Princeton University graduate, served as Wood County's prosecuting attorney in 1860 and held the rank of Lieutenant Colonel in the 113th Regiment of Virginia Militia for Wood County.[4] His brother, John Jackson, Jr., operated a law office in Parkersburg and represented Wood County in the Virginia Assembly.[5] A third son, Jacob Beeson Jackson, had succeeded William L. Jackson as prosecuting attorney for neighboring Pleasants County. Jacob Jackson also maintained a law office in Parkersburg.[6]

William Lowther Jackson, John Jay Jackson's first cousin, his former law student, and a classmate of James Monroe Jackson, also exercised considerable power in Wood County. As judge of the Nineteenth Circuit of the Virginia Superior Court, Jackson controlled administration of justice in Wood County. If Virginia chose to secede from the Union, Jackson would have the responsibility for enforcing the state's decision. His power of enforcement, however, depended upon the cooperation of John Jay Jackson, Sr. and James Monroe Jackson and the support of John J. Jackson, Jr. Dissension among these powerful members of the Wood County Jackson clan created chaos and confusion among Wood County's residents when the secession crisis descended on the area in 1861.

All of the Jackson men attended a hastily convened political meeting in Parkersburg on New Year's Day, 1861. Wood County voters, apprehensive over national politics since passage of the South Carolina Secession Ordinance in December 1860, turned out in large numbers for the meeting at the Wood County courthouse. The only topic for discussion was Virginia's role in the increasingly volatile secession crisis. The Parkersburg meeting was non-partisan and had no clear leader. No one spoke strongly in favor of secession, although several men voiced the opinion that secession was legal. After much discussion the informal gathering passed a resolution which included the statement that "the doctrine of Secession of a State has no warrant in the Constitution, and that such doctrine would be fatal to the Union and all the purposes of its creation."[7]

As political and military leaders in Wood County, John Jay Jackson, John J. Jackson, Jr., James Monroe Jackson, and William Lowther Jackson attended the January meeting in Parkersburg, but only John Jay Jackson spoke to the gathering. Other speeches were delivered spontaneously by Arthur I. Boreman and J. M. Stephenson, Parkersburg attorneys and outspoken unionists.[8] Local newspapers did not record what the speakers at the meeting said, but the Jacksons, like everyone else in attendance, were confused over the issues and divided in their loyalties. All of the Jackson men were intensely loyal to the state of Virginia, but all of them also held public office under the ultimate authority of the United States government. Philosophically the Jacksons were nationalists, but the secession issue complicated their loyalty by presenting the possibility of multiple nations. Uncertain of where their allegiance lay, John Jay Jackson and his sons awaited developments on the state and national scene before taking sides. William Jackson had no uncertainties about where he owed allegiance. He had made his position clear in his speech to the Virginia Assembly ten years earlier in support of James Mason's nomination to Congress: "When the Union ceases to be a blessing and becomes an instrument of oppression and injustice, . . . every true son of the South will know his place."[9]

SECESSION

Virginia governor John Letcher, who owed his election in 1860 to support from northwestern Virginia, wanted southern states to compromise with Washington and resolve the secession crisis. Letcher opposed both secessionist and abolitionist points of view, and he believed that a national conference of states would discourage other southern states from following South Carolina's example.[10] While Letcher encouraged reason and compromise, six other southern states seceded between 9 January and 11 February 1861. Letcher's proposed peace convention met in Washington on 4 February, but the seven seceded states – South Carolina, Mississippi, Florida, Alabama, Georgia, Louisiana, and Texas – did not attend.[11] Forced to face political reality, the Virginia Assembly issued a call for a special convention to meet in Richmond on 13 February 1861. Publicly the purpose of the convention was to discuss tax reform for the state. Privately everyone knew that the convention would be plotting Virginia's course in the secession crisis.[12]

In a special election on 4 February 1861 Wood Countians elected John Jay Jackson, Sr. to represent the county's interests at what became known as the Virginia Secession Convention.[13] In Richmond, Jackson joined with other northwestern Virginia unionists in opposition to Virginia's secession from the Union. Jackson, John S. Carlile, Waitman Willey, Chester Hubbard, and George Summers addressed the convention and spoke strongly against secession. At one session of the increasingly frustrated convention, Jackson addressed the assembly and proclaimed, "So help me, God, I will not go with South Carolina under any circumstances!"[14] As late as 4 April 1861 the Virginia Secession Convention still voted eighty-five to forty-five against secession.[15] The following day, 5 April, John Jay Jackson shocked even some of his fellow western Virginia delegates by delivering a speech in which he announced that, "If it is the purpose of this Convention to take Virginia out of the Union on the pretext of coercion applied to seceding states, I am ready to raise the banner of revolt and secede with my people from the State of Virginia!"[16] Despite this ominous threat from Jackson, secessionists merely postponed a final vote while events farther south pushed the crisis beyond inflammatory rhetoric. On 12 April 1861 South Carolina artillery fired on Fort Sumter in Charleston Harbor. Three days later President Lincoln issued a call for 75,000 state militia troops to assemble under federal authority to enforce the laws of the United States in South Carolina. Virginia received orders to supply its share of militia to suppress rebellion in South Carolina, but on 16 April Governor Letcher refused to comply with Lincoln's order.[17]

The following morning former Virginia governor Henry Wise, representing his native Accomac County at the Secession Convention, addressed the assembly. Laying a loaded pistol on the table before him, a visibly agitated Wise harangued the convention about the sovereign rights of states. Wise then announced to his astounded audience that even as he spoke Virginia military forces had seized control of the federal arsenal at Harper's Ferry and the United States navy ship yards at Norfolk.[18] A few hours later the Virginia Secession Convention voted to secede. Following John Jay Jackson's lead, thirty-two of the delegates from northwestern Virginia counties voted against the secession ordinance.[19]

Anti-secession delegates from northwestern Virginia stayed in Richmond for a few days following passage of the Secession Ordinance. On the evening of 20 April, John Jay Jackson convened a meeting of northwestern men at the Powhatan Hotel. The delegates concluded that they could do nothing further in Richmond to stem the swelling tide of secessionism, and they made arrangements to return to their homes. Most of them left Richmond on 21 April determined to lobby in their home counties for rejection of the secession referendum scheduled for 23 May 1861.[20] As his train pulled out of Richmond, John Jay Jackson did not know that civil war already had broken out in the Jackson family in Wood County.

THE PARKERSBURG RIOT

News of Virginia's decision to secede from the Union was received in the telegraph office of the Northwestern Virginia Railroad on Ann Street in Parkersburg on 18 April 1861. A crowd gathered near the telegraph office as rumors flew about town. As unionists and secessionists alike stood around discussing what secession might mean for Wood County, a second telegram from Richmond arrived. Addressed to James M. Jackson, Colonel of the 113th Wood County Militia, the telegram came from James L. Morehead, commanding general of the Virginia State Militia. Morehead ordered Jackson to proceed at once to the Parkersburg armory and take possession for the State of Virginia all of the armaments stored there.[21]

Colonel Jackson hesitated to comply with his orders. In the absence of his father who had not returned yet from Richmond, James M. Jackson commanded the Wood County Militia, a Virginia military organization. The armaments stored in the Parkersburg armory had been supplied to Wood County by the state of Virginia and clearly were the property of Virginia. However, Jackson also was aware that the Virginia Militia was under the authority of the United States government. In fact, the federal army organizing at that time was drawn from state militia regiments throughout the northeast and midwest. James Jackson did not support secession, and he knew that his father felt even more strongly about preserving the Union. Both Jacksons believed that secession was the work of a few hotheads and that most Virginians had no desire to leave the Union. At the same time, Jackson was reluctant to disobey orders sent directly to him by the commanding general of Virginia militia under whose authority he held his appointment as colonel of militia.

Colonel Jackson had no time to rationalize conflicting emotions. He had his orders, the increasingly boisterous crowd knew he had his orders, and he had a responsibility to do something. Jackson noted that several members of the Wood County militia were present in the crowd milling around the telegraph office. He ordered them to fall in, and around two dozen unarmed militiamen haltingly obeyed. With Jackson in the lead the men marched from the telegraph office up Ann Street two blocks and made a right angle turn onto Court Street. The Wood County armory shared a building with the county jail on the corner of Court Street and Market Street. By the time the militia turned onto Court Street, the crowd following them had grown in numbers and boisterousness. [22]

The Wood County armory held two brass cannons and several boxes of Mexican War vintage muskets supplied by the State of Virginia following John Brown's raid at Harper's Ferry in 1859. The weapons had been stored in the county jail because the jail was convenient to the militia regiment's drilling ground behind the courthouse. As Jackson and his hesitant troops marched along Court Street to secure the cache of weapons, the men discussed the constitutionality of secession. By the time the group arrived at the jail several shoving matches had occurred among unionist and secessionist members of the militia. Hostility among the militiamen affected the crowd of civilian followers and a few fistfights broke out. Colonel Jackson ignored the altercations in the crowd, but when he arrived at the jail he discovered a more serious problem that could not be ignored.

When the squabbling militia and their nervous commander reached the armory they found William Lowther Jackson, judge of the Nineteenth Virginia Circuit Court, in possession of the building's entrance. Colonel James M. Jackson may have had questions about where he owed allegiance, but Judge Jackson had none. He represented judicial authority for the State of Virginia in Wood County. The Wood County courthouse and jail were Virginia property as were the armaments stored in the jail. From Judge Jackson's point of view, removing Virginia-owned property from the armory and placing that property under jurisdiction of any government agency other than Virginia was illegal and unconstitutional. Colonel Jackson ordered Judge Jackson to allow him to execute his orders and take possession of the armory. Judge Jackson asked him under whose authority he intended to seize the armory. Colonel Jackson's reply was ambivalent, and Judge Jackson refused to move. James M. Jackson and William L. Jackson had been law students together under John Jay Jackson's tutelage in 1845. Now the cousins and former classmates faced each other on the steps of the Wood County jail and debated the merits of each other's position while the crowd behind them grew increasingly partisan.

With clearly identified leaders at hand, the militia under Colonel Jackson's command quickly took sides. States rights supporters lined up beside Judge Jackson, while unionists formed behind their colonel. More fistfights and shoving matches broke out in the crowd. Parkersburg's only policeman, George Creel, stood beside his niece's husband, Judge Jackson, while events surged beyond his control. Colonel Jackson momentarily abandoned his argument with the judge and sought the advice of Peter Van Winkle, Parkersburg's leading unionist spokesman and an interested observer in the proceedings. Van Winkle suggested that a local home guard company, an unofficial paramilitary pro-Union organization, be pressed into service to secure the armory. The home guard commander, Captain John Kiger, had been watching developments from the street. Colonel Jackson and Van Winkle approached Kiger and asked him to take charge of securing the armory. Kiger pointed out that his company had no official status and that he had no legal authority to do anything. He agreed to release his command to the authority of Rathbone Van Winkle, Peter Van Winkle's son and major of the 113th Virginia Militia, but not to Colonel Jackson whose loyalty Kiger questioned. Colonel Jackson, deeply insulted by Kiger but unable to reach an alternative solution, relinquished his command to Major Van Winkle. The unionist members of the militia supplemented by several home guards confronted Judge Jackson and Police Chief Creel. Creel persuaded the judge to allow Van Winkle to occupy the armory. Van Winkle and his men entered the armory, equipped themselves with militia weapons stored inside, and mounted guards around the building securing it in the name of the United States government.[23]

Judge William Jackson, outraged over his failure to protect what he believed to be Virginia property, marched to the courthouse to seek a legal method to recover control of the militia's armory. Colonel James Jackson, angered over his cousin's obstreperous conduct and humiliated by his failure to resolve the confusion at the jail, confronted the judge at the courthouse steps. The two former classmates argued loudly about the correctness of each other's course of action. Frustrated beyond endurance, Colonel Jackson suddenly struck Judge Jackson in the face. James Jackson and William Jackson were both thirty-six years old, over six feet tall, and weighed more than two hundred pounds. Both possessed the combativeness of their grandfather, George Jackson, and the ensuing brawl between two of Parkersburg's leading citizens brought the riot among the town's lesser roustabouts to a standstill. Everyone watched in amazement as the judge of the Nineteenth Virginia Circuit pummeled the Colonel of the 113th Regiment of Virginia Militia into submission.[24] Despite Judge Jackson's pugilistic victory over his cousin, the Wood County armory remained under control of Parkersburg unionists.

A CITY DIVIDED

During the last two weeks of April and the first two weeks of May 1861, tension continued to grow among citizens of Parkersburg. Secessionists believed that federal troops gathered on the Ohio side of the river soon would be sent to occupy Parkersburg. They feared that federal occupation meant confiscated property and arrest of anyone who spoke out for secession. A Confederate recruiting station on Market Street continued to enlist Parkersburg men for the southern army despite rumors of federal occupation of the city. Unionists in town feared a Confederate attack, especially from numerous partisan bands that were rumored to be circulating through the countryside of rural Wood County. Efforts to organize pro-Union military companies failed due to the absence of federal authority to legitimize the companies. Several unofficial companies of unionists organized to protect themselves against an anticipated attack.[25] As excitement from the events of 18 April waned, unionists in Parkersburg grew more confident. One observer noted in a local newspaper that union men did not "hesitate to avow their feelings and express their devotion to the stars and stripes."[26] On 5 May, Parkersburg unionists prevented Leonard S. Hall, a Virginia Assembly delegate from Wetzel County who had voted in favor of Virginia's secession, from speaking at the Wood County courthouse. Hall escaped threats of physical violence by locking himself in a railroad car and hiding under the seats.[27] Hall's treatment may have been influenced by earlier events. Hall had been elected from Wetzel County to attend the Secession Convention as a unionist. Once in Richmond he became an outspoken proponent of secession. One western Virginia newspaper editor commented that if "Judas Iscariot and L. S. Hall were to run for the same office in Wetzel County tomorrow, Judas would beat Hall by more than two hundred votes."[28]

In late April 1861, Robert E. Lee—commanding general of Virginia state troops—issued a general order to mobilize militia units in counties through which the Baltimore and Ohio Railroad passed. The militia had orders to guard the railroad against an anticipated federal invasion of northwestern Virginia. General John J. Jackson, home from the Secession Convention and back in command of the Wood County militia, ignored Lee's order. He directed his son, Colonel James Jackson, to keep the 113th Wood County Militia in a state of readiness, but he did not direct them to deploy anywhere. Judge William Jackson learned of Lee's order and attempted to persuade secessionist members of the 113th Regiment to mobilize and station themselves along the railroad outside Parkersburg to prevent Union troops from seizing control of this vital transportation link with the eastern part of

northwestern Virginia. Although Jackson tried to convince the men that
they were mobilizing for the protection of Wood County, they countered his
argument with the fear that they would be sent east to join the regular Confederate force organizing at Grafton under the direction of Colonel George
Porterfield. None of the members of the 113th Wood County Militia were
willing to leave home to fight for the Confederacy.[29]

FEDERAL OCCUPATION

On 26 May 1861 General George B. McClellan, United States Commander of the Department of Ohio, ordered Colonel James B. Steedman at
Marietta to cross the Ohio River and occupy Parkersburg with the Fourteenth Ohio Infantry regiment.[30] The next day Steedman and his regiment
left Marietta on a steamboat for Parkersburg thirteen miles downstream.
The steamboat pulled up to the Parkersburg wharf shortly before noon. The
Ohio soldiers expected trouble, but instead Parkersburg Mayor James Cook
and a relieved Parkersburg Safety Committee greeted them at the wharf and
pledged complete cooperation.[31]

Colonel Steedman established his headquarters in Parkersburg at the
railroad station and telegraph office on Kanawha Street. General John Jay
Jackson offered Steedman the use of his farm on Prospect Hill as a campsite
for the Fourteenth Ohio Infantry. The regiment marched through Parkersburg
city streets to Prospect Hill guided by Jackson's twelve-year-old granddaughter, Lily Irene Jackson.[32] Steedman did not accompany his troops to Prospect Hill. He stayed at the railroad depot to organize his command center,
and that was where a frantic railroad employee found him a few hours later
to report that rebels had been spotted at the Worthington Creek bridge a few
miles east of Parkersburg. Steedman had been warned that partisans in the
Wood County countryside had plans to burn railroad bridges to prevent
federal troops from using the railroad. He immediately dispatched a company of men to the bridge to investigate. The soldiers found A. C. "Doc"
Kennedy, Theodore Boyd, Bun Wheeler and June Stephenson sitting under
the bridge playing cards.[33] They arrested the four men and brought them
back to Parkersburg under guard. Steedman drew up charges of bridge burning against the men and confined them in the Wood County jail to await
transportation to Wheeling and trial in federal court.[34]

Word of the arrest of Kennedy, Boyd, Wheeler and Stephenson quickly
reached Judge Jackson. Jackson approached Steedman and demanded that
the prisoners be released to civil authority. Steedman insisted that federal
authorities had jurisdiction because his orders instructed him to secure and
safeguard the railroad for transportation of federal troops and supplies. Jackson countered that the railroad was private property and the federal govern-

ment had no jurisdiction over it. Steedman's orders from McClellan to occupy Parkersburg included an admonition to cooperate with local authorities. When Jackson produced a writ of *habeas corpus* demanding custody of the prisoners, Steedman capitulated.

JUDGE JACKSON CHOOSES SIDES

The trial of the four accused bridge burners hastily convened the following morning, 28 May 1861. The Wood County courtroom filled quickly with partisans supporting both the unionist and secessionist points of view. Outside in the court square, dozens of the town's residents gathered to hear the outcome of the trial. The Wood County prosecutor, James M. Jackson, still showing bruises from his fistfight with Judge Jackson ten days earlier, read the charge to the court: Kennedy, Boyd, Wheeler and Stephenson, known secessionists, had attempted to burn the Northwest Virginia Railroad bridge over Worthington Creek. Judge Jackson asked the prosecutor to call his witnesses. Prosecutor Jackson aggressively stated that he had no witnesses, but that none were needed since everyone in the courtroom knew what the accused had planned to do. Judge Jackson addressed the open court and invited anyone who had witnessed a crime at the Worthington Bridge or who had information about a crime being planned there to come forward and testify. No one moved. Judge Jackson then announced that there were no witnesses to a crime and no evidence that a crime had been committed. He banged his gavel and dismissed charges against the four defendants.[35]

Before Judge Jackson could adjourn court, prosecutor James Jackson launched an anti-secession diatribe, implying that the judge himself had secessionist sympathies. Judge Jackson ordered the prosecutor to cease and desist, but James Jackson, encouraged by sympathetic mutterings among the courtroom crowd, continued to condemn all secessionists in general and Judge Jackson in particular. Unintimidated by the growing chaos in the courtroom, Judge Jackson calmly ordered Wood County sheriff Henry Dils, an uncompromising unionist, to arrest the prosecuting attorney for contempt of court. Sheriff Dils refused to comply with the judge's order. Pistols suddenly appeared in the hands of both unionist and secessionist partisans in the crowd but no shots were fired. A group of secessionists, including the four released defendants, formed a human shield around Judge Jackson and escorted him from the courtroom.[36] Judge Jackson's impromptu bodyguard escorted him to his home on Ann Street and stood guard outside while he discussed the situation with his wife and children. Convinced that Union authorities would arrest him if he remained in Parkersburg, Jackson hurriedly threw a few belongings into saddlebags, mounted his horse, and rode eastward out of town toward Grafton. Jackson's concern that Union authorities would arrest him understated the real threat he faced. Commenting on the trial fiasco the following day, the Unionist editor of the Marietta *Intelligencer* warned that Judge Jackson should beware. "We are at war," the editor declared, "and there will be no Traitors left in the rear. Our soldiers are not to be molested or trifled with. They will hang a Judge who is a traitor as promptly as the poorest rebel wretch."[37]

Among the papers William Jackson hurriedly stuffed into his saddlebags before his precipitate departure from Parkersburg was a copy of a letter James Jackson would have given a great deal to possess earlier in the day. Written by Major Francis Boykin of the Virginia Volunteers and addressed to Robert E. Lee, commanding general of Virginia volunteer forces, the letter recommended that William L. Jackson be appointed commander of Confederate forces at Parkersburg. Boykin concluded his letter with the comment, "I have recently had a conversation with him and he will accept the command if tendered to him." The date on the letter was 10 May 1861.[38]

4

LAUREL HILL

With expectations of receiving a commission as colonel of Virginia state troops tucked securely in his saddlebags, William L. Jackson started eastward on the Parkersburg and Staunton Turnpike on the evening of 28 May 1861 in search of a Confederate regiment to command. Virginia governor John Letcher had ordered militia brigades in northwestern Virginia to rendezvous at Fetterman Station near Grafton, Taylor County, in early May. George A. Porterfield, a Virginia Military Institute graduate and Mexican War veteran, had been assigned the task of organizing the militia into an effective army to meet an anticipated federal invasion of northwestern Virginia. Jackson's promised commission as an officer of Virginia Volunteers would not take effect until he reported for duty to Porterfield. William Jackson had seen the orders for northwestern Virginia militia regiments to report to Grafton for assignments, and that was his destination on 28 May. Robert E. Lee, commander of Virginia state troops, preferred that Jackson remain in Parkersburg, take command of the Wood County militia, and prevent federal troops from seizing the western terminus of the Northwest Virginia Railroad.[1] The occupation of Parkersburg by Union troops on 27 May 1861 and the uproar in the town created the following day by the trial of partisans accused of plotting to burn the railroad bridge at Worthington persuaded Jackson to leave town. Jackson started for Grafton but had been on the road less than twenty-four hours when he received news that Porterfield had conceded the town to superior federal forces. Porterfield withdrew to Philippi, Barbour County. [2]

Porterfield established defensive positions around Philippi while he awaited reinforcements. Between 29 May and 2 June his little army grew to around eight hundred men, but basic military supplies still reduced the effectiveness of the force. Porterfield fired off a steady stream of telegrams to authorities in Richmond demanding supplies and more troops. He received promises for both, but events moved faster than Porterfield anticipated. During the night of 2 June a torrential rainstorm struck the Philippi area. Convinced that the weather was too severe to allow troop movements, Porterfield's pickets guarding the roads to Philippi from Grafton and

Clarksburg abandoned their posts to seek shelter from the rain. At four thirty in the morning on 3 June, Union artillery placed on a hill overlooking Philippi during the night opened fire. Within twenty minutes Porterfield's entire army had poured onto the Beverly road. The troops did not stop until they reached Beverly nearly forty miles away.[3] Porterfield's panicked soldiers finally halted at Huttonsville five miles south of Beverly. That was where William L. Jackson found Porterfield when he reported for duty on 11 June 1861.[4]

Porterfield was pleased to see Jackson. He had been dissatisfied with his officers during the Philippi fiasco, and in Huttonsville they continued to demonstrate evidence of incompetence. Drilling troops and establishing military discipline were done in a desultory manner if at all. Porterfield complained to Richmond authorities that he could not even get an accurate count of the men under his command.[5] When Porterfield acknowledged to Richmond that Jackson had reported for duty, he remarked, "He (Jackson) has been very active, and will become a most useful officer."[6]

Porterfield did not elaborate on how Jackson had been "very active" in Confederate service prior to 11 June, but Jackson's reputation clearly proceeded him. Major Francis Boykin, whose endorsement of Jackson to Robert E. Lee in early May had led to Jackson's commission as colonel of Virginia Volunteers, remarked that Jackson was "a gentleman of great personal popularity not only with his own party but with those opposed to him politically."[7] Although subsequent events in Parkersburg contradicted Jackson's popularity with "those opposed to him politically," Porterfield probably was aware of Jackson's previous distinction as a leader of Virginia Democrats and a partisan Virginia politician. Porterfield also may have been aware of political maneuvering centering on Jackson in nearby Lewis County. Weston attorney William B. Lively, a dedicated secessionist, had received permission from General Henry A. Wise to recruit two companies of Virginia partisans in Lewis and Gilmer counties. Lively understood from his communications with Wise that his companies would form the nucleus of a new regiment of Virginia troops with William L. Jackson as colonel and Lively as lieutenant colonel. The Gilmer County court appropriated three thousand dollars to arm and deploy local soldiers to defend the county against any federal invasion, and Lively, who maintained a law office in Glenville, was given access to these funds to further his recruiting efforts. Lively opened a recruiting office in Weston and was engaged in enlisting Lewis County men for Confederate service when the Seventh Ohio Infantry appeared suddenly in town on 2 July. Lively was arrested, charged with treason against the United States, and sent under guard to military prison at Grafton.[8] Jackson and Lively probably held discussions in Weston about the formation of a central western Virginia regiment between the time Jackson left Parkersburg and the time he reported for duty at Huttonsville. Porterfield kept informed of local events in the area of his command through a network of civilian informants, and he undoubtedly knew of Jackson's association with William Lively.

On 6 June 1861, five days before William L. Jackson arrived at Huttonsville, Robert E. Lee approved the appointment of Robert S. Garnett to command the Army of Northwestern Virginia, superseding the beleaguered George Porterfield.[9] Immediately after his arrival in Huttonsville on 14 June, Garnett implemented plans to hold the Confederate line along the Tygart's Valley River. Prior to Garnett's arrival, Porterfield had assigned Jackson the task of organizing the Virginia militia at Huttonsville into companies. When Garnett arrived for duty, Jackson had organized six companies with one hundred men assigned to each. Garnett ordered Jackson to form four additional companies to create a regiment composed of ten companies and one thousand men. Garnett appointed Jackson colonel of the new regiment and designated it the Thirty-first Virginia Infantry.[10] The Thirty-first Virginia was the first Confederate regiment organized in northwestern Virginia.[11]

Garnett faced a daunting task in Tygart's Valley. Robert E. Lee expected Garnett to either regain control of the Baltimore and Ohio Railroad or render it useless for Union troop movements. Concurrent with his effort to regain control of the railroad or destroy it, Garnett was expected to establish a defensive line to prevent further federal encroachment on Virginia territory. To accomplish these tasks Garnett had in his command around six thousand poorly trained and ill-armed citizen soldiers, few of whom had ever experienced combat. Most of the troops carried weapons brought with them from their homes. Food supplies were scarce, and other basic equipment such as rifle cartridges, cartridge boxes, and canteens were non-existent. The men had little concept of military movements or discipline, and they had little time to acquire any training. Garnett assessed his prospects in a telegram to Lee in which he noted that his army was "wholly incapable, in my judgment, of rendering anything like efficient service."[12]

Union General George B. McClellan arrived at Grafton on 22 June 1861 with his well-armed and equipped army, and put in motion a slow and cautious advance against Garnett's forces. Garnett had limited options in defending his position. Two main roads entered Tygart's Valley from the north. The Parkersburg-Staunton Turnpike wound its way from Buckhannon across the imposing bulk of Rich Mountain to Beverly. A second road entered the valley from Grafton by way of Belington and through a narrow mountain pass at Laurel Hill seventeen miles north of Beverly. Garnett decided that defending the passes at Rich Mountain and Laurel Hill could at least contain the federal advance until he received reinforcements. He concluded that Laurel Hill offered the most likely avenue of attack. Garnett sent William Jackson and his Thirty-first Infantry to construct fortifications on the high ground and to cut trees across the road in front of their position. Jackson discovered a dried up millrace, which bisected the road at the foot of Laurel Hill. He positioned men in the natural trench, and he and his men sat around waiting for federal troops to appear. For nearly two weeks William L. Jackson and his ten companies of ill-prepared infantrymen were all that stood between twenty-thousand Union troops concentrated at Grafton, Clarksburg and Buckhannon and Virginia's vital Shenandoah Valley and the Virginia Central Railroad. Reinforcements arrived during the first few days of July, and Garnett stationed them at Laurel Hill. The new units included the Twenty-third and Twenty-seventh Virginia Infantry regiments and the First Georgia Infantry.[13]

On top of Rich Mountain where the Parkersburg and Staunton Turnpike passed through a low gap, Garnett stationed the Twenty-fifth Virginia Infantry, a regiment organized by Colonel Jonathan M. Heck of Monongalia County a few days after Jackson organized the Thirty-first Infantry. Heck constructed Camp Garnett at the top of the mountain and manned his position with his entire regiment of 695 men. On 7 July Colonel John Pegram and his Twentieth Virginia Infantry arrived at Beverly, and Garnett sent Pegram to Rich Mountain. Pegram's commission predated Heck's, and he assumed command at Camp Garnett much to the disgust of Heck. General Garnett established his headquarters at Laurel Hill, where he expected the main federal thrust to occur.[14]

Garnett desperately needed cavalry to keep him appraised of federal movements and to provide an early warning of a federal advance. On 3 July three cavalry companies reported for duty. Much to the delight of William Jackson, his brother, George Jackson, was in command of the companies. George Jackson carried a note from Robert E. Lee to Garnett confirming his commission. Lee wrote, "I have ordered G. Jackson to report to you for duty with the cavalry. His commission will entitle him to precedence over officers of the same grade in the volunteer service. He is a cavalry officer of some experience." [15]

Federal troops finally appeared in front of Laurel Hill on 7 July. An artillery barrage was directed at William Jackson's troops entrenched in the abandoned millrace, but the Confederates held their position.[16] George Jackson and his cavalry scouted the federal force, and he reported to Garnett that the Union troops appeared to be approximately equal in number to Garnett's forces at Laurel Hill. Garnett had reliable information on the total number of federal troops collected by McClellan, but he did not find it remarkable that such a small fraction of McClellan's force was attacking the Laurel Hill position. Over the next three days Union forces shelled the Laurel Hill camp with artillery, sniped at exposed Confederates from long range, and several times formed battle lines only to suddenly withdraw without attempting to advance.[17] Not until the afternoon of 11 July did Garnett finally realize the significance of the modest Union force arrayed against him and its eccentric behavior.

Around noon of 11 July Confederates at Laurel Hill could hear sounds of heavy firing in the distance toward Rich Mountain. Couriers began arriving at Garnett's headquarters advising him that Pegram and Heck were under attack by a significant federal force. In the meantime, federal troops in front of Laurel Hill continued their odd behavior with sporadic bursts of artillery, sniper fire, and an occasional sortie, which always withdrew before getting too close. Late in the afternoon a frantic courier arrived from Colonel William C. Scott, whose late arriving Forty-fourth Virginia Infantry had been stationed at Beverly as a reserve. The courier informed Garnett that Pegram and Heck had been flanked on Rich Mountain and that the entire command was trapped between federal forces on both the north and south slopes of Rich Mountain. Garnett realized that he had been duped. The federal demonstration at Laurel Hill had been nothing more than a diversion; the main Union assault had been directed at the undermanned position on Rich Mountain.[18]

Garnett had been slow to recognize McClellan's strategy, but when it became clear what had happened he took decisive action to minimize the disaster. Garnett ordered William Jackson and the Thirty-first Infantry to direct a heavy fire at federal positions below Laurel Hill and give an impression that a Confederate attack was imminent. While the Thirty-first Virginia kept the federals pinned in their positions, the remainder of Garnett's command hastily packed supply wagons and prepared to move out. As night fell, Garnett ordered the men to light campfires. With George Jackson and his cavalry companies leading the way, Garnett's army began to withdraw down the road toward Beverly, hoping to reach the Parkersburg and Staunton Turnpike before federal troops seized it. Jackson and his men continued to fire in the direction of the federal positions until daylight began to fail. Withdrawing a few men at a time, the Thirty-first Infantry joined the retreat. Jackson hoped that the burning campfires implied that the skirmishers had simply returned to camp because of darkness.[19]

A steady rain during the previous two days had turned the road to Beverly into a quagmire. By seven o'clock on the morning of 12 July Garnett had covered only nine miles. A courier from the Forty-fourth Virginia met the column three miles from Beverly and informed Garnett that federal troops had already seized the turnpike south of the town.[20] Garnett ordered his column to reverse its course and head east over a poorly maintained trace known as the Leading Creek Road. This road crossed Cheat River at a place called Corrick's Ford and continued to Red House, Maryland where it intersected the Northwestern Turnpike to Romney. Orders were sent down the line to William Jackson who commanded the rear guard. Jackson was ordered to take the lead. His brother, George Jackson who had been leading the retreat with his cavalry, became the rear guard of Garnett's column.[21]

Almost immediately the retreat degenerated into a logistical nightmare. The heavily laden supply wagons churned the narrow Leading Creek Road into a sea of mud. A few wagons slipped over the edge of the slick, muddy track and toppled over precipitous mountainsides. Other wagons were too heavy to drag through the mud and had to be abandoned. Cast off equipment and wagons soon cluttered the road and further complicated progress of the wet, hungry, and dispirited soldiers. The army paused at four o'clock in the morning along Shaver's Fork River, but two hours later pursuing federals opened fire on the rear guard. The weary Confederates resumed their march. Jackson led his men across Corrick's Ford without incident and headed for Horseshoe Run of Cheat River. Firing continued behind them. A short time later a distraught cavalryman caught up with Jackson and informed him that a sniper at Corrick's Ford had killed General Garnett. The retreat became a disorganized rout. Soldiers got lost in the dense forest, the rain intensified and temperatures dropped, and all semblance of order and discipline disappeared. Jackson somehow managed to keep his regiment together. The exhausted troops marched for two days and nights without stopping to eat, and five days after abandoning Laurel Hill they straggled into Petersburg, Hardy County. Jackson got his men across the rain-swollen South Branch of the Potomac, then waited to see if his pursuers would risk crossing the river. Federal scouts appeared on the north bank of the South Branch, but the river had risen higher since Jackson's men had crossed and the federals halted their pursuit.[22] After resting for a few hours, Jackson prodded his men back onto the muddy road to Monterey, Highland County, where the Virginia government had established a supply depot.

GREENBRIER RIVER

William Jackson and the Thirty-first Infantry arrived at Monterey on 22 July 1861. His ranks thinned by the capture of several men and a large number of men "missing" from the frantic retreat from Laurel Hill, Jackson rested only three days at Monterey. The Thirty-first Infantry was assigned to a new brigade under the command of General Henry R. Jackson of Georgia. The new commander of the Army of Northwestern Virginia, William W. Loring, ordered General Jackson's brigade to establish defensive positions on the Parkersburg and Staunton Turnpike at the top of Allegheny Mountain, twelve miles north of Monterey. On 25 July General Jackson moved his brigade to Camp Allegheny. The Thirty-first Virginia and Colonel Jackson accompanied the brigade. From their new position, on a clear day the Confederate troops could see the new federal fort erected at Cheat Summit fourteen miles away.[23]

Late in July Robert E. Lee came to Monterey to try to salvage the desperate Confederate situation in northwestern Virginia. Lee met with General Henry Jackson at Monterey, then rode on to Huntersville, Pocahontas County, where General Loring had established his headquarters. Lee and Loring met with Loring's brigade commanders, Samuel R. Anderson, Daniel Donelson, Albert Rust, Henry Jackson, Jesse Burks and William Gilham on 8 September. At Rust's insistence an elaborate four-pronged attack on federal positions in Tygart's Valley was scheduled for 12 September. Colonel Albert Rust and his Arkansas regiment, supplemented by William L. Jackson and the Thirty-first Virginia Infantry, had the key assignment for the attack. Rust and Jackson would assault and capture the Cheat Summit fort, removing the only federal force concentrated between the Confederate positions and Tygart's Valley. At the sound of the first volley from Rust's command, the other Confederate units already in position would strike federal positions at Elkwater, Huttonsville and Beverly.[24]

Lee, Loring, and the other brigade commanders waited in vain for Rust's volley. Rust sent Company C of the Thirty-first Virginia around the Cheat Summit fort to blockade the road leading west from the fort to Huttonsville. At daybreak a small wagon train left the fort and headed west. Company C ambushed the train and captured all of the Union soldiers accompanying it. The prisoners were taken through the woods to Rust, who questioned them about the fort's occupants. The prisoners informed Rust that there were three thousand soldiers stationed at the fort,[25] that the fort's commander was aware of the impending attack, and that he had telegraphed to Huttonsville for reinforcements which were already on their way. Despite Confederate intelligence that there were only around three hundred soldiers at the fort and that the telegraph wire linking Cheat Summit to Huttonsville had been cut earlier in the morning, Rust decided to call off his assault.[26] Rust neglected to send a message to Lee and Loring informing them of his decision, and nine thousand Confederate troops waited in the rain for nearly four hours listening for Rust's volley. Not knowing what calamity may have befallen Rust, Lee cancelled the attack around ten o'clock in the morning.[27]

Lee remained in the Huntersville area for another week, but incessant rain and premature cold weather demoralized his officers and troops to the extent that he abandoned plans for a new offensive. Lee realized that while his troops could not move forward, the muddy roads and swollen streams in the area also prevented the federal troops from moving against Confederate positions. General Henry Jackson was entrusted with holding the Confederate line at the Greenbrier River, and on 20 September Lee departed for the Kanawha Valley. He ordered General Loring to follow him with the other four brigades under his command.[28] After Loring moved his brigades out of Pocahontas County, Henry Jackson had fewer than two thousand troops to

block more than five thousand federals on Cheat Mountain from invading
the Shenandoah Valley and threatening the Virginia Central Railroad at
Staunton.[29]

Following the botched assault on Cheat Summit, General Henry R. Jackson moved his brigade to the Greenbrier River. In the narrow valley, where
the Parkersburg and Staunton Turnpike crossed the river, he established Camp
Bartow. William Jackson and the Thirty-first Infantry were bivouacked on a
point of land overlooking the intersection of the Greenbank Road and the
turnpike.[30] Jackson took advantage of the momentary lull in action to have
Major Francis Boykin instruct the regiment's company officers in the manual
of arms. The soldiers kept busy building breastworks and digging gun emplacements for the two guns of Anderson's Battery on the high ground above
Jackson's camp.[31]

Around six o'clock on the morning of 3 October 1861 a company of
pickets made up of men from both the Thirty-first Virginia and the Third
Arkansas regiments were fired on by what they thought was a company of
federal skirmishers. For nearly two hours the handful of Confederates fought
the Union soldiers while grudgingly withdrawing nearly a mile from their
original position. As more blue coated soldiers kept appearing from the direction of Cheat Summit, the skirmishers finally realized that they were fighting something much larger than a skirmishing party. The long awaited federal assault on Camp Bartow had finally begun.[32]

The defiant action of the pickets gave General Henry Jackson time to
deploy his undermanned brigade to meet the federal assault. General Jackson placed Colonel William L. Jackson and the Thirty-first Infantry behind
breastworks on the left wing of the Confederate line overlooking the vital
Greenbank road. Colonel Albert Rust and his Third Arkansas Infantry joined
the Thirty-first along with the Ninth Virginia Battalion, a regiment greatly
depleted by illness. The Ninth Battalion's commander, Colonel George
Hansbrough, was ill and unable to command. Captain James A. Robertson
commanded the weakened regiment. General Jackson placed Colonel Rust
in command of the left wing with orders to make certain that Union infantry did not flank his position.[33]

Union General Joseph J. Reynolds started his assault on the Confederate
positions at Camp Bartow with an artillery barrage. The Confederate artillery, outnumbered and deficient in firepower, answered the federal guns with
surprising effect. Around nine-thirty, an hour and a half after the artillery
duel began, the Fourteenth Indiana Infantry regiment commanded by Colonel Nathan Kimball attempted to flank the position manned by Jackson,
Rust and Robertson. Rust ordered his command to lie flat behind their breastworks until he gave the order to stand and fire. The Indiana troops crossed
the river and deployed into a battle line. Just as they began their advance,

Rust ordered his men to stand and give them a volley. The ensuing volley had little effect because the Confederates failed to allow for the downhill angle at which they were shooting. Most of the bullets passed harmlessly over the heads of the Indiana soldiers. However, despite lack of actual damage, the Confederate volley produced panic in the Indiana ranks. They turned and fled back across the Greenbrier without firing a single shot at the Confederates.[34] No further infantry attacks were made against Rust's position during the day, but federal artillery continued to shell the trenches. One solid shot struck near the top of the embankment and dislodged an enormous pile of dirt and mud, which momentarily covered Colonel William L. Jackson completely. The men of Company I of the Thirty-first dug out their colonel and listened with amusement while he raged against the federal artillerists.[35]

The Battle of the Greenbrier lasted until half past two o'clock in the afternoon. The federals had expended huge quantities of ammunition and made no progress in forcing the Confederates out of their positions. Reluctantly General Reynolds ordered a withdrawal. At the end of the day both armies rested on the same ground they had held when the battle began six hours earlier. General Reynolds and General Jackson made inflated claims of success in the Battle of the Greenbrier. Reynolds claimed to have killed and wounded at least three hundred Confederates. Henry Jackson claimed that his men had killed between two and three hundred Unionists. In reality, Reynolds had eight men killed and thirty-five wounded while Jackson reported six men dead and twenty-nine wounded. William L. Jackson reported two men of the Thirty-first Infantry killed and two wounded.[36] Jackson also reported nine members of his regiment missing, but the missing men turned out to be members of the picket squad who had initiated the battle early that morning. These men had been cut off from their lines as they tried to withdraw while holding off Reynolds's entire army. They had spent the day hiding on the mountainside overlooking the battle site. They all returned to camp later that evening.[37]

During the first week of December 1861, the Confederate Army of the Northwest underwent administrative reorganization. Henry R. Jackson resigned command of his brigade to accept an appointment as Major General of Georgia Volunteers and went home to Atlanta.[38] Edward Johnson, colonel of the Twelfth Georgia Infantry, replaced Jackson in command at Camp Bartow.[39] In October, when Robert E. Lee ordered General William Loring to join him in Fayette County to assist General Floyd in the Kanawha Valley, Loring left Colonel William Gilham and the Twenty-first Virginia Infantry in Pocahontas County to occupy the Huntersville line thirty miles south of Camp Bartow. In the reorganization of the Valley District Army in December, Gilham's regiment was ordered to report to General Thomas J. Jackson at Strasburg. The regiment left immediately.[40] On 1 December William L. Jackson was relieved of command of the Thirty-first Virginia Infantry. His replacement was Francis M. Boykin, Major of the Thirty-first Infantry, who had originally recommended Jackson to Robert E. Lee for an appointment as colonel of Virginia Volunteers. [41]

After relinquishing his command, William L. Jackson disappeared during the first three weeks of December 1861. In light of subsequent events, he probably went to Richmond to lobby for the formation of a regiment of western Virginia men who would operate exclusively in northwestern Virginia counties. Jackson's antipathy toward the reorganized government of Virginia at Wheeling and the movement to form a loyalist state west of the Alleghenies at times approached fanaticism. Throughout the war every reference Jackson made to Wheeling authorities or "West" Virginia regiments was prefaced with the word "bogus." Around 20 December, Jackson returned to the Thirty-first Infantry in its camp on top of Allegheny Mountain between the Greenbrier River and Hightown, Highland County. In the interim he had been promoted from lieutenant colonel to full colonel. Jackson remained with the Thirty-first Infantry for only a few days. On 26 December General Edward Johnson assigned Jackson command of the Huntersville line. [42]

THE HUNTERSVILLE LINE

For unknown reasons Jackson did not assume command at Huntersville until mid-January 1862. In the hiatus between Jackson's appointment to command at Huntersville and his appearance at his new post, disaster struck the tiny mountain town. Huntersville, county seat of Pocahontas County, played an important part in Confederate strategy during the first six months of warfare. The small town lay on the Huttonsville-Warm Springs road, fifty miles south of Huttonsville and twenty-five miles north of Warm Springs. The only bridge in the region that crossed the Greenbrier River was located seven miles north of Huntersville at Marlin's Bottom. William Loring established his headquarters at Huntersville when he was placed in command of northwestern Virginia forces after Robert Garnett's death in July 1861. The town became the major depository for army supplies shipped there by Confederate quartermaster Alfred Ward Davis in Lewisburg. When the brigade of Colonel William Gilham was ordered to join General Thomas J. Jackson in the Shenandoah Valley in early December, protection for Huntersville and its tons of supplies for Edward Johnson's army at Camp Allegheny became the responsibility of Pocahontas County militia and partisans.

During the fall and winter of 1861, Federal troops at Huttonsville never penetrated Pocahontas County farther than Big Springs, a small community

Map of the Huntersville Line Commanded by Col. Wm. L. Jackson

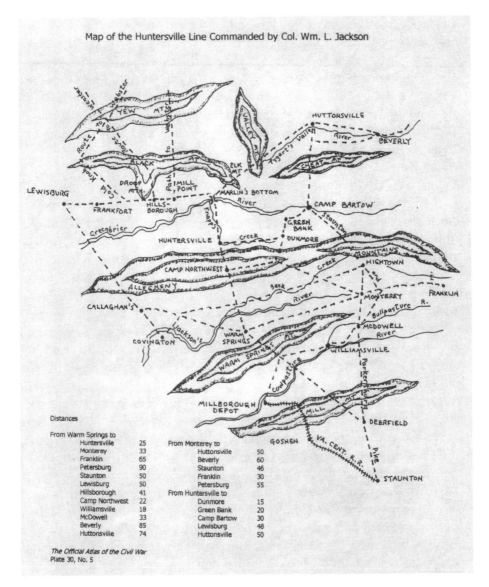

Distances

From Warm Springs to

Huntersville	25
Monterey	33
Franklin	65
Petersburg	90
Staunton	50
Lewisburg	50
Hillsborough	41
Camp Northwest	22
Williamsville	18
McDowell	33
Beverly	85
Huttonsville	74

From Monterey to

Huttonsville	50
Beverly	60
Staunton	46
Franklin	30
Petersburg	55

From Huntersville to

Dunmore	15
Green Bank	20
Camp Bartow	30
Lewisburg	48
Huttonsville	50

The Official Atlas of the Civil War
Plate 30, No. 5

twenty miles north of Huntersville. At the base of Elk Mountain, fifteen miles north of Huntersville, Gilham's men felled trees across the Huttonsville road to forestall any federal movement toward Huntersville and Warm Springs. On top of Elk Mountain, Gilham constructed rifle pits and artillery emplacements with a commanding view of the road. When Gilham's regiment transferred to the Shenandoah Valley, the Elk Mountain camp was abandoned. Local informants advised the federal garrison at Huttonsville in early December that regular Confederate troops guarding the supply depot at Huntersville had pulled out, leaving only militia in their place. Federal commanders jumped at the opportunity. Under the command of Major George Webster of the Twenty-fifth Ohio Infantry, a federal force numbering nearly eight hundred men began an advance on Huntersville on 31 December 1861. Webster's men reached the barricaded section of the road on the evening of 2 January 1862. Leaving the road and advancing over footpaths to the abandoned Confederate positions on top of Elk Mountain, Webster's men descended on the Greenbrier River bridge early in the morning on 3 January.

Word of the federal troops' approach preceded them. Militia and partisan soldiers rushed to the Greenbrier bridge to block the Union advance. Although Gilham's men had dug rifle pits and placed two pieces of artillery around the approaches to the bridge, none of the Pocahontas militia who responded to the emergency knew how to fire the big guns. Webster's men fired one volley at the bridge's nervous defenders, and most of the citizen soldiers fled without returning fire. Webster captured the bridge with no casualties. Webster ran into slight opposition twice during the seven mile dash from the Greenbrier bridge to Huntersville, but each time the handful of Confederate defenders fled when Webster sent flanking parties out to cut off their retreat. When Webster's men poured into Huntersville they found the town deserted and a barn filled with army supplies on fire. The federals ransacked every house in Huntersville and destroyed flour, beef, salt, sugar, coffee, rice, bacon, clothing and other supplies intended for Johnson's army at Camp Allegheny. Two hours after seizing the town, the federal troops left to return to Huttonsville.[43]

A few days after Webster's raid, William Jackson arrived in Huntersville to assume his new command. He found most of the town in ashes and the civilian population in a state of rebellion against the Confederacy. Jackson reported to General Johnson at Camp Allegheny that the commissary had lost property valued at over ten thousand dollars, the quartermaster's office had lost over two thousand dollars worth of goods, and damage to private dwellings in the town amounted to three thousand dollars.[44] A public meeting had been scheduled for 16 January at the courthouse, one of the few buildings in Huntersville still standing. Alfred Ward Davis, Virginia quartermaster from Lewisburg, had been expected to speak at the meeting, but when Davis failed to appear Jackson took his place. An experienced and eloquent orator, Jackson relished the opportunity to address a public gathering. He advised the concerned citizens that their help was essential to prevent a repetition of the 3 January raid. He urged them to form companies of men to keep watch for federal movements toward Pocahontas County and to give early warning of federal incursions to Confederate authorities. He condemned Union soldiers as invaders and traitors to Virginia. He particularly railed against the federal Second Virginia Cavalry, which contributed a company to the Huntersville raiding party. Most of the Union soldiers in the company were western Virginia men. Although the citizens at the public meeting passed a resolution pledging to form early warning companies, Jackson had little confidence in their ability to comply with their resolution. "I am promised such assistance," he wrote to Johnson on 18 January, "but as the county is sparsely settled, with two volunteer companies in the service, I do not expect much assistance from that source."[45]

When Jackson left Camp Allegheny for Huntersville in January, Johnson allowed him to take one company of the Thirty-first Infantry with him. He selected Company F, a group of men from Randolph and Pocahontas counties commanded by Jacob Currence. Jackson chose this company because most of its members lived in neighboring Randolph County and were intimately familiar with the area around Huntersville. Currence's men not only knew all of the roads and trails in the area, they also were familiar with the identity of local unionists. Jackson was determined to suppress union supporters whom he viewed as traitors. In his report to Johnson, Jackson noted:

> *There is considerable disloyalty in the county. The report was in circulation that the Confederate government was willing to treat for peace with the loss of Northwestern Virginia. This I stigmatized as false in the speech which I made. But the fear, while it makes some neutral, makes others false. By some means heretofore, every transaction in the camp has been communicated to the enemy. In the course of my speech I announced that no one except on particular business should come into my lines, and as I had the names of the suspected, none such should return if found inside. I allowed the meeting, as that was necessary, but since, I am enforcing rigid rules.*[46]

Jackson closed his letter to Johnson with a warning about a "Mr. Kerr" who lived near Camp Allegheny. Jackson claimed that local informants had told him that Kerr had been passing information on Confederate strength at Camp Allegheny to federals at Cheat Summit.[47]

William Jackson accepted his assignment to Huntersville, but he did not want to be there. Only a few days after arriving in Huntersville, Jackson wrote to Johnson and related that a Pocahontas civilian whose brother served in the Thirty-first Infantry had told him that most of the men in the regiment intended not to re-enlist when their enlistments expired in May. The civilian told Jackson that the men intended to return to their homes and fight as partisans rather than serve in a regular Confederate unit. "To change this determination is my desire, and to exert myself for the object I should be present with the regiment," Jackson wrote. "Owing to the peculiar relation I have always borne to the regiment, I believe I can do more to procure the re-enlistment desired than anyone else."[48] Evidently Jackson believed that the men of the Thirty-first Infantry owed a personal allegiance to him. He had reasons for believing that his men held him in esteem. He recruited them personally at Beverly, and they held the distinction of being the first regular Confederate regiment organized in northwestern Virginia. He led them on the nightmarish retreat from Laurel Hill and delivered them safely to Monterey with only minimal losses. The regiment's combat record had been laudable if not exceptional.[49] Johnson considered Jackson more valuable in his post at Huntersville, and he left him there in command. Johnson did order three companies of the Twenty-eighth Virginia Infantry to Huntersville and he supplied Jackson with two cavalry companies. Although Jackson wanted more men, he used what he was given to good effect. During his tenure at Huntersville federal forces made no attempt to raid in Pocahontas County. The road to Warm Springs was secure.

AIDE DE CAMP

When the Confederate government reorganized forces in northern Virginia in October 1861, Thomas J. Jackson, already known as "Stonewall," was placed in command of the Valley District Army. Jackson soon discovered that his additional responsibilities required an expanded personal staff. Stonewall Jackson, suspected by many Confederate officials of being an eccentric overachiever with dangerous tendencies to do rash things, was exceptionally cautious in selecting officers to serve him. In interviewing potential staff members, Jackson had a habit of questioning applicants about their personal lives and habits. He was interested only in men who clearly demonstrated intelligence, faithfulness, and industriousness. Furthermore, Jackson required all members of his staff to be willing to get out of bed early in the morning.[50]

Alfred H. Jackson, captain of Company I, Thirty-first Virginia Infantry, was William L. Jackson's first cousin and a first cousin once removed to Thomas J. Jackson. Alfred Jackson was an 1857 graduate of Washington College in Lexington, Virginia. During his three years in Lexington as a student he became intimately acquainted with Thomas Jackson, an instructor at neighboring Virginia Military Institute. Alfred Jackson formed a company known as the Lewis County Rangers at the outbreak of the war in May 1861. William L. Jackson mustered the Lewis Rangers into service with the Thirty-first Virginia Infantry in June 1861. Alfred Jackson, head of his class at Washington College and a successful Weston attorney, met General Thomas J. Jackson's standards as a staff member. On 11 October Thomas Jackson sent a letter to Alfred at Camp Allegheny: "My Dear Alfred: If agreeable to you, please join me at once as a member of my staff. Please give my kindest regards to William L. Jackson."[51] Alfred Jackson resigned his captain's position with Company I, and on 12 November 1861 he was appointed Assistant Adjutant General and assigned to General Jackson's staff.[52] Alfred Jackson served his cousin intelligently, faithfully, and industriously from the beginning of December 1861 until the end of April 1862. During that time he demonstrated a character flaw which General Jackson could not ignore; Alfred Jackson refused to get out of bed early in the morning. In February 1862, General Jackson alerted Alfred Jackson's brother-in-law, Jonathan M. Bennett, of Alfred's tendency to oversleep.[53] Shortly afterwards, Alfred Jackson was asked to resign from General Jackson's staff. General Jackson then offered the Assistant Adjutant General position to Bennett, but Bennett had just been elected to a second term as Virginia State Auditor. He had no desire to trade his executive position in Richmond for the uncertain rigors of campaigning with Stonewall Jackson.[54] General Jackson selected staff member Major Robert Dabney, a Presbyterian theologian, to replace Alfred Jackson as chief of staff.[55] Dabney's appointment did not alleviate General Jackson's need for experienced and reliable staff members. As his army increased the frequency and scope of its operations in the Shenandoah Valley, Jackson remembered his cousin whom he thought at one time would restore the dignity and honor once accorded the Jackson family in northwestern Virginia. He decided to offer a position on his staff to William L. Jackson, but events began unfolding in the Valley in March 1862, which required Stonewall's full attention. Appointing William Jackson to his staff was delayed.

Boredom and frustration plagued William L. Jackson during his tour of duty guarding the Huntersville line. In what amounted to little more than garrison duty, Jackson had no opportunity to expend his considerable energy in campaigns against federal positions or to satisfy his ambition for promotion and subsequent high command. The force under his command at Huntersville was inadequate to mount offensive operations against Union positions in Tygart's Valley. After their January raid on Huntersville, federal commanders were content to remain close to their bases at Elkwater, Huttonsville and Beverly.

While William Jackson fretted over lack of action in his narrow theater of the war, farther east his cousin Thomas Jackson had more action than he could handle. On 23 March 1862 Jackson engaged Union forces at Kernstown south of Winchester. The Battle of Kernstown occurred spontaneously, and results of the battle demonstrated lack of planning. Jackson's forces, including his beloved Stonewall Brigade, were forced to retreat after a chaotic daylong battle.[56] Confusion in delivering and interpreting orders played a major role in Stonewall Jackson's defeat at Kernstown. Following the battle he decided to recruit some new staff members whose reliability and integrity met his exacting standards. One of the men he contacted was his cousin, William L. Jackson.

No record exists documenting whether or not William L. Jackson solicited an appointment to Thomas J. Jackson's staff. Stonewall Jackson carefully considered his staff appointments. He wanted men around him who would execute his commands efficiently and promptly. He also wanted staff members who possessed sufficient initiative and judgment to take control of any battlefield situation where decisiveness was necessary.[57] Although William L. Jackson had not achieved distinction on the battlefield during the first year of the war, he had performed efficiently. His leadership during the disastrous retreat of Robert Garnett's army from Laurel Hill in July 1861 impressed General Jackson. William Jackson had guided his regiment through difficult terrain under nearly impossible conditions and emerged with the regiment intact. More importantly to Stonewall Jackson, William had kept his men moving despite the most adverse of conditions. Stonewall had firsthand knowledge of William's remarkable achievement from his former adjutant, Alfred H. Jackson, who had commanded a company of the Thirty-first Infantry during the retreat from Laurel Hill. Whether or not William Jackson asked Stonewall Jackson to be assigned to his staff, Jackson did recommend his cousin for a position. On 4 June 1862 William L. Jackson was appointed volunteer aide-de-camp to General Thomas J. Jackson.[58]

William Jackson reported to his new assignment at Jackson's headquarters in the tiny Rockingham County community of Port Republic. He started on his duties as an administrator immediately. Only two days after his appointment as aide-de-camp became official, William issued his first general order under his own name. Issued from "Headquarters, Valley District," and dated 6 June 1862, the terse message read:

> *The commanding general directs that your trains with baggage be sent to the rear to-morrow morning at dawn; the troops to remain in camp. If you have not one day's rations already cooked, have it done at once and put in the haversacks of the men.*
>
> **Wm. L. Jackson**
> **Colonel and aide-de-camp**[59]

General Jackson had established his headquarters in the home of Dr. George Kemper at the upper end of Port Republic's main street. His army was camped on the north side of the South Fork of the Shenandoah River. A narrow bridge across the river at the end of Port Republic's main street linked the general and his army. Around nine o'clock on the morning of 8 June, William L. Jackson and other aides were standing with General Jackson in Kemper's front yard when federal troops suddenly appeared at the lower end of town and opened fire on them. Guards around Kemper's house returned the fire while the general and his staff collected their horses. Disdaining the flurry of bullets whistling past him, Stonewall Jackson mounted his horse and rode directly at the federal troops who were between him and the bridge. William Jackson rode beside, him followed by the rest of the staff. Miraculously, neither of the Jacksons was hit as they charged for the bridge. Two of the staff members were captured, but the rest of the staff safely crossed the bridge. The Jacksons and other aides rode to the top of a small hill overlooking Port Republic. General Jackson wanted to know what the federal troops in the town were planning, and he sent Colonel Jackson back down to the bridge to scout the situation. As William Jackson sat on his horse at the north end of the bridge, federal troops appeared suddenly at the south end and fired at him through the bridge. None of the shots took effect, and Colonel Jackson returned to report to General Jackson that the Yankees apparently planned to attack.[60]

The Battle of Port Republic on 8 June and the Battle of Cross Keys the following day resulted in victories for Stonewall Jackson's army. Reports of the battles did not make clear what role William L. Jackson played during the action, but in Jackson's report on the Port Republic battles he cited William L. Jackson for "valuable assistance in the transmission of orders."[61] With a rank superior to Stonewall's other staff members, William Jackson may have coordinated the transmission of orders rather than carry orders himself.

The battles at Port Republic and Cross Keys were victories for Stonewall Jackson's army, but not to the extent the general wished. He had hoped to inflict crushing defeats on the Union armies of John C. Fremont and James S. Shields, who had been trying to trap him between their two armies since the Battle of Kernstown in March. Not only had Jackson failed to crush either army, he barely eluded personal capture. Nevertheless, Jackson believed that he had the federals in the Shenandoah Valley where he wanted them — out of the valley. Jackson had spent the entire month of May and the first two weeks of June distracting three federal armies to prevent their reinforcing Union General George B. McClellan on the Virginia peninsula. McClellan had landed at Hampton Roads, Virginia on 4 April with over one hundred thousand troops. Opposing him was a Confederate force under General Joseph Johnston consisting of around sixty thousand men. McClellan had moved along the James River at a snail's pace, constantly appealing to war planners in Washington to send him reinforcements from the Shenandoah Valley. Jackson had prevented reinforcements from reaching McClellan, and his series of victories at McDowell, Front Royal, Winchester, Port Republic, and Cross Keys had forced Union strategists in Washington to withdraw all forces from the Shenandoah Valley to guard against a possible attack on the national capital. With most Union forces out of the Shenandoah Valley, Jackson was free to move his army to Richmond. [62]

The first engagement of the Peninsular Campaign did not occur until 31 May at Fair Oaks. The battle was a draw, but General Johnston was wounded and replaced by Robert E. Lee. McClellan's and Lee's armies continued to probe at each other during the first two weeks of June, while Stonewall Jackson was fighting Shields and Fremont at Port Republic and Cross Keys in the Shenandoah Valley. Lee concluded that he did not have enough men to stop a determined assault by McClellan, and on 8 June he wrote to Jackson and asked him to bring his army to Richmond if possible. Since Jackson's successful Valley Campaign had been conducted partly to make such a move possible, Jackson prepared to march to Richmond. To avoid alerting federal spies that he was moving his army from the Valley, Jackson maintained almost complete secrecy of his intentions. The only member of Jackson's staff who knew about the move to Richmond before the army began to fall in was William L. Jackson. On the evening of 17 June General Jackson distributed secret orders to his brigade commanders to start the army moving at midnight eastward to Waynesboro. At ten o'clock that night, the general mounted his horse and rode to Staunton, twenty miles west of the army's encampment at Weyer's Cave, Augusta County. Of his staff members, he took only William L. Jackson with him to help plan logistics of the move to Richmond.[63] Much to their disgust, the remainder of the staff spent the next day looking for their general.[64] During the long march to Richmond, William Jackson often spent the night wherever his commander chose to sleep.[65]

William L. Jackson accompanied Stonewall Jackson throughout the grueling Peninsula Campaign from 25 June to 1 July 1862. Like Jackson's other aides, William spent his time dodging artillery shells and sweltering in the heat and humidity of the Virginia peninsula. The campaign ended with Stonewall Jackson's reputation damaged due to his presumed failure to move his army quickly and efficiently at critical times. Blame for Jackson's failure to perform to expectations in the Peninsula again focused on the inability of his staff to transmit orders expediently and accurately. The most serious breakdown in communication between Jackson and his staff occurred at Gaines's Mill on 27 June 1862. In an inexplicable series of miscommunications, Jackson's army took wrong roads, misunderstood orders, and arrived late at the front. The most critical error occurred when Stonewall entrusted his most important message of the day— the order for generals Chase Whiting and Sidney Winder to bring their divisions forward to launch an assault on federal positions at Gaines's Mill— to Major John Harman, Jackson's quartermaster. Harman, unaccustomed to carrying verbal orders on a battlefield, informed Whiting and Winder that General Jackson wished them to remain where they were. The resulting delay and confusion prevented Lee's forces from quickly overwhelming an undermanned federal army at Gaines's Mill. Lee's forces suffered huge casualties at Gaines's Mill, many of which would not have occurred had Stonewall Jackson's divisions been in place on time. Why Jackson entrusted such an important message to a staff member with no experience in transmitting orders never was explained.[66] Evidently trusted and reliable staff members such as William Jackson, Sandie Pendleton and Henry Kyd Douglas were not available to carry the critical orders to Whiting and Winder, but records of the battle did not indicate where they were or what they were doing.[67] Chief of staff Major Henry Dabney commented later that the near disaster was the result of "wretched, disjoined staff service."[68]

Despite Stonewall Jackson's disappointing performance during the Peninsula Campaign, when word reached Robert E. Lee on 12 July that yet another federal army had appeared in the Shenandoah Valley and was inching southward he did not hesitate to detach Jackson's forces from his army and send Jackson to deal with the new threat. Due to battle casualties and illness Jackson's army amounted to only eleven thousand men, eight thousand less than he had brought with him to Richmond. Facing him in the Valley was a new federal army of fifty thousand soldiers under the command of General John Pope. Before Jackson could dispatch John Pope, he had to deal with an old nemesis, Nathaniel Banks.

On 9 August 1862, just three weeks after leaving Richmond, Stonewall Jackson's army collided with a detachment of Pope's new Army of Virginia at the intersection where roads from Madison Courthouse, Orange Courthouse, and Culpeper converged, near a low hill the locals called Slaughter's Mountain. Because a small creek known as Cedar Run curled around the north base of Slaughter's Mountain, the battle that occurred there became the Battle of Cedar Mountain. As was the case in many of the battles fought by Stonewall Jackson, the battle of Cedar Mountain developed in a series of small confrontations, each of which grew larger as more troops responded to the sound of the guns, until finally a major conflagration exploded. Jackson won the day only because of the timely arrival of reinforcements from Ambrose Powell Hill.[69]

William L. Jackson again was cited by his commanding general for his efficient conduct in transmitting orders under fire.[70] However, the hard fought victory was achieved at high personal cost to both Thomas and William

Jackson. Alfred H. Jackson, Stonewall's former chief of staff and a company commander in the Thirty-first Infantry under William, had returned to the Thirty-first Infantry after resigning from Stonewall's staff. He had been promoted to Lieutenant Colonel of the regiment and was seriously wounded at the height of the action at Cedar Mountain. His wound never healed and he died from its effects after being bedfast for nearly a year.[71] Another close associate of both Jacksons who suffered serious injuries was Richard Snowden Andrews, Stonewall Jackson's artillery division chief and a pre-war business partner of William Jackson. Andrews recovered from his extraordinary injuries and later returned to his artillery unit.[72]

The remainder of William Jackson's service as aide-de-camp to Stonewall Jackson passed without remarkable occurrences. Three weeks after the Battle of Cedar Mountain, William was cited by Stonewall for efficient conduct at the Second Battle of Bull Run.[73] He accompanied Jackson throughout the Antietam Campaign in September 1862, and he was with Jackson at Fredericksburg on 13 December 1862. When Jackson's army established its winter camp along the Rappahannock River in late December 1862, William Jackson asked for leave to go to Richmond on a military mission. Approval by Thomas J. Jackson of a request for leave during the winter of 1862-1863 was a rare event. Jackson believed that once a man was in the army he should stay in the army until the army's work was completed. He set an example by never taking a leave from the army from the day he left for his first assignment at Harper's Ferry in April 1861. Jackson offended several of his officers during January 1863 by refusing their requests for leave.[74] However, Stonewall apparently granted leave to William Jackson. During the first week in January 1863, William was in Richmond making the rounds of politicians' offices.

INDEPENDENT COMMAND

From the outset of the Civil War, William Lowther Jackson wanted an independent command in western Virginia. In his discussions with Francis Boykin, the energetic and far-sighted organizer of Virginia militia units in the period between Virginia's secession and the invasion of Virginia by Ohio troops, Jackson expressed his willingness to take charge of Virginia Volunteers in the Parkersburg area. Jackson sought a command like the one given to George A. Porterfield at Grafton. Although Jackson had no military background, his administrative experience as a Virginia legislator, commonwealth attorney, and circuit judge probably convinced him that he had the ability to manage a brigade. Military experience could be learned in the field. William Jackson's absence from Richmond during the critical month of April 1861 probably cost him an opportunity to secure a general's commission like those

of his political colleagues Henry Wise and John Floyd. Considering the ca-
lamitous careers of Wise and Floyd as Confederate generals, Jackson probably was fortunate not to have been appointed to high rank early in the war.

In December 1861, Jackson had been promoted from lieutenant colonel
to full colonel.[75] His assignment to command the Huntersville line, while
important to overall Confederate strategy in western Virginia, did not satisfy
Jackson's desire to take charge of an effort to regain Virginia's control of her
western counties. As part of Edward Johnson's brigade, Jackson commanded
a mere skeleton force at Huntersville. His responsibility simply was to scout
the Huttonsville-Warm Springs road and report any federal movement in
the direction of Warm Springs. He did not have sufficient manpower to
mount any offensive movements against federal garrisons at Elkwater and
Huttonsville. In the event of a federal advance on the road, Jackson would
have been obligated to send for reinforcements from Johnson at Camp Allegheny. In his spare time Jackson tried to convince civilians along the
Huntersville line that the Confederate government in Richmond had not
abandoned them. Isolated in a backwater outpost on the Virginia line of
defense, Jackson was not so certain that Confederate authorities had not
forgotten him. Jackson had jumped at the opportunity to serve on Thomas
J. Jackson's staff in the spring of 1862.

William Jackson served on Stonewall Jackson's staff from June 1862 until
January 1863. During that time he accompanied the Confederacy's most
accomplished and nearly legendary field commander on some of his most
famous campaigns. Jackson was beside Stonewall at Port Republic and Cross
Keys when he exulted in victory, and he accompanied him through the dis-
mal days of the Seven Days Battle on Virginia's peninsula. He stood by his
cousin and commander during critical victories at Cedar Mountain, Groveton,
Bull Run, and Chantilly, and he was present with Jackson on the right at
Fredericksburg when the Army of Northern Virginia crushed the Army of
the Potomac under Burnside. During the six months William Jackson was
associated with his famous cousin, he learned much about Stonewall's philosophy of war. Stonewall Jackson believed that the surest road to success lay
in mystifying, misleading, and surprising the enemy. He believed that once
the enemy had been overcome and put to flight, he should be pursued re-
lentlessly and destroyed so he could not recoup and fight again another
day. Stonewall also avoided fighting against heavy odds. Instead, he recommended that a wise commander would seek out the weakest part of his enemy and crush it, then move on to the next weakest part until the enemy had
been annihilated in piecemeal fashion. The only rule for cavalry, Jackson
maintained, was to pursue a retreating enemy. If the enemy turned to fight,
the infantry had the responsibility to do the fighting.[76]

William Jackson was an attentive student, but by January 1863 he still had no command to demonstrate how well he had learned his lessons. Records do not indicate that Stonewall Jackson ever considered appointing William Jackson to command one of the units included in his corps, despite numerous openings that occurred during the time William served on Stonewall's staff. Nothing in Stonewall's correspondence indicated that he lacked confidence in William Jackson as a field officer. A more likely explanation for William Jackson's lack of promotion to command in Stonewall's corps lay in the fact that Stonewall almost certainly knew of William's desire to command a brigade in western Virginia. Stonewall probably regarded his cousin as an ideal commander for a northwestern Virginia regiment or brigade due to his pre-war popularity in the region. Events in Richmond in January and February 1863 created the possibility of William Jackson finally fulfilling his ambition for a western brigade. It was probably for that reason that Stonewall Jackson granted his cousin a furlough to go to Richmond in January 1863, when no one else in his corps could get leave for any reason. Whatever the circumstances that persuaded the duty-obsessed Stonewall Jackson to approve leave for William Jackson, William was in Richmond through January and February 1863.

From his days as a Virginia legislator, state auditor, and lieutenant governor, William L. Jackson had many political contacts in Richmond. In particular he had strong friendships with two men who wielded extraordinary power in the Confederate capital: Virginia State Auditor Jonathan M. Bennett, and Confederate Secretary of State Robert M. T. Hunter. Jackson was also personally acquainted with Virginia Governor John Letcher. However, the pre-war Jackson-Letcher friendship had become strained since the beginning of the war. Letcher's efforts in 1861 to keep Virginia in the Union and his lukewarm support for secession did not find favor with a firebrand secessionist such as William L. Jackson. Despite Letcher's appointment of Jackson as lieutenant colonel of Virginia Volunteers in May 1861, Jackson believed that Letcher was responsible for denying him an important field command in late 1861 and early 1862.

Jonathan M. Bennett was a native of Lewis County. Ten years older than William Jackson, Bennett had been involved in Lewis County politics and the business community of northwestern Virginia since the late 1830s. In 1846 Bennett married Margaret Elizabeth Jackson, a daughter of George W. Jackson and a first cousin of William Lowther Jackson. Lewis County sent him to the Virginia Assembly in 1852, where he worked tirelessly to bring economic improvements to western Virginia. Bennett was a Democrat, but he was not a hard line party supporter in the William Jackson mold. He was not a supporter of slavery, although he owned slaves. States rights, the rallying cry of southern Democrats in the 1850s, received only his token support. In the Virginia Assembly, Bennett worked closely with Jackson, the delegate from Wood and Pleasants counties, to push the charter for the Northwest Virginia Railroad through the legislature. A moment of discord arose in 1852 over Jackson's outspoken support for the re-election of Robert M. T. Hunter to the United States Senate. Because of Hunter's persistent opposition to internal improvements in western Virginia, his candidacy did not find favor with Bennett. Bennett was one of only half a dozen delegates who refused to vote for Hunter. [77]

Most often the two assemblymen from the northwest supported each other. In 1855 Jackson worked for Bennett's nomination as lieutenant governor of Virginia on the Democratic ticket with gubernatorial candidate Henry A. Wise.[78] Although Bennett lost that political battle, in 1857 he returned to Richmond as Virginia's State Auditor. In 1860 Bennett used his considerable political influence in central western Virginia to help William Jackson win election as judge of the Virginia Court of Appeals. The candidate Jackson defeated in the judicial election was Mathew Edmiston, a bitter political enemy of Bennett.[79] When William Jackson appeared in Richmond in January 1863 seeking authority to form a regiment in western Virginia, he went to Jonathan M. Bennett first. He could not have chosen a more propitious time to approach the State Auditor with his problem.

In January 1863, Bennett was embroiled in a controversy concerning the Virginia State Line corps. Created by the Virginia Assembly in May 1862, the purpose of the Virginia State Line was to recover the western part of Virginia from federal control and to protect the salt mines in the Kanawha Valley. Former governor John B. Floyd resigned from Confederate service and had authority to raise five volunteer regiments of two thousand men each. Only men between the ages of thirty-five and forty-five and those under eighteen years of age were eligible to enlist in the State Line regiments.[80] The Assembly appropriated over two million dollars to finance the organization and maintenance of this state army. The appropriation of state monies to finance the Virginia State Line caught the attention of the State Auditor, Jonathan M. Bennett. The proposed ten thousand man Virginia State Line corps did not appear to be cost effective, and Bennett suspected that the original two million dollars appropriated for the corps would fall far short of actual costs. In December 1862, Bennett submitted a report to the Assembly compiled by a committee of accountants which calculated the actual cost of maintaining one soldier for one year in the Virginia State Line to be seven hundred and ninety-three dollars. If the State Line achieved its goal of enlisting ten thousand men, the expected annual cost to the state of Virginia would be nearly eight million dollars. Bennett asked the legislature to abolish the State Line Corps and relinquish the companies already recruited to the Confederate States government. Despite editorials in the *Richmond Examiner* castigating Bennett as an "odorous emanation of a bit of carrion, which we hope to see one day disinterred and affixed to the gibbet where it belongs," Bennett did not waver from his determination to shed the state of its responsibility for the Virginia State Line. In February 1863, the Assembly voted to authorize Governor Letcher to transfer without delay the Virginia State Line troops to the national army.[81]

Word of the impending dissolution of the Virginia State Line provided William L. Jackson with the opportunity for which he had been waiting. Before leaving Stonewall Jackson's camp for Richmond, Jackson persuaded the officers of the Twenty-fifth Virginia Infantry, a regiment with which Jackson had been closely associated since the beginning of the war, to sign a letter recommending Jackson for command of any regiment formed from the dissolved Virginia State Line.[82] When Jackson arrived in Richmond he visited the offices of two prominent Trans-Allegheny politicians, Charles W. Russell, a member of the Confederate Congress from Tyler County,[83] and Thomas S. Haymond, former Brigadier General of the Third Division of the Virginia Militia and a member of the Virginia Military Advisory Council.[84] Haymond's support was critical. As a member of Virginia's Advisory Council on the conduct of the war, he had a close working relationship with Confederate Secretary of War James Seddon and Judah Benjamin, Secretary of State for the Confederacy.[85] Both Russell and Haymond gave Jackson letters supporting him as commander of a western Virginia regiment created from the Virginia State Line.[86] With these endorsements, Jackson visited Jonathan M. Bennett and presented his case for the creation of a new Trans-Allegheny regiment composed of the companies from the soon to be dissolved Virginia State Line. Bennett and Jackson visited Confederate Secretary of War James Seddon and explained the possibilities and potential of a new regiment permanently stationed in western Virginia. On 17 February 1863 Seddon's office issued a directive:

> *Authority is hereby granted to William L. Jackson to raise a regiment for the Provisional Army within the lines of the enemy in Northwestern Virginia; the same, when completed, to be mustered into the service of the Confederate States, and the muster rolls forwarded to this office.*[87]

William L. Jackson had his regiment. All he lacked were soldiers to fill its ranks, and the Virginia Assembly soon would make numerous soldiers available for Jackson to recruit.

MOUNTAIN SOLDIERS

The Virginia Assembly dissolved the Virginia State Line regiments on 31 March 1863. Governor Letcher wrote to Secretary of War Seddon that most of Floyd's troops had gone home and only one or two hundred soldiers remained to form a new regiment.[88] Governor Letcher underestimated William L. Jackson's determination to form a cavalry regiment of western Virginia men. Jackson had been in the field for at least one month enlisting State Line companies for his new cavalry regiment prior to the Assembly's transferal of Virginia State Line troops to Confederate Service. On the same day that the Assembly abolished the State Line, Jackson wrote to General Samuel Jones, commander of the Department of Western Virginia, informing him that he had raised "eleven or twelve" companies for his regiment.[89] Most Virginia regiments contained only ten companies of one hundred men per company. Since Jackson reported that he had raised "eleven or twelve" companies, he already was working on organizing a second cavalry regiment that would become the Twentieth Virginia Cavalry in August 1863.

Jackson recruited seasoned and hardened veterans for the Nineteenth Cavalry. All of his recruits were veterans of the Virginia State Line, and most of them had served in partisan ranger companies prior to the organization of the State Line regiments. Nearly all of the soldiers were natives of the central counties of northwestern Virginia. These men had not been subjected to rigid military discipline, even while serving in Floyd's State Line regiments. The companies and their captains were accustomed to acting independently, often without orders. During their service as part of the Virginia State Line, Floyd complained to the Secretary of War's office that he could not get an accurate accounting of the number of men actually under his command. When the Assembly abolished the State Line the numbers of troops affected by the dissolution of the regiments was unknown to Virginia authorities.

Between the end of February and the middle of March 1863, William Jackson recruited the ten companies which would comprise the Nineteenth Virginia Cavalry. Eight of the companies had served previously as part of the Third Virginia State Line regiment. One company captained by Jacob Marshall of Randolph county, claimed service with the First Virginia State Line. A second company, led by William L. McNeel of Pocahontas County, had been attached to the Second State Line regiment. The companies of Marshall and McNeel joined Jackson's new regiment with conditions attached. Both companies had been in the field since the summer of 1861. Although officially attached to the command of John B. Floyd, neither served under the direction of any commander other than their company captains. Both companies operated in their home counties, Marshall in Randolph and McNeel in Pocahontas. Apart from occasional skirmishing with federal scouting parties, they had served primarily as scouts reporting on federal troop movements along the Parkersburg and Staunton Turnpike and the Huttonsville-Huntersville Pike. All of the men in the two companies were mounted, some on horses brought from home when the war began, others on horses captured from United States Army herds or confiscated from suspected unionist civilians. Marshall explained that unique circumstances applied to his and McNeel's companies in a letter to Secretary of War James Seddon on 14 February 1864. "My company," Marshall wrote:

> *was principally formed and organized for the purpose of scouting the roads leading to Beverly, on the right of Gen. Loring's Command then on the Kanawha line, likewise to be used as a police guard in the counties of Bath, Pocahontas & Highland counties. The company was used for this purpose until Col. Jackson came with authority to recruit a command to operate on this the Huntersville line. My company agreed to join his command. When the 19th regt. was ready to be organized we agreed to get into the regt. with the understanding and promise from Col. Jackson that as soon as other companies could be organized to supply our places in the 19th Regt. that Capt. McNeels Co. and my company should be detached or taken out of the Regt.[90]*

The other eight companies recruited by William Jackson for service with the Nineteenth Virginia Cavalry included two companies of men mostly from Roane County, one each of soldiers drawn largely from Marion and Kanawha counties, and four companies composed almost entirely of men from Braxton, Gilmer and Webster counties.

Two of Jackson's companies enjoyed reputations of infamous notoriety. A company captained by George Downs of Calhoun County had been in the field since the summer of 1861 under the name "Moccasin Rangers." Under the direction of Downs, the Moccasin Rangers maintained a reign of terror throughout Calhoun and Roane counties during the autumn of 1861 and the spring of 1862. The partisans fought against companies of the Eleventh Virginia Infantry (USA) in Roane and Calhoun counties, and pillaged and terrorized the civilian population.[91] Captured at Big Bend, Calhoun County, in July 1862, Downs spent two months as a prisoner of war. Exchanged in September 1862, Downs enrolled his company in the Third Virginia State Line.[92] George Downs and his company was the first company William Jackson recruited for the Nineteenth Cavalry. They were organized as Company A, George Downs, Captain, and Jackson reported that he had mustered them into his regiment for Confederate service on 1 March 1863.[93]

The second company recruited by Jackson for the Nineteenth Cavalry enjoyed a reputation for brigandage second to none. The company was organized in Braxton County during June 1861 under the leadership of John S. Sprigg, son of a prominent miller near Sutton. Sprigg's command competed with another Braxton County partisan company led by Salt Lick Creek farmer, Andrew Jackson Chewning[94]. Both partisan bands roamed the countryside in Braxton, Nicholas and Webster counties, seizing private property ostensibly in the name of the Confederacy, and harassing Union outposts in Sutton, Bulltown and Summersville. In December 1861, the commands of Sprigg and Chewning cooperated in a raid on Sutton which resulted in the destruction by fire of a large part of the town.[95] When the Virginia State Line was formed in the summer of 1862, Sprigg enlisted his company with the Third Regiment. Chewning and his small group joined Sprigg's company, but Chewning's men continued to call him "captain" and often conducted raids independent of Sprigg's authority as the commissioned captain of the company. When Jackson enlisted Sprigg's company in the Nineteenth Cavalry on 7 March 1863 as Company B, Sprigg was elected captain and Chewning served as the company's first sergeant. When Sprigg resigned his command in September 1864, Chewning replaced him as captain of Company B.[96] A federal raiding party captured John Sprigg and Marshall Triplett, a captain in the Twenty-second Virginia Infantry, at Callaghan's Station in Alleghany County in May 1862. Sprigg and Triplett became objects of a political debate with potentially serious repercussions. Union authorities charged the two men with being bushwhackers not enlisted in regular military commands, and threatened to hang Sprigg and Triplett as common criminals. Virginia Governor John Letcher came to their defense and claimed that both men were commissioned officers in Virginia Volunteer forces. Before the issue was resolved, Confederate authorities selected two Union prisoners among captives held in Richmond to hang in retaliation if Sprigg and Triplett were executed. George McClellan and Robert E. Lee exchanged hostile letters, and Abraham Lincoln intervened personally. Neither Sprigg nor Triplett were hanged, but they spent six months in federal military prisons until exchanged in December 1862.[97]

Company B typified the composition and character of the men who served under William L. Jackson in the Nineteenth Virginia Cavalry. During the two years that Company B existed, twelve mountain counties of western Virginia contributed soldiers. Seventy-five percent of the troops came from Braxton and Webster counties. Before the war all of these men who served in Company B, including its captain, were farmers or farmhands. Most of them were uneducated, and many existing documents, which required signatures, were signed with marks. None of the men who served in Company B wrote diaries or journals while they served in the Nineteenth Cavalry, and none of them published post-war memoirs. Many of the Braxton and Webster men who served in Company B were related either by blood or by marriage.

Most of the Braxton and Webster men in Company B served for the entire four year period of the war, first as the Braxton Volunteers, then as Company B of the Third Virginia State Line, and finally as Company B of the Nineteenth Virginia Cavalry. While the larger issues of the Civil War may not have been recognized by the Braxton and Webster men, all of them probably believed that they were defending their families, homes, and property from northerners who wanted to take these things from them. David Poe of Taylor County, a member of the Twentieth Virginia Cavalry also organized by William L. Jackson, began his Civil War memoirs in 1911 with the statement, "The beginning of the Civil War in Northwestern Virginia . . . was brought about by a threatened invasion of several thousand troops from the states of Ohio and Indiana into that part of Virginia."[98] Men in central West Virginia responded to the "threatened invasion" by volunteering to fight in Virginia state forces. Recruiting announcements influenced them with inflammatory rhetoric. George Hansbrough's recruiting poster circulated throughout Taylor and Barbour counties in April 1861 appealed to both patriotism and fear:

> War is upon us. Virginia has been driven from the Union formed by our fathers and so long cherished by their descendants. She has now no other alternative but to make common cause with her sister States of the South. Lincoln is sending New England soldiers to Norfolk, Alexandria, and Harper's Ferry. Men of Taylor, arouse, from your torpor. Show the world that the spirit of '76 still burns in your bosoms. Come forward and enlist as Volunteers for the defence of the State that gave you birth. Our brothers east of the Mountains are gathering for the fray. O, let us not be laggards when danger menaces the liberties of our Country, the lives of our citizens, the sanctity of our hearths and homes, and the safety of our wives and little ones.[99]

Braxton and Webster County soldiers felt obligated to protect their families and farms from what they considered to be an invasion by foreigners. They had a sense of duty to their native state not shared by secessionists in all regions of western Virginia.[100] They were willing to fight in defense of Virginia as a whole, but they preferred repelling Yankee invaders from northwestern Virginia. Impassioned pleas such as George Hansbrough's recruiting poster appealed to central western Virginia farm boys and raised issues they understood. Although they were willing to travel to the Shenandoah Valley to fight, when western Virginia soldiers learned in advance that their regiment had been ordered to Maryland or Pennsylvania, desertions increased at alarming rates. Often when the regiment returned to locations near their homes, many of the deserters returned to their companies. Because of William Jackson's constant need for soldiers to fill his regiments, disciplinary action was seldom taken against men who had been absent without leave. This independent and casual approach to military service kept many Braxton and Webster men in the field long after other companies of the Nineteenth

Cavalry abandoned the cause and went home. Of the one hundred and eight men from Braxton and Webster counties who served in Company B, only eight were listed on company rolls as deserters between 1863 and 1865. However, nearly all of them at various times were absent without leave, some for extended periods of time. None of them surrendered at Appomattox, and only nineteen of them accepted paroles at the end of the war.[101]

The men recruited by William Jackson to serve in the Nineteenth Cavalry possessed one attitude that caused Jackson problems throughout the regiment's career. The soldiers possessed an extremely independent approach to military discipline, often to the detriment of battle plans devised by Jackson. Company captains often disregarded orders from Jackson or interpreted orders to fit their own preconceived ideas of a course of action. On several occasions entire companies left camp without leave and returned to their homes for provisions and to check the well being of their families. Usually such massive absences were explained as independent scouting missions. If William Jackson was aware that his men used scouting mission assignments to return to their homes for lengthy visits, his reports on his companies' activities never indicated prior knowledge. On other occasions companies raided federal outposts or homes of unionist sympathizers without prior knowledge of their colonel. Straggling plagued Jackson after every major operation involving the Nineteenth Cavalry. The fact that the men nearly always returned to their regiment after visits home or straggling during a march finally forced Jackson to surrender to the inevitable. By late 1864, the colonel of the Nineteenth Cavalry encouraged his troops to go home at their leisure and re-equip themselves for the spring campaign.

An attitude of independence particularly prevailed among the Braxton and Webster soldiers of Company B. Union scouting parties captured numerous members of Company B between 1863 and 1865 at their homes during times when the Nineteenth Cavalry was involved in actions far from Braxton or Webster counties. S. W. N. Feamster of the Fourteenth Virginia Cavalry recounted one typical example of independence by a Webster County soldier in a 1908 memoir. Feamster accompanied Robert E. Lee on his trip from Cheat Mountain to join Wise's command in the Kanawha Valley in September 1861. At Frankford, Greenbrier County, Lee expressed interest in knowing the latest news from Sewell Mountain. Feamster noticed Thomas Reynolds, a volunteer scout from Webster County, in the camp. Feamster knew Reynolds personally and knew that he had been employed to scout for General Wise. Certain that Reynolds could update Lee on events at Sewell Mountain, Feamster called out to Reynolds to join him and Lee. When Reynolds approached them, Lee, without waiting for an introduction, asked Reynolds for news from Sewell Mountain. Reynolds, who had been ordered to report only to General William Loring, asked Lee, "Is that any of your business?" Feamster experienced difficulty convincing Reynolds that activities at Sewell Mountain were indeed Robert E. Lee's business. Reynolds explained that he was reluctant to communicate any intelligence about military operations to a man he did not know personally.[102]

5

A WESTERN VIRGINIA REGIMENT

William Lowther Jackson had a single goal in mind when he envisioned the formation of a cavalry regiment; he wished to recover northwestern Virginia for the Confederacy. He intended to accomplish his goal by recruiting a regiment manned by northwestern Virginians whose home territory was occupied by Union forces. Jackson believed that a regiment of northwestern Virginia men would fight harder and more effectively to reclaim their homes than would troops from eastern Virginia or other states. He planned to go on the offensive with his home grown regiment and destroy Unionist influence among northwestern Virginians. The feasibility of taking offensive action against federal soldiers and unionist civilians had been demonstrated in August and September 1862 by Albert G. Jenkins, Jackson's brigade commander. Jenkins had led five hundred and fifty cavalrymen on a reconnaisance raid through the central counties of northwestern Virginia and into Ohio. He had encountered only token resistance, and William Jackson, among other Confederate commanders in the region, believed that federal authority in the western Virginia region had weakened fatally for unionists.[1] Jenkins, a former United States Congressman from Virginia, and Jackson, a former lieutenant governor of the state, were strongly opposed to the Virginia government in Wheeling and the movement to form the new state of West Virginia. In reports submitted to superiors Jenkins and Jackson always prefaced any reference to the loyalist Restored Government of Virginia and Union military organizations designated as "Virginia" regiments with the word "bogus." [2]

William L. Jackson was not the only Confederate officer with ambitions of recovering western Virginia for Virginia and the Confederacy. Thomas J. Jackson had sought command of the northwestern Virginia theater at the beginning of the war, but had lost the appointment to Robert S. Garnett. Some western Virginia politicians believed that the Confederate government's failure to appoint Jackson to the western command cost the Confederacy control of the region.[3] Despite his disappointment at not receiving the northwestern Virginia command, Thomas Jackson did not lose interest in the region. During the summer of 1862 Jackson recommended to the Confederate War office that Colonel John D. Imboden, whose improvised artillery work at Manassas Junction in July 1861 had helped Jackson turn a Confederate rout into victory, be given command of a brigade of partisan ranger units in northwestern Virginia. Jackson hoped that a western Virginia brigade made up of western Virginian soldiers would keep the Baltimore and Ohio Railroad in a state of disrepair and block federal movements from the west against Jackson's forces in the Shenandoah Valley. In October 1862 Imboden received a commission as Brigadier General with instructions to recruit his brigade among partisan units operating in the western Virginia mountains. Imboden established his headquarters at Moorefield, Hardy County.[4]

Before the outbreak of the Civil War, John D. Imboden had been a successful attorney in Staunton. His parents lived on a prosperous farm near the Braxton-Lewis County line. From the beginning of the war in 1861, they had suffered numerous indignities because three of their sons were in Confederate service. Motivated by harassment of secessionist families living in western Virginia and convinced that Union forces in the region were weak, Imboden proposed an operation to Robert E. Lee in early spring 1863 that met with Lee's approval. On 2 March 1863, Imboden wrote a letter to Lee outlining an audacious raid into northwestern Virginia. Imboden declared that he could destroy the Baltimore and Ohio Railroad from Oakland, Maryland to Grafton. He claimed that federal garrisons at Beverly, Philippi and Buckhannon were undermanned and could easily be defeated and captured. Once these outposts were removed, Imboden claimed, there were no other Union forces between them and the Ohio River. Imboden believed that the citizens living within the area were hostile to occupying Union forces and the Wheeling government. He suggested that a strong Confederate presence in the region would encourage local citizens to overthrow unionist authorities and replace them with officials loyal to Virginia and the Confederacy.[5]

Although John D. Imboden received credit from historians for organizing and carrying out the Jones-Imboden Raid in northwestern Virginia in April and May 1863, at least one contemporary observer felt otherwise. Writing more than forty years after the event, John A. McNeel, a participant in the raid, claimed that, "the man who planned and did more to execute the 'Imboden Raid" than any other one person was William L. Jackson."[6] Exactly how much planning Jackson provided for the raid cannot be determined. At a meeting in the home of Pocahontas County Militia Colonel Paul McNeel around 1 March 1863, Jackson presented an outline of a proposed raid to colonels McNeel and Winston Fontaine which suggested that Jackson, if not the originator of the plan, at least had been privy to planning

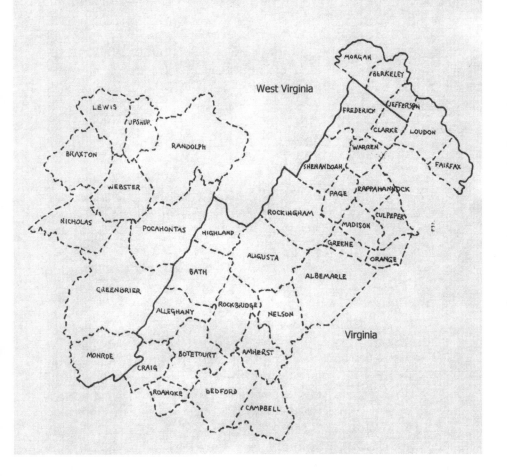

Area of Operations of William L. Jackson's Brigade, April 1863 – April 1865

sessions.[7] Jackson advised McNeel and Fontaine that he had just arrived in Pocahontas County from General Lee's headquarters on the Rappahannock, and that Lee had presented Jackson with an idea to raid northwestern Virginia to capture cattle for Lee's army. Jackson did not mention to McNeel and Fontaine the broader goals outlined in Imboden's 2 March letter to Lee. Regardless of who planned the Jones-Imboden raid, Robert E. Lee appointed Imboden to command the expedition. However, during the course of the raid from 20 April to 12 May federal dispatches concerning movements of the Confederate force always referred to the rebels as the men of "Imboden and Jackson." Union officers, at least, believed that William L. Jackson was co-commander of the raid.[8]

John A. McNeel's memoir of his experience as a soldier on the Jones-Imboden Raid contained the only wartime description of William L. Jackson known to exist. McNeel, an impressionable seventeen year old at the time he met Jackson, retained a precise mental picture of Jackson forty-three years after meeting him for the first time. Jackson, McNeel wrote:

> *had on a beautiful uniform of new Confederate gray cloth, with three stars on the collar, that told he held the rank of colonel. General Jackson would have weighed fully two hundred pounds and was at least six feet in height. He had unusually fine shoulders, head and face, and the most animated man that I had ever seen in conversation. His hair and whiskers were the deepest red that I had ever seen on the head and face of any man. In reply to a question from my father, he stated that he was forty-two years old. . . . He seemed to be perfectly informed of all matters, both civil and military, relating to the Confederacy. A good deal of the time that night, during the conversation, he walked the floor, although he had made a long horseback ride the day he reached my father's.[9]*

The Confederate War Department assigned the Nineteenth Virginia Cavalry to a brigade commanded by Albert Gallatin Jenkins, William L. Jackson's rival for the Democratic nomination to Congress in 1856. Jenkins' brigade, in turn, formed part of the Department of Western Virginia commanded by Major General Samuel Jones. From the beginning of the organization of the Nineteenth Cavalry, Jones took a special interest in the regiment. Although nominally part of Jenkins' brigade, nearly all preserved orders directing the Nineteenth Cavalry to make military movements came from Jones personally. In May 1863, Jones transferred Jenkins' brigade to the Army of Northern Virginia, but he retained the Nineteenth Cavalry under his own command. Jones recognized that it was only the Nineteenth Cavalry that blocked Union troops at Beverly and kept the Union from invading the Shenandoah Valley. Jones believed that the knowledge of the terrain and the personal stake in the war's outcome held by Jackson's men made the regiment's presence vital on the Huntersville line.[10]

THE JONES-IMBODEN RAID

The first order for action by the Nineteenth Virginia Cavalry as an organized regiment came from Jones on 4 April 1863. Jackson met with Jones at department headquarters in Dublin, Pulaski County, on 3 April. During their meeting Jones advised Jackson of the details of Imboden's planned raid into northwestern Virginia. For the first time Jackson learned that a second raid, led by General William E. Jones, would operate concurrently with Imboden's movements. The following day Samuel Jones ordered Jackson to report to Huttonsville with his regiment no later than 15 April and join Imboden's command on the expedition to Beverly. Jones pointed out that Imboden ranked Jackson and that he was to act under Imboden's orders.[11] On 7 April Jones detached the Thirty-seventh Virginia Battalion under Colonel Ambrose Dunn and ordered Dunn to report to Jackson to supplement his command for the Imboden raid. A prescient footnote to Dunn's order from Jones stated that "you are specially instructed to enforce strict discipline in your command, and prevent all marauding and depredations by your men."[12] In the meantime Imboden changed the rendezvous point and date. Jackson left his regimental headquarters at Warm Springs, Bath County, on 20 April and joined Imboden at Hightown, Highland County on 21 April. He brought with him around one thousand five hundred men, including Dunn's battalion, for Imboden's command.[13]

Robert E. Lee cautioned Imboden to keep his plans for an invasion of northwestern Virginia secret, and Jones warned Jackson to keep knowledge of the raid's plan "strictly confidential."[14] When the army of Imboden and Jackson prepared to move at Hightown on the bright spring morning of 22 April 1863, the soldiers had no idea where they were going. Most of the soldiers gathered at Hightown suspected they would be moving into the Shenandoah Valley to support Lee's attempt to block the advance of the Army of the Potomac under Hooker. When the army began to move on the morning of 22 April, the soldiers could not contain their pleasure when they realized they were moving west. John A. McNeel, soon to become a private in Company F, Nineteenth Virginia Cavalry, described the scene:

> *The soldiers were still bewildered as to their movements, but when the command began to move west over the Parkersburg and Staunton Turnpike you could see joy in their faces. First came General John Imboden, at the head of his brigade, composed of the Sixty-second Virginia Infantry, the Eighteenth Virginia Cavalry, some independent companies and*

*one good battery of four pieces of artillery. The Sixty-second Regiment . . .
was immediately behind General Imboden's staff, and with fife and drum
they moved out. Next came Colonel Patton, as true a knight as ever put
lance to rest, at the head of the Twenty-second Regiment. Next came
William L. Jackson, whose face was beaming with joy, at the head of the
Nineteenth Regiment of Cavalry. Next Colonel Dunn, at the head of his
batalion (sic); next Colonel John Higginbotham, at the head of the
Twenty-fifth Virginia Infantry . . . Next came that war worn veteran,
Colonel John S. Huffman, at the head of 'the old Thirty-first.'. . . The
scene was too much for my young rebel heart, . . . and I am glad that no
one saw me just then.*[15]

The euphoria and spectacle of the warm, sunny spring morning start to
the Imboden expedition gave way to reality the following day. The army left
old Camp Bartow at dawn on 23 April in a cold rainstorm. By the time the
men reached the top of Cheat Mountain, six inches of snow had turned the
previous day's martial extravaganza into a wet, cold and hungry mass of discomfort.

Imboden's grand plan to recover northwestern Virginia for the Confederacy began coming apart almost immediately. After routing the small federal garrison at Beverly on 24 April, Imboden planned to move from Beverly
to Philippi, but the mud churned up by retreating federals prevented him
from using the Philippi road. He decided instead to take back roads over
Rich Mountain and aim for a location on the Buckhannon-Philippi road
midway between the two towns. A captured federal order revealed to Imboden
that six Union regiments were being rushed to Philippi. Unable to establish
communications with William Jones, Imboden concluded that Jones' attempt to disrupt the Baltimore and Ohio Railroad had failed. Concerned
that his small army could be cut off and destroyed by superior federal forces,
Imboden and his colonels, including William L. Jackson, decided that withdrawal was their best option. Before the order to turn back was issued, a
scouting party returned from Buckhannon and informed Imboden that the
large federal force there had destroyed its stores and artillery and retired to
Clarksburg leaving the town without soldiers. Imboden occupied Buckhannon
on 28 April. With no federal forces on his flanks, Imboden decided to advance on Philippi and had his army moving in that direction on 2 May when
a courier from William Jones suddenly appeared with information that Jones
had succeeded in destroying the critical Baltimore and Ohio bridge at
Fairmont. Around the same time Jones' courier arrived at Buckhannon, a
detachment of the Nineteenth Cavalry returned to camp and reported that
it had destroyed all of the railroad bridges west of Fairmont. A scouting
party came in a short time later with the information that several thousand

federal soldiers were entrenching at Lost Creek near Clarksburg anticipating an attack. Imboden received intelligence on 1 May that the federal garrison in Weston had evacuated that town and retired to Clarksburg. He decided to move to Weston instead of Philippi and await the arrival of Jones and his brigade. Jones rode into Weston on 4 May. The two commanders considered their options and decided that the federal force at Lost Creek was too strong to attack. Imboden complained that desertions, illness and fatigue had reduced his effective force to slightly more than two thousand men and that Jones had only around one thousand men with him. The federal army at Lost Creek had been reported to be between six and eight thousand men. Imboden and Jones decided that withdrawal was the only prudent course of action. Jones took his command westward to destroy the Northwestern Virginia Railroad, left undefended by the concentration of federal troops at Lost Creek, while Imboden retired south to Summersville in charge of the large herds of captured cattle and horses and nearly seventy wagons loaded with supplies. The federal force at Lost Creek waited in vain for the Confederate attack.[16]

The Nineteenth Cavalry's participation in the Jones-Imboden Raid established a pattern of behavior for the regiment and public perception of the regiment's character. William Jackson had filled the roster of the Nineteenth Cavalry with ten companies when the raid began. He also had recruited four other companies that formed the nucleus of the Twentieth Virginia Cavalry. However, of the more than one thousand men mustered into cavalry service by Jackson, only four hundred of them owned horses. The remainder served as dismounted cavalry and would continue in that capacity until they obtained horses. Jackson eagerly lobbied for inclusion of the Nineteenth Cavalry with Imboden's army to provide his dismounted soldiers an opportunity to seize horses suitable for cavalry service from the well-bred stock in central western Virginia. Although the Nineteenth Cavalry performed military duties under Imboden's command, the primary objective of Jackson's men was to appropriate horses, preferably from federal herds, but from the civilian population if military horses could not be taken in sufficient quantities. Imboden hoped that his army's success in northwestern Virginia would recapture the allegiance of the civilian population, and he realized that the seizure of private property would negate this objective. Imboden, aware that many of the dismounted soldiers under his command intended to seize horses for their personal use, issued an order to the army forbidding seizure of private property and required anything, including horses and cattle, to be paid for with Confederate banknotes. His order provoked two hundred men in Ambrose Dunn's Thirty-seventh Battalion to desert at Buckhannon.[17] No record documented objections to Imboden's orders by members of the Nineteenth Cavalry, but many of the regiment's soldiers who left Hightown on foot returned to Warm Springs on horseback. Along with their new horses, the men of the Nineteenth Cavalry and their commanding officer carried reputations as horse thieves.

One action by William Jones on his raid against the Northwestern Virginia Railroad had serious post-war consequences for William Jackson. On 9 May Jones and his raiders struck the newly opened oil field at Burning Springs, Wirt County. According to Jones' report, "the wells are owned mainly by Southern men, now driven from their homes, and their property is appropriated either by the Federal Government or Northern men. . . . All the oil, the tanks, barrels, engines for pumping, engine-houses, and wagons – in a word, everything used for raising, holding, or sending it off was burned."[18] William L. Jackson was one of the "Southern men" who owned a share of the Wirt County oil field before the war. When Jones' raiders destroyed the oil producing facilities in 1863, Johnson N. Camden, one of the wealthiest men in Parkersburg, owned the entire oil field.[19] After the war Camden exacted retribution for the destruction of the oil field on William Jackson.

BEVERLY

William L. Jackson and his exhausted soldiers returned from the Imboden campaign on 23 May 1863. They had ridden and marched over four hundred miles in thirty-seven days. Jackson had about four hundred new recruits and an undetermined number of cavalry horses as a consequence of the expedition.[20] The regiment camped at Huntersville while Jackson crossed Allegheny Mountain to his headquarters at Warm Springs. Throughout June the regiment recuperated. Jackson split his command into small detachments for scouting duty along the Huntersville line. Samuel Jones ordered Jackson to especially watch for any Union movement on the Parkersburg and Staunton Turnpike toward Staunton.[21] Jackson found himself once again on garrison duty along the Huntersville line. Jackson, however, had no intention of passively patrolling the border. Since his return from the Imboden campaign, Jackson worked to develop a plan for another raid against the same targets in Tygart's Valley and westward.

On 15 June 1863 the Tenth (West) Virginia Infantry stationed at Beverly received orders to report to Grafton for immediate transfer to the Shenandoah Valley.[22] Only a skeleton force composed of cavalry scouts remained to man the Beverly garrison. Jackson probably received word that Beverly had been emptied of most of its defenders within hours after the garrison had departed for Grafton. Jackson had at his disposal the largest regiment in Samuel Jones' department in June 1863. The new recruits gathered in the Imboden raid were organized into four companies and designated the Twentieth Virginia Cavalry. Jackson also still had Dunn's depleted Thirty-seventh

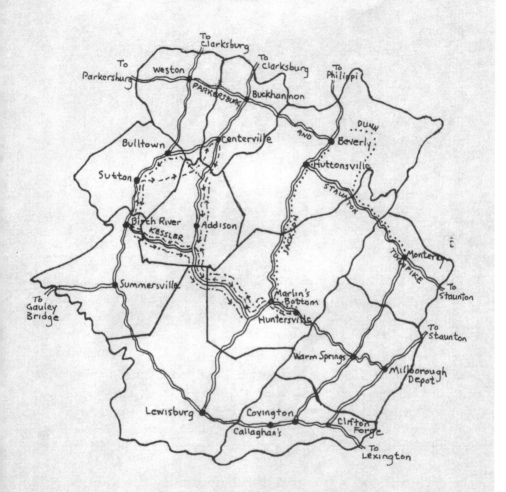

Offensive Operations of the Nineteenth and Twentieth Virginia Cavalries

June – October 1863

. . . . . Beverly, Randolph County, 3 July 1863
_ _ _ Centerville, Upshur County, 12 September 1863
_ . _ . Bulltown, Braxton County, 13 October 1863

Battalion under his command. Altogether he had nearly twelve hundred men who could be used for a new raid into northwestern Virginia. By the middle of June, Jackson believed that the time was right to strike Union positions in Tygart's Valley. Jackson sent a request to his new brigade commander, General John Echols, for two pieces of artillery and as many ambulance wagons as he could spare.[23]

Jackson could have captured Beverly in mid-June 1863 by riding into town and pitching his tent in the middle of the nearly deserted federal camp. However, Jackson did not want to simply occupy Beverly. He did not have enough men to station a permanent garrison at the town, and he knew that any Confederate attempt to establish a base at Beverly could be overwhelmed easily by Federal forces from Clarksburg. Jackson intended to inflict a military defeat on the Beverly garrison and capture the entire force stationed there. Removal of a hostile enemy force on his flank would enable him to march westward in relative security and raid in any direction he chose. On 20 June, the day West Virginia officially was admitted to the Union as a loyalist state, General Benjamin F. Kelley, Brigadier General of the newly created federal Department of West Virginia, ordered the Tenth West Virginia Infantry to return to Beverly and reestablish the federal garrison evacuated a week earlier. Under the command of William Jackson's former Harrisville neighbor, Colonel Thomas M. Harris, the Tenth Infantry had nearly one thousand men to occupy the camp.[24]

Jackson did not know that his plan for a raid into northwestern Virginia had the endorsement of Robert E. Lee before Lee was even advised that such a plan was contemplated. On 20 June 1863 Lee had written to Samuel Jones and suggested that an attack be made into western Virginia to relieve pressure against the Army of Northern Virginia as it moved north into Pennsylvania. About the same time Jones received Lee's communication, Echols forwarded Jackson's request for artillery along with Jackson's letter outlining his planned attack against Beverly. Jones enthusiastically endorsed Jackson's plan and instructed Echols to send Jackson the artillery he needed. Jones also sent a supportive letter to Jackson, closing with the comment, "Indeed, you have only anticipated my wishes."[25] By 29 June Jackson was ready to move west in the first independent operation conducted by the Nineteenth Virginia Cavalry.

William L. Jackson's plan to capture the federal garrison at Beverly should have succeeded beyond Jackson's expectations. However, in circumstances reminiscent of Lee's debacle at Cheat Mountain in 1861, the expedition failed to achieve any of its objectives. Jackson designed a plan to surround the garrison at Beverly and capture the entire force. His plan required precise coordination among three separate commands. Success depended on blocking the only two avenues of escape for the federals, the Rich Mountain road to Buckhannon on the west of the federal encampment, and the Philippi road that ran north from Beverly. Responsibility for closing off the Rich Mountain road was assigned to Major John B. Lady and two companies he had raised in Rockbridge County. Lady's men were in position by the evening of 1 July without revealing their presence to the federal garrison in Beverly. Jackson dismounted the cavalry companies of John Sprigg and Jacob Marshall and positioned them directly in front of the federal camp on the south side of the burned bridge over Files Creek. Their job was to keep federal troops from breaking out of the trap Jackson designed for them. Jackson posted Major David B. Stewart and six companies among heavily wooded slopes on the east side of the federal encampment. Stewart's companies had the responsibility for launching the actual attack on the Union camp.[26] The most critical assignment in Jackson's battle plan went to Colonel Dunn and his Thirty-seventh Battalion. Dunn marched from Hightown at the same time Jackson left Huntersville. Dunn followed the Back Allegheny Road north from Bartow to a point that brought him onto the Philippi road six miles north of Beverly. Dunn did not communicate with Jackson during the three-day march, but he carried with him explicit instructions from Jackson that the Thirty-seventh Battalion should assault the rear of the federal camp at Beverly on 2 July at the moment Jackson's artillery opened fire. Not only would Dunn's attack be unexpected, it also would cut off the federal's line of retreat to Philippi.[27]

Everyone was in position by two o'clock on the afternoon of 2 July except Dunn. From his vantage point on a knoll west of Beverly, Jackson had a clear view of the Philippi road, but Dunn was not in sight. Unwilling to delay the attack, Jackson ordered the artillery to commence firing. However, he sent orders to Sprigg, Marshall and Stewart to delay their assault until Dunn appeared. A federal attempt to break through the Confederate line at the Files Creek bridge was repulsed by Sprigg and Marshall. Stewart skirmished with pickets on the eastern side of the camp. Dunn failed to make an appearance. Jackson's two-gun battery dueled with federal artillery mounted on a hill to the rear of the Union encampment until nightfall, but to little effect. Jackson later complained that only one in fifteen of the shells fired by his artillery exploded. Jackson sent Major Lady and his companies around the base of Rich Mountain to a new position near the Philippi road. In case Dunn should appear, Lady was ordered to add his forces to Dunn's Battalion for an assault the next day.[28]

The following morning, with Dunn still not in sight and scouts unable to locate him, Jackson decided to assault the federal camp without him. Sprigg, Marshall and Stewart, who had held their positions from the previous day, received orders to advance. Stewart engaged in a furious firefight with elements of the Tenth West Virginia Infantry as he maneuvered into position for the attack. While that skirmish was in progress, Jackson noticed federal reinforcements arriving on the Philippi road. Major Lady spotted the same reinforcements. He sent a message to Jackson advising him that perhaps seven hundred federal cavalrymen had arrived to reinforce the Union infantry in Beverly. Lady, whose one hundred and fifty men were dismounted, withdrew back toward the Rich Mountain road. Jackson, convinced that Dunn would not appear, called off the attack and ordered Sprigg, Marshall and Stewart to withdraw. Jackson's army retired back up Tygart's Valley and camped for the night at the Crouch farm on the Huntersville road a short distance south of Huttonsville.[29]

As Jackson withdrew from Beverly, a detachment of mounted men from Dunn's Battalion commanded by Major James R. Claiborne caught up with him. Claiborne's company had been on detached duty when Dunn set out from Hightown to meet Jackson at Beverly. Informed that the expedition had left without him, Claiborne on his own initiative hastened over the Huttonsville and Warm Springs road to add his one hundred mounted men to Jackson's command. Since Claiborne's men and horses were comparatively fresh, Jackson assigned them to protect his army's rear as it withdrew to the Crouch farm.[30]

On the morning of 4 July the cavalry reinforcements that had arrived at Beverly the day before moved out on the Huntersville road in pursuit of Jackson's army. The federal force included the Fourteenth Pennsylvania Cavalry and the First and Third West Virginia mounted infantries. General William Averell, newly appointed commander of the Fourth Separate Brigade of the Department of West Virginia commanded them.[31] Averell's pursuit of Jackson's army at Beverly on 4 July marked the first instance of conflict between these two volatile personalities. In the months to follow, Jackson and Averell met frequently in head to head confrontations, each narrowly missing several opportunities to destroy the other's brigade.

While still camped at Crouch's, Jackson received a dispatch from Dunn advising Jackson that he had retired as far as George Stype's rooming house near Cheat Mountain Pass. Jackson sent Claiborne to find Dunn and deliver orders for a new plan of battle. Jackson intended to withdraw slowly from Averell's force along the Huntersville road while trying to lure the cautious Union cavalry commander farther away from Beverly. Dunn was ordered to bring his battalion back along the Parkersburg and Staunton Turnpike to Huttonsville, then attack Averell from the rear while Jackson assaulted him from the front. John Sprigg and Company B had the task of skirmishing with Averell to keep his attention while drawing the Union cavalry farther up the Huntersville road. Claiborne reached Stype's only to find that Dunn had withdrawn to Camp Bartow and was too far away to come to Jackson's assistance. Claiborne returned to Jackson's position below Huttonsville to advise him that Dunn could not be located. Averell mistook Claiborne's arrival as a new Confederate force of unknown strength, and he broke off the engagement. As Averell withdrew north of Huttonsville, an infuriated Jackson followed him and spent the night in camp again at Crouch's. Averell camped a mile north of Jackson's position.[32]

Rain had fallen intermittently throughout the weeklong campaign. On the morning of 5 July rain fell in such torrents that creeks throughout Tygart's Valley began rising at an alarming rate. Fearing that his weary army would not be able to cross the creeks in case a retreat became necessary, Jackson reluctantly ordered a general withdrawal to Huntersville.[33] On the other side of Huttonsville Averell reached the same conclusion. He withdrew to Beverly.[34] The Jackson raid was over, but the Jackson rage was just beginning. On 11 July Jackson wrote to Major Charles S. Stringfellow, Samuel Jones' Assistant Adjutant to report on the Beverly expedition. Near the end of the report, Jackson stated grimly:

> *Lieut. Col. A. C. Dunn, it appears from his own dispatches, was in position at the time appointed. He was ordered to make a vigorous attack upon the rear of the enemy whenever he heard my signal. This it was impossible for him to avoid hearing. I am reliably informed that, instead of advancing and attacking, as ordered, he fell back when my signal was heard. His dispatches are contradictory in the attempt to explain this singular retrograde movement. I have felt it my duty to order him under arrest, and will prefer charges. Maj. J. R. Claiborne is now in command of the battalion.[35]*

As a consequence of Jackson's charges against Dunn, a court martial in November 1863 tried the Georgia-born colonel. Found guilty of disobeying orders and implicated in a scheme to sell fraudulent discharge papers, Dunn was cashiered from the Confederate Army on 6 November 1863. However, President Jefferson Davis reinstated him in June 1864 and he resumed command of the Thirty-seventh Battalion.[36] William Jackson would encounter Ambrose Dunn again before the end of the war.

Other problems for William Jackson arose as a consequence of his July raid on Beverly. One of Jackson's greatest assets in the eyes of the Confederate War Department in Richmond was his popularity among the people in northwestern Virginia. Jackson was well known throughout the region because of his political prominence before the war. His high profile position as a circuit judge made him a familiar figure in county seats from Weston to Parkersburg. Two events associated with the attack on Beverly called Jackson's popularity into question. The first incident occurred on the march to Beverly. Jackson rode with his infantry and artillery on the southern route to Beverly

across Valley Mountain. As the long column approached a farm near the
foot of the mountain, a young girl ran out from the house and handed a
letter to Jackson. As she returned to her home, shots rang out from the woods
near the house. The assassins aimed too high and their volley whistled over
the heads of Jackson and his aides. Several infantrymen nearby immediately
returned the fire and charged the woods. One of the assailants was killed and
the others routed. Jackson placed the girl and her family under arrest and
posted a guard at their home until he withdrew from Beverly after the battle.[37]

The second episode concerned public relations. Jackson's success at Beverly
depended not only on perfect coordination among three widely dispersed
units but also on a sudden appearance in force before the federal camp at
Beverly before the camp was aware that it was under attack. To achieve the
element of surprise, pickets had to be captured before Jackson's army could
advance. John Righter and Company D of the Nineteenth Cavalry drew the
assignment to capture the pickets. Righter and his men had discovered the
federal picket post near Huttonsville on 1 July. Concealed in the dense forest
near the road, Righter noted the time when the pickets were relieved. Near
the end of their shift at dawn on 2 July, the fourteen federal pickets, blithely
unaware that a large Confederate force was only a few miles south of their
position, were quickly and silently surrounded and captured by Righter's
men. Fourteen of Righter's men took the blue jackets from the captured
pickets, put them on, and sat around waiting for the relief detachment to
arrive at dawn. When the relief appeared on schedule, they also were captured without a shot being fired.[38] Capturing pickets was a routine proce-
dure and ordinarily would have excited no comment beyond the fact that
pickets needed to be more vigilant. In this instance, a rumor started almost
immediately that Jackson had lined up the twenty-eight prisoners and executed them. The civilian population in the area readily accepted the truth
of the rumor. Sirene Bunton, a unionist living in Buckhannon, entered in
her diary for 6 July; "The secesh surrounded our pickets at Beverly, took
them prisoners and then killed them in cold blood. The pickets belonged to
Co C 10th Va. The rebels are perfect savages to kill men that way. I hope they
will get their pay for it before they get out of West Va."[39] Clearly, in the
public mind, William Jackson's regiment was no "Stonewall Brigade." The
Nineteenth Cavalry was perceived as a collection of blood thirsty killers and
marauders who deserved extermination.

WILLIAM AVERELL

William L. Jackson's first encounter with William W. Averell along the
Tygart's Valley River on 4-5 July 1863 began a long and deadly series of
confrontations between the two cavalry commanders. Averell, a native of

New York, was a career soldier. He was an 1855 graduate of West Point and a veteran of western Indian wars in the late 1850s. Once the Civil War began, Averell quickly moved upward in the military hierarchy. He began the war as a first lieutenant in the Third United States Cavalry, but by August 1861 he had risen to the rank of Colonel in command of the Third Pennsylvania Cavalry. He directed his regiment in defenses around Washington, D. C. between October 1861 and March 1862. In September 1862 he was promoted Brigadier General and placed in command of the Second United States Cavalry Division.[40] In March 1863, Averell led an attack on Confederate cavalry positions at Kelly's Ford, Culpeper County, Virginia. At Kelly's Ford, Averell demonstrated a command characteristic that would cause him problems in future campaigns. Despite a three to one numerical superiority, Averell exercised such extreme caution that he failed to dislodge the undermanned Confederates. Although he claimed a tactical victory, his superiors questioned Averell's aggressiveness.[41] At Chancellorsville in May 1863, Union General Joseph Hooker, desperately seeking scapegoats to explain his humiliating defeat by undermanned and outgunned Confederates, accused Averell of non-aggressiveness and removed him from command. Hooker's complaint focused on the fact that in three days of fighting Averell's brigade had suffered only five casualties.[42] Soon after his disappointing performance at Chancellorsville, the Union high command offered Averell an opportunity to redeem his reputation. They sent him to northwestern Virginia to organize a strategy to contain Confederate raiders.

The ease with which the cavalry units of William Jones and John Imboden moved about northwestern Virginia during the Jones-Imboden raid of April and May 1863 forced federal strategists to reexamine their strategy in the western Virginia mountains. Throughout 1862 and the spring of 1863, federal infantry troops manned dozens of small outposts in the mountain region. The foot soldiers scouted the countryside for rebel activity, fighting occasional skirmishes with partisans, and harassing civilians suspected of secessionist leanings. With few cavalry companies stationed in the mountains, Union mobility was limited. The inadequacy of the system became apparent when William Jones's cavalry regiment raided with impunity as far north as Morgantown. The spectacle of federal infantry chasing Jones's cavalry clearly indicated that changes needed to be made. A change in Union commanders in western Virginia also proved desirable. During the first few days of the Jones-Imboden raid, Union general Benjamin S. Roberts, commander of the Fourth Separate Brigade at Clarksburg, complained to General-in- Chief Henry Halleck that his forces could not contain the two Confederate raiders because roads in the area were impassable. Halleck replied that he did not understand "how the roads there are impassable to you, when, by your own account, they are passable enough to the enemy. If you cannot drive the enemy out, we will seek some one who can."[43] On 26 June 1863 William W. Averell replaced Roberts as commander of the Fourth Separate Brigade. Averell immediately began turning the numerous infantry regiments assigned to defend the western Virginia mountains into cavalry regiments. Averell also decided that his command would carry the war into the Greenbrier Valley instead of sitting in isolated base camps reacting to Confederate raids.[44] Only three days after assuming command he had an opportunity to test his new mounted infantry when he was ordered to rescue the Tenth West Virginia Infantry at Beverly from an assault by William L. Jackson. Although he failed to inflict a battlefield defeat on Jackson's army, Averell believed that the appearance of his cavalry regiment saved Beverly from being overrun.[45]

Averell's report of his confrontation with William Jackson at Huttonsville indicated another problem for Averell's superior officers. He exaggerated his success to such an extent that superior officers distant from the scene of action often were misled about the reality of the situation in western Virginia. Averell reported to General Kelley at Clarksburg that he had driven Jackson's army "from their position and across the Elk Water, the enemy showing very little disposition to fight. . . . Had Colonel Harris furnished me with timely warning of the approach of the enemy, I should have killed, captured, or dispersed his entire command."[46] In reality, Jackson's army "showing very little disposition to fight" was a tactic of strategic withdrawal designed to draw Averell's forces well beyond Huttonsville where Jackson intended to strike him from the front and the rear simultaneously.[47] Only the failure of Ambrose Dunn to obey Jackson's orders prevented Averell's command from possibly suffering a devastating defeat.

ROCKY GAP

William Jackson and the Nineteenth Cavalry returned to Warm Springs, Bath County, following the failed attempt to capture Beverly. For the remainder of July and the first weeks of August, Jackson dispersed the companies under his command to watch for federal movement on roads leading from Tygart's Valley toward Staunton, a major Confederate storehouse for military supplies. Jackson's Nineteenth Cavalry at Warm Springs and the disgraced Dunn's Thirty-seventh Battalion at Hightown were the only Confederate forces between Staunton and the Union concentration in Tygart's Valley. Throughout July rumors circulated through the mountains along the Huntersville line that Averell and his new federal cavalry brigade intended to break through Confederate defenses and attack Staunton.

Jackson's scouts on the Parkersburg and Staunton Turnpike and the Huntersville road reported no unusual federal activity until 21 August. A courier from William W. Arnett, newly elected colonel of the Twentieth Virginia Cavalry, awakened Jackson early that morning at Camp Northwest on

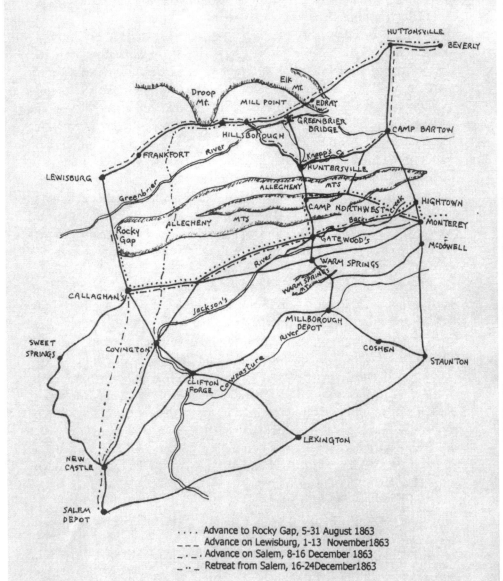

Routes of William W. Averell's Raids

August – December 1863

.... Advance to Rocky Gap, 5-31 August 1863
_ _ _ Advance on Lewisburg, 1-13 November1863
_._. Advance on Salem, 8-16 December 1863
_.._ Retreat from Salem, 16-24December1863

Allegheny Mountain between Huntersville and Warm Springs.[48] Arnett reported that Averell had appeared suddenly in Monterey the preceding day with a large number of cavalry and infantry. The federals had slipped undetected into Monterey on a back road from Franklin, Pendleton County, surprised a meeting of the Highland County circuit court, and arrested all Highland County officials attending the court session. Jackson immediately concluded that the anticipated assault on Staunton had begun.[49]

The surprise appearance of a large number of federal cavalry in Highland County caught Jackson ill-prepared to contend with a major attack. Jackson's primary responsibility was to block any federal movement against Staunton, and he had dispersed his companies to various posts throughout Pocahontas and Highland counties to watch for federal activity on the Parkersburg and Staunton Turnpike and the Huntersville road. Faced with a federal force whose numbers were uncertain, Jackson had in camp only around four hundred men, most of them dismounted. Jackson dispatched orders to his far-flung companies to rendezvous immediately at Camp Northwest.[50]

While Jackson collected his companies during the early morning hours of 21 August, Colonel Arnett attempted to delay Averell's advance toward Huntersville. Arnett had less than two hundred men to dispute the progress of Averell's cavalry along the Back Creek road. Convinced that Averell was preparing to advance against Staunton, Jackson rushed dispatches to Colonel John Nadenbousch at Staunton and to John Imboden at Moorefield warning them that an attack was imminent. He also sent a dispatch to Colonel George Patton at Lewisburg explaining that while he thought the federal attack was aimed at Staunton, Patton should also watch the approaches to Lewisburg.[51] Having warned everyone whom he thought might be the object of the federal advance, Jackson set about dealing with his own situation.

By the time his scattered companies had gathered at Camp Northwest, Jackson had around one thousand men to meet whatever force Averell sent against him. Lack of reliable intelligence left him guessing exactly what he faced. Trying to prepare for every eventuality, he stationed one company at Gatewood's at the foot of Little Mountain where the Back Creek road joined the road to Warm Springs. Arnett had reported skirmishing with an undetermined number of cavalry along the Back Creek road. Jackson, with two companies of cavalry, waited at Camp Northwest. He ordered his infantry to gather near Warm Springs and await developments. Arnett discovered that the federal infantrymen had crossed Little Mountain west of Back Creek and were advancing along the Knapp Creek road. At three o'clock on the afternoon of 21 August a courier from Arnett advised Jackson that infantry was pressing him down the Knapp Creek Road toward Huntersville. This information convinced Jackson that Staunton was not the object of the federal invasion, and he sent dispatches to General Samuel Jones at Dublin and

Colonel George Patton at Lewisburg suggesting that Lewisburg was the target.[52] Jackson's conclusion about the federal destination was correct, but not in his wildest imaginings could he have guessed the reason for Averell's sudden appearance. On 12 August and again on 14 August, Averell received orders from General Kelley instructing him to go to Lewisburg and confiscate the law library of the Virginia Court of Appeals stored there. Kelley claimed that the new West Virginia government in Wheeling considered the library to be the property of the new state, and that new state judges needed them. While Confederate officers and quartermasters in Staunton frantically made preparations to defend their essential military supplies, William Averell continued on his quest to capture a law library at Lewisburg.[53]

Arnett failed to appear in Jackson's camp the following morning, and Jackson sent a company of cavalry toward Huntersville to find him and to determine federal movements. Jackson moved with his cavalry companies to Gatewood's to organize a defense at the point where Back Creek cut through the Warm Springs road. The scouting company, around forty men, ran into the Tenth West Virginia Infantry coming from Beverly to reinforce Averell's cavalry. The scouts withdrew while skirmishing with the advance elements of the federal infantry. Late in the afternoon they discovered that the federals were attempting to flank Jackson's position at Gatewood's. Jackson retired to establish a new defensive line along Jackson's River four miles west of Warm Springs. Jackson concluded that the federal assault against him intended to clear him out of the way while the main federal army moved toward Lewisburg. To be absolutely certain that Staunton was not the federal target, he sent Major Joseph Kessler and sixty mounted troops more than thirty miles to McDowell to check for Union movement on the Parkersburg and Staunton Turnpike and to blockade the road from Monterey to McDowell.[54]

By the morning of 23 August, federal troops still had not appeared at Gatewood's, but Captain Arnett and his missing skirmishers had straggled into camp after spending a day and two nights in the dense forest between Knapp's Creek and Jackson's River. Suspecting that the Union force had turned to the right to move south toward Covington and Lewisburg on the Indian Draft road, Jackson placed Arnett in command of a cavalry company and sent him back up the road toward Gatewood's to locate the federals. Arnett advanced a short distance west of Gatewood's and encountered the entire federal infantry advancing carefully toward Warm Springs. Jackson ordered his infantry forward to contest the advance and they spent the day skirmishing with the advancing federals while the Union commander, Colonel Thomas Harris, tried to estimate the strength of the Confederates in front of him. At ten o'clock in the morning, Harris launched a full assault on Jackson's position. Jackson's four hundred infantrymen managed to hold the federal advance for an hour, but when scouts discovered large Union detachments moving to flank him on both sides of his line, Jackson hastily withdrew to Warm Springs. Consulting with his company commanders, Jackson concluded that Warm Springs was untenable due to roads into the town from both northern and southern directions. Having insufficient men to fight on three lines and fearing that he would be surrounded, Jackson abandoned the town and established a new position on Warm Springs Mountain, which he did not think was susceptible to flanking movements. Harris and the Tenth West Virginia Infantry occupied Warm Springs around noon on 24 August, and Jackson observed the federal troops again positioning themselves for a three pronged advance which would surround Jackson's position if successful. For the first time since the campaign began on 21 August, Jackson was able to determine correctly the number of federal troops facing him. The nearly four to one advantage held by the Union force convinced Jackson that he could not hold any position for long. He sent a dispatch to General Jones advising him that he intended to fall back to Panther Gap near Goshen and await reinforcements. Earlier Jackson had received a communication from General Francis H. Smith, superintendent at the Virginia Military Institute, advising him that Smith and a corps of cadets were coming to reinforce Jackson. They were bringing with them a battery of artillery. Jackson sent his infantry to Bath Alum on the south side of Warm Springs Mountain, but through a misunderstanding the infantry continued an additional six miles to Millboro Springs. Advised of the error, Jackson—realizing that his foot soldiers already were exhausted—simply ordered them to stay where they were.[55] By leaving his infantry nearly fifteen miles from Warm Springs, Jackson reduced his force at the front to less than three hundred mounted men.

Early on 26 August, Jackson sent Arnett to the top of Warm Springs Mountain to reconnoiter federal movements in Warm Springs. Kessler had returned from McDowell and Jackson sent him and his travel weary company to look for federal activity on the roads south of Warm Springs. Arnett reported that the federals had withdrawn from Warm Springs and had gone into camp at Gatewood's. Kessler discovered that the entire Union cavalry appeared to be heading for Covington on the Hot Springs road. A dispatch arrived from General Smith informing Jackson that he was at Goshen with a battery. Jackson concluded that the attack against him on the preceding days had been a mere diversion to mask the real intention of the invading force to attack Lewisburg with cavalry. The Tenth West Virginia Infantry, he decided, had been left at Gatewood's to secure the rear of the federal cavalry and to keep the Huntersville road open for an eventual withdrawal once the cavalry raid ended. Jackson recognized that he had an opportunity to inflict a damaging blow on the Tenth Infantry and block the avenues of retreat for the federal cavalry headed for Lewisburg. He dispatched an order to Smith to bring up his artillery and directed his infantry at Millboro Springs to move back to Warm Springs. The infantry was slow to respond and did not return to Warm Springs until the afternoon of 27 August. In the meantime, Smith advised Jackson that the troops and the artillery under his command were the property of the Virginia Military Institute, not Virginia or the Confederacy, and he had decided conditions were too uncertain to risk the loss of either by bringing them to Warm Springs. Jackson and his small contingent of cavalry waited without artillery support at Warm Springs for reinforcements and information throughout the day.[56]

At three o'clock on the morning of 28 August, Jackson received a dispatch from Kessler advising him that the federal cavalry had been defeated at Rocky Gap and were falling back toward Warm Springs. Jackson concluded that the retreating federals would be returning to Gatewood's and he began moving his entire force of less than one thousand men in that direction hoping to intercept them. He did not move quickly enough. Arnett arrived at Gatewood's in time to fire on the rear guard of Averell's men as they moved quickly toward Huntersville. Jackson started his small army in pursuit, but at Huntersville he discovered the Tenth West Virginia Infantry established in a defensive line to cover the retreat of Averell's cavalry. With evening coming on and much of Jackson's infantry still on the march from Millboro Springs, Jackson halted to evaluate the situation. With no artillery, only part of his infantry, and no reinforcements in sight, a direct attack against the Union position was imprudent. He decided to wait overnight while the rest of his infantry came up. He directed Arnett to take his cavalry company by way of the Clover Lick road and get ahead of the retreating federals on the Huttonsville and Warm Springs road. Jackson hoped that Arnett could blockade the road at Big Springs while Jackson and his main force assaulted the federals from the rear. Arnett left at two o'clock in the morning on 29 August.[57]

During the night of 28 August, Jackson received a dispatch from Colonel James Corns at Gatewood's. Corns had pursued Averell's retreating cavalry from the battlefield at White Sulphur Springs with the Eighth Virginia Cavalry and the Thirty-seventh Virginia Battalion, but had failed to overtake them. Jackson ordered Corns to bring his men up to the front line. Corns arrived shortly after Arnett departed for Big Spring, and Jackson requested that he send two hundred of his men to reinforce Arnett. Corns decided that his horses were too tired to make the trip and he refused to honor Jackson's request. As daylight dawned on 29 August, Jackson discovered that the Union line at Huntersville had dissolved during the night. Scouts informed him that the federal army had crossed the Greenbrier River at Marlin's Bottom and was moving rapidly north on the Huttonsville road. Jackson and Corns rode to the bridge and Jackson asked Corns to pursue the fleeing Federals and attack their rear guard. Corns informed Jackson that his horses were unable to raise a trot, then turned his men onto the Millpoint road and rode off toward Lewisburg.[58] As Corns was leaving, Major Kessler and his cavalry company arrived from their scouting trip toward Covington. Jackson ordered Kessler to pursue the federal rear guard while he brought up the infantry. Kessler and his tired men and horses set out on the long climb up Elk Mountain. Jackson followed with his exhausted infantry. By the time Jackson reached Edray, six miles up Elk Mountain, he concluded that his infantry was in no condition to continue the pursuit. Kessler continued trailing the federal force hoping to attack them if Arnett succeeded in blocking the road at Big Spring, but blockades thrown across the road north of Elk Mountain prevented him from making contact.[59] Arnett actually reached Big Spring ahead of Averell's cavalry. His men cut some trees across the road, but with less than one hundred men he could do little more than direct sniper fire at Averell's men while they cleared the blockade.[60]

Although Averell had failed to capture the law library at Lewisburg, his August raid through Highland, Bath and Alleghany counties illustrated both the strengths and weaknesses of William L. Jackson's command along the Huntersville line. Jackson demonstrated that he could make command decisions in the field with expediency and efficiency. Faced with a vastly larger enemy, Jackson managed to keep his small army out of harm's way while at the same time forcing the enemy to fight for every mile gained. While Jackson's force did little damage to Averell's cavalry or Harris's infantry during the raid, he did delay Averell's progress for five days, enabling a Confederate force to gather at Rocky Gap near White Sulphur Springs and prevent Averell's advance to Lewisburg. Most importantly, Jackson's army survived intact to fight another day. Jackson reported that during the campaign none of his soldiers had been killed and less than twenty had been wounded.[61] The light casualty list indicated a judicious use of available manpower. Jackson wanted to instigate a battle with the federal army, but he demonstrated a grasp of reality which convinced him that the few men he had under his command could not stand against more than three times their number. The only complaint registered against Jackson's conduct during the campaign came from Colonel James Corns, cavalry commander of George Patton's First Brigade. In explaining to Patton why he had failed to overtake Averell's retreating command, Corns stated,

> . . . the enemy had left Callaghan's about 2 o'clock in the night, I pushed on rapidly with the hope that Colonel Jackson . . . would so blockade the roads and otherwise delay the enemy's retreat as to enable me to come up with him; and it is the opinion of all of my officers and myself that had 100 men been thrown down the road leading from the Warm Springs turnpike to Gatewood's that they could have so obstructed the road in

two hours' time as to have compelled the enemy to abandon all of his transportation and cannon, and perhaps to surrender his entire command.[62]

Corns' belief that Jackson had failed to act in a timely and efficient manner may explain his unwillingness to comply with any of Jackson's requests for assistance during the pursuit of the withdrawing federals beyond Huntersville.

The weaknesses of Jackson's position on the Huntersville line also showed clearly during Averell's August raid. Jackson did not have enough men to adequately defend the area assigned to him. His scouts gave timely warning of the federal presence on the Parkersburg and Staunton Turnpike and the Huntersville Road, but beyond that there was little Jackson could do with the manpower available. However, Jackson had nearly twice as many soldiers on his regimental rosters at the time of Averell's raid than he was able to put into the field. The reason for Jackson's shortage of available men in August 1863 was a continuing problem for him: many of his men, including the entire companies of George Downs, John Sprigg, Jacob Marshall, and William McNeil, nearly half the regimental strength of the Nineteenth Cavalry, were scattered throughout central western Virginia on independent raids. Sprigg was harassing federal outposts in Braxton, Nicholas and Webster counties; Marshall and McNeel were raiding in Pocahontas, Randolph and Tucker counties; and Downs' whereabouts were unknown. Records do not reveal whether or not Jackson was aware of the locations of these companies, but he was aware that they were not in the immediate area. He issued no orders calling those companies in to Camp Northwest when Colonel Arnett first informed him that Union cavalry was moving toward the camp on 21 August. Jackson had difficulty keeping track of his companies throughout the time he manned the Huntersville line. Several complaints were registered against him for failing to control the independent actions of his men, especially the companies of Downs and Sprigg. The Confederate War Office complained to Samuel Jones in early August 1863 that Jackson's command was out of control and that "even some of the officers of his regiment have been permitted to remain absent several months at a time."[63] Jones excused Jackson's lack of discipline by explaining that the regiment was new and that many of the reports of absentees probably were men "employed recruiting and collecting men from within the enemy's lines."[64] However, following Averell's raid, Jones wrote to Jackson and ordered him to collect his stragglers and deserters. Jackson replied that he was doing so, but absenteeism continued to plague Jackson's command.[65]

Another problem for William Jackson became evident during the Averell raid of August 1863. Although Jackson was a student of his legendary cousin,

Stonewall Jackson, he was not Stonewall. Other Confederate commanders demonstrated a lack of willingness to cooperate with him when cooperation may have meant the difference between victory or a meaningless exercise in which nothing was gained or lost. Francis Smith's refusal to send his artillery to Jackson at Warm Springs cost Jackson an opportunity to attack the Tenth West Virginia Infantry with superior firepower. James Corns' refusal to use his cavalry detachment to help Arnett block the federal withdrawal at Big Spring or to pursue the rear of the federal army at Marlin's Bottom allowed Averell and Harris to escape virtually unscathed. The failure of Jackson's own company commanders to follow orders caused his infantry to be moved so far to the rear of the front lines that by the time the infantry returned to action the men were exhausted and unable to attack the retreating federals.

Adding to Jackson's lack of respect among his fellow commanders was the unfortunate appellation "Mudwall" which became attached to William L. Jackson as a consequence of the August 1863 raid. This ignominious nickname was associated with Jackson for the rest of the war and the immediate post war period. John A. McNeel explained how Jackson acquired the derogatory nickname. During the August raid, the Tenth West Virginia spent several days camped in Huntersville waiting for Averell's return from Greenbrier. During their idle time at Huntersville, McNeel noted,

> *Some wag of a fellow wrote a doggerel verse on the inside walls of the old Courthouse, entitled 'Mudwall Jackson,' the principal feature of which was a complaint that 'Mudwall Jackson' would not fight. The writer saw this writing a few days after the retreat of the Federals, and it was understood by the Confederate soldiers as having been put there by a Yankee soldier, and as we Confederates understood it at the time, the animus of the verse was because the dead 'Stonewall' had been so hard on the Yankees, and the live 'Mudwall' had escaped their net.*[66]

The Confederate high command considered the victory over William Averell and his Union cavalry at Rocky Gap a significant achievement. Major General Samuel Jones, writing to Confederate Adjutant General Samuel Cooper on 30 August 1863, claimed that Averell's troops "have been severely punished, and when they reach Beverly will not, I think, be fit for service for several weeks."[67] William L. Jackson, frustrated over his inability to deliver a crushing blow to Averell's defeated forces, knew better. He knew that casualties among the federal troops had not been great, and that a few days rest in Beverly would find both Averell's cavalry and the Tenth West Virginia fully recovered and ready to take the field again. Jackson intended to strike a blow at Unionists somewhere in central northwestern Virginia, not only to impress upon the citizens of the central counties that the Confederacy was still strong in the area, but also to quiet criticism of his conduct during Averell's raid. Jackson's leadership ability had been questioned by Colonel Corns' charge that he had failed to block Averell's retreat, and General Jones, responding to complaints from citizens and soldiers alike, had ordered Jackson to collect his stragglers and restore order in his command.[68] Jackson replied to Jones' reprimand on 2 September 1863 in detail. He informed Jones that he had pursued Averell's men as far as Crouch's fortifications, a few miles south of Huttonsville, that he was gathering in his stragglers, and that Arnett's company had "killed a number of the enemy at Big Spring."[69] In each instance Jackson's reply to Jones' criticism was less than truthful. In his own report of his movements during the Averell raid Jackson stated that his pursuit was called off at Edray, thirty-five miles south of Crouch's. He also declared that Arnett had fired on the enemy at Big Spring, "but with his small force could do nothing more."[70] In his report of his encounter with Arnett's men at Big Spring, Averell mentioned no casualties and stated that while his men worked to clear the blockade Arnett had thrown across the road, his cavalry foraged their horses in nearby fields.[71] As for collecting stragglers, Jackson could do little because most of the "stragglers" were companies of the Nineteenth Cavalry that had been on detached assignments since the middle of July. All he could do to collect them was to wait and hope that they returned to camp. Around the first of September, one group of "stragglers" did return. These were the men of Company B under the command of John S. Sprigg.

CENTERVILLE

Sprigg and his men left Camp Northwest in Pocahontas County around the middle of July 1863. Officially the men were on a scouting mission to Braxton, Webster and Nicholas counties to assess federal strength in those areas. Unofficially, the men were on furlough visiting their homes and families, tending to farm chores and refitting for the fall campaign. When Sprigg finally returned to Jackson's headquarters in early September, he reported that Sutton was garrisoned by one company detached from the Tenth West Virginia Infantry, that a small force of infantry with no artillery was stationed at the federal fort at Bulltown on the Little Kanawha River, and that there were no federal garrisons in Webster County. Jackson, smarting under the thinly veiled criticism implicit in Corns' report and Jones' communication, quickly recognized that Sprigg's information provided him an opportunity to recover lost prestige and reestablish Confederate respectability in the central region of the new union state of West Virginia. On 2 September 1863, he dispatched Major Joseph Kessler and two hundred dismounted men to attack and capture the federal garrison at Sutton.[72]

John Eagle, only recently enlisted in the Twentieth Virginia Cavalry, volunteered to guide Kessler to Sutton over back roads and trails. A native of Pendleton County, Eagle's parents settled in Upshur County near Buckhannon during the 1850s. The Eagle family was one of a large group of Pendleton and Highland County migrants who relocated in northern Webster County and southern Upshur County in the 1850s. In 1862 Upshur County farmers in the southern end of the county bordering secessionist areas in Webster and Lewis counties organized a militia company for their own protection against Confederate raiders. John Eagle, his father and his older brother were members of the militia, although the family evidently harbored secessionist sympathies. During the summer of 1863, John Eagle left his home in Upshur County and returned to his childhood home in Pendleton County. On 15 July 1863 he enlisted in Company D of the Twentieth Virginia Cavalry at Hightown.[73] Because of his familiarity with the area and his personal knowledge of union sympathizers in the region, Eagle volunteered to guide Kessler's company to Sutton over a route that would get them into the area undetected.

Kessler and his men reached Sutton around 9 September, only to discover that the federal garrison there had been recalled to Clarksburg. Unwilling to return to camp with nothing to show for his effort, Kessler scouted around for a new target. Eagle suggested a likely opportunity. The Upshur County Militia, Eagle said, met every Saturday at Centerville to train and drill.[74] Eagle suggested that Kessler attempt to capture the entire command. When Eagle explained that the Upshur Militia had only seventy men on its roll and that the men drilled with unloaded muskets, Kessler agreed that an attack on the militia held great possibilities for success. On the evening of 11 September, Kessler and his men reached Centerville on back trails and took up positions in the woods surrounding the drill field. The Confederates waited quietly and patiently in the dense forest while the unsuspecting Upshur Militia gathered at Centerville early on Saturday morning, 12 September. Many of the militia members brought their families with them for a day of socializing and trading at the stores in Centerville. The militia drill sergeant, Loyal McAvoy, assigned pickets for the day and distributed loaded weapons to them. The rest of the militia shouldered their unloaded muskets and organized into ranks on the drill field. Before McAvoy could give a command to the assembled men, shots rang out from the woods surrounding the field. To the astounded eyes of the militiamen, their armed pickets fell to the ground and gray clad rebels began pouring from the woods on all sides. One militiaman attempted a dash to the nearby armory to secure ammunition only to find the building already in the possession of rebels who had set it on fire. Daniel Gould, captain of the Upshur Militia, recognized the hopelessness of his company's situation. Quickly tying a white handkerchief to his musket barrel, he surrendered the entire command without firing.[75]

Kessler had achieved in a few minutes the single greatest achievement of

William Jackson's command during the two years the Nineteenth and Twentieth cavalries existed. He captured the entire Upshur militia with the exception of four men who managed to flee through the woods during the confusion, and he accomplished his victory without a single casualty among his own troops. He rounded up every horse in the Centerville vicinity, looted the stores of all of the goods his men could carry, and destroyed what remained. Early in the afternoon he started his long train of eighty-seven prisoners down the road toward Hacker Valley.[76] Marching over the rugged and unpatroled roads of Webster County, Kessler, his loot and his captives, reported to Jackson at Warm Springs on 15 September.[77]

BULLTOWN

Kessler's success at Centerville pleased William Jackson, but the intelligence Kessler brought back about the unprotected condition of the central West Virginia area excited him even more. Jackson began planning an audacious raid into Braxton County. He planned to send a battalion of men to demonstrate in front of Huttonsville to divert the attention of the Tenth West Virginia Infantry. In the meantime Jackson intended to march his main force through Webster County and surprise the Union garrison at Bulltown on the Gauley Bridge and Weston Turnpike. Once Bulltown was taken, no other federal garrison existed between the Little Kanawha River and the Ohio Valley. Jackson envisioned replicating the success of Albert Jenkins in 1862 and William Jones in 1863, both of whom had wreaked havoc in western Virginia and created panic in Wheeling and Washington with cavalry raids. Exactly what Jackson planned to do once he captured Bulltown was never committed to paper.[78] However, Bulltown was the only federal garrison in the path of Confederate raiders between the headwaters of the Little Kanawha River in Randolph County and the Ohio River at Parkersburg. Once Bulltown was overcome, the only federal troops who could contest a Confederate raid had to be detached from Clarksburg or Charleston, both of which were several days march away from the Bulltown area.

The force assembled by Jackson for the raid against Bulltown consisted of companies drawn from both the Nineteenth and Twentieth cavalry regiments, several companies of mounted partisan rangers, six infantry companies, and two artillery pieces assigned to Jackson's command after the Averell raid in August. Warren S. Lurty, Jackson's chief adjutant, who had no previous artillery experience, commanded the battery. Jackson had around seven hundred men in his command. According to Kessler's scouting report, the Bulltown garrison had around one hundred men permanently assigned to the fort, and no artillery to support them. Jackson concluded that capturing the Bulltown garrison was not a problem, provided he could approach it in complete secrecy. His plan was to overrun the fort before the federals were aware that he was in the area. Jackson selected John Sprigg's company, all of whose members were natives of the Webster and Braxton County area, to lead his force through Webster County to the Little Kanawha River upstream from Bulltown. Webster County's sparse but fiercely secessionist population guaranteed that Jackson could reach Bulltown undetected.

Jackson's small army set out from Huntersville around 9 October. At Edray they turned onto a barely cleared track known as the Straight Creek road. This road took the army across Williams River, over Tea Creek Mountain, and down to Gauley River near its headwaters. John R. Coger, a forty-two year old private in Company B, directed the army over Cold Knob and into Addison, the county seat of Webster County. At Addison, Lewis Weese, a young farmer from Holly River, took over guide duties and led the army through the Holly country to Hacker Valley. Jack Chewning, first sergeant of Company B, whose home was on Salt Lick Creek five miles downstream from Bulltown, took charge at that point and directed Jackson's force through a torturous maze of mountain trails to emerge at Falls Mill on the banks of the Little Kanawha River early in the evening on 12 October. Jackson's entire force was two miles upstream from the Bulltown fort, and no one at the fort knew the army was in the area.[79]

The Bulltown fort lay on a promontory overlooking the Gauley Bridge and Weston Turnpike. The only practical approach to the fort lay on its northern side where a hayfield belonging to Moses Cunningham gradually sloped up to the fort's main entrance. Earthen walls had been constructed around that part of the fort that rested on the edge of the precipice. The northern face of the fort consisted simply of trenches and rifle pits. About fifty yards in front of the trenches, a barricade of trees cut from the forest at the edge of Cunningham's hayfield were stacked lengthwise to form a porous barrier. Pickets were posted at the tree barricades and along the road at the foot of the cliff, which formed the fort's southern face. Jackson planned to attack the fort from two directions. One force would approach the north side of the fort through Cunningham's hayfield. The other force would make its way around the face of the steep cliff on the south side and attack from both sides of the cliff. Jackson would locate his artillery across the river from the fort and keep the fort's defenders pinned down while his troops scaled the hillsides.[80]

To maintain the crucial element of surprise, Jackson sent a squad of men dressed in blue jackets to capture all pickets posted that night. The pickets were speedily and quietly removed. Jackson sent Major Kessler and most of his infantry through the Cunningham fields north of the fort where they hid in the forest until daylight. With the remainder of his men and his two piece battery, Jackson took a back trail to the top of a hill across the Little Kanawha

River from the Bulltown fort. From this vantage point Jackson mounted his artillery in such a way that the guns could shoot down at the fort. He sent Lieutenant Colonel William P. Thompson and the remainder of his troops to the river, with instructions to cross and assault the cliff below the fort. While the hill directly in front of the fort was too steep to be climbed, the slopes on either side of the promontory could be scaled. A single cannon shot at four-thirty in the morning on 13 October would be the signal for simultaneous assaults by Kessler from the north and Thompson from the south.[81]

Major Kessler and his men had been in position for several hours and grew impatient waiting for the signal to attack. Kessler checked his watch and noted that it said four-thirty. Figuring that something had gone wrong with the artillery, Kessler ordered his troops to advance. At this point, the Bulltown garrison seemed ripe for plucking. No alarm had been given, all of the pickets had been captured, and Kessler should have been able to simply walk into the fort and announce that everyone there was his prisoner. However, one overly zealous company commander, while leading his men at a trot through the early morning mist, discharged his pistol into the air and shouted "Charge!"[82]

The federal troops inside the Bulltown garrison were veterans of the Sixth and Eleventh West Virginia Infantry regiments. They were under the command of William H. Mattingly, captain of the Sixth Infantry's Company G. Surprised but not panicked by the sudden appearance of a screaming horde of rebels charging directly at them, the seasoned federal soldiers, most of them in their underwear, quickly grabbed their rifles and dove for the trenches and rifle pits. The charging rebels presented only the briefest of targets in the low-lying fog of dawn, but the federal troops poured a withering fire in the general direction of Cunningham's hayfield. Although only two Confederates were hit in the initial volley, the volume of fire forced the charging line to stop its advance and reconsider. Some of the men moved forward cautiously and penetrated the barrier of downed trees, only to be driven back by rapid firing from the entrenched federals. Kessler's assault had been stopped in its tracks.[83]

Meanwhile, across the river Jackson's two gun battery had gone into action. Not until the first few rounds had thudded harmlessly into the earthen walls of the fort did Jackson realize that someone had made a critical error. The shot for the two six-pound guns, laboriously dragged over the mountains from Huntersville, was mostly solid shot. Jackson had ordered canister shells, but no one had checked the supply to determine that that was the type of shell supplied with the cannons. The solid shot had no effect on the dirt walls of the Bulltown fort. At the foot of the hill, Thompson's attempt to scale the sides of the cliff to reach the fort also failed. The Confederates quickly discovered that their rifles did not have sufficient range to reach federal defenders at the top of the cliff. On the other hand, the Yankees' Enfield rifles had more than enough range to reach the attacking Confederates at the bottom of the hill. Kessler encountered this same problem on his end of the attack. His troops were forced to move out of range of the federal rifles, but when they did, they discovered that their rifles did not have enough power to reach the fort's trench works.

With his infantry reduced to the role of spectators, Jackson's artillery continued to lob shells at the fort. Around six thirty in the morning Jackson sent a message to Captain Mattingly requesting that he bow to superior force and surrender. Mattingly returned a message saying, "Come and take us."[84] Jackson resumed his artillery bombardment and occasional sniping at exposed federal soldiers. At some point during the morning Captain Mattingly was struck in the thigh by a bullet. Captain James L. Simpson of the Eleventh Infantry assumed command. Around three o'clock in the afternoon Jackson sent another message to the Union garrison, demanding that it surrender in the name of humanity. Captain Simpson, noting that his men had suffered only one casualty, replied that the fort would fight until Hell froze over, then retreat on the ice if necessary.[85] Frustrated beyond endurance, Jackson continued shelling the fort until he ran out of ammunition around four thirty in the afternoon. He ordered his troops to disengage and began to withdraw south toward Sutton. Jackson left behind on the battlefield seven dead soldiers and six others too badly wounded to move.[86] Mattingly reported no casualties other than his wound.[87]

Jackson withdrew his weary army to Salt Lick Bridge, five miles south of Bulltown on the Weston and Gauley Bridge Turnpike. The army camped overnight only to be rudely awakened the following morning when a detachment of the Fourth West Virginia Cavalry charged into their midst. Believing that they were attacking Jackson's rear guard, the forty men of the Fourth Cavalry quickly realized that they had ridden rashly into the middle of Jackson's entire army. Outnumbered twenty to one, the federal cavalrymen hastily retreated, but not before one of the federal troopers seized the reins of a mule loaded with one of Jackson's artillery pieces and led it away. Fearful that a larger federal force was in the wake of the impetuous cavalry company, Jackson started his army moving southward. On the afternoon of 14 October, Jackson rode into Sutton and scattered the slight opposition threatened by the Braxton Home Guard company. He confiscated enough supplies in Sutton to feed his men while they fled the area. The army marched on to Birch River where a small federal detachment sent from Summersville to block its retreat was dispersed. Guided by George and Lewis McElwain, two Webster County farmers who were members of Company B, the army turned up the Birch River road, crossed the mountain to Laurel Creek, and continued to Webster Glades. Just after the army started up Laurel Creek, the remaining mule carrying Lurty's surviving six pounder suddenly balked. Repeated attempts to force the mule to move failed, and Jackson ordered the gun abandoned. The McElwains carried the gun to their nearby farm and buried it.[88] At the Glades the exhausted army camped. The rear guard reported that no pursuit was in sight. The federal commander at Clarksburg, Benjamin Kelley, had his own problems. Kelley reported that Jackson was retreating up Bryant's Fork on the Little Kanawha River toward Addison, Webster County. Jackson was retreating up Birch River, and the federal cavalry sent after him was misdirected to a road nearly thirty miles northeast of Jackson's actual position.[89]

A disgruntled William Jackson and his dispirited army straggled back into Camp Northwest around 20 October. Instead of the anticipated triumphant return from a spectacularly successful raid, Jackson had to deal with rumors that he, Lieutenant Colonel Thompson and Major Kessler had all been drunk at the time of the attack on Bulltown. On 22 October Jackson tried to dispel these rumors in a letter to Captain Jacob Marshall, whose company had been part of the diversionary force sent to Huttonsville and was not present at Bulltown. Jackson wrote to Marshall, "No one can escape slander. I am however surprised at the talk . . . the charges are utterly without foundation both as regards Lt. Col. Thompson and myself. I am sure nothing has emanated from Maj. Kessler to justify what they say."[90] Rumors of drunkeness at Bulltown among Jackson and his officers persisted into the post-war period, but no official inquiry at the time was made.[91]

DROOP MOUNTAIN

Jackson quickly put the disappointment of the Bulltown adventure behind him. Rumors abounded that Averell planned to strike at Lewisburg, and Jackson increased patrols along the Huttonsville road and the Parkersburg and Staunton Turnpike. Jackson established his headquarters at Millpoint, seven miles south of Marlin's Bottom on the Lewisburg road. While in camp at Millpoint on the evening of 3 November 1863, Jackson received a dispatch from Lieutenant George Siple, commander of Company F, Nineteenth Virginia Cavalry, from his outpost at Dunmore between Huntersville and Camp Bartow. Siple reported that federal cavalry had appeared in force on the Greenbank road. Jackson immediately dispatched couriers to recall companies stationed throughout the area. Messages were sent to Colonel Arnett at Marlin's Bottom and to Jacob Marshall at Edray instructing them to meet Jackson at Millpoint, seven miles south of Marlin's Bottom on the Lewisburg road. A courier was also sent to recall Joseph Kessler and William Thompson, who were on their way to raid Nicholas County with over one hundred and twenty mounted men. Jackson sent a dispatch to Siple ordering him to determine the size of the federal force and the direction in which it seemed to be moving. After sending this vital intelligence to Jackson, Siple had orders to withdraw to Millpoint along the Beaver Creek road— which led from Huntersville to Millpoint— and to blockade the road as he retired. In case the federal movement was the long anticipated drive to Lewisburg, Jackson sent a dispatch to General John Echols at Lewisburg advising him that a federal force of around one thousand men was advancing on Huntersville.[92]

Jackson waited throughout the early morning hours of 4 November for information from Lieutenant Siple detailing the strength of the invading federals. He waited in vain. While trying to estimate Union strength near Greenbank, Siple and his company were cut off and forced to circle far to the north to avoid capture. Siple's absence alarmed Jackson. Colonel Arnett had been stationed at Marlin's Bottom with the Nineteenth and Twentieth cavalry's supply train. Jackson ordered Arnett to start the wagons moving immediately to Millpoint and to send scouts to Huntersville to report on the enemy's progress. Around noon scouts reported to Jackson that federal infantry was moving down the Beaver Creek road towards Millpoint. Jackson sent William Thompson, who had arrived in camp only an hour earlier after being recalled from his Nicholas County raid, to blockade the Beaver Creek road and hold it until Arnett and the wagon train passed the Beaver Creek intersection with the Lewisburg road. With only eighty men Thompson frantically ordered that trees be cut across the road. His men took positions behind their freshly cut barricade just as federal troops came into view. Thompson's men stopped the federal advance in its tracks with a steady and effective fire. For over three hours Thompson kept the intersection clear until Arnett passed safely through around dusk. Thompson then pulled his men back, one squad at a time, to the base of Droop Mountain.[93] David Poe of Company A, Twentieth Cavalry, was in charge of the last squad withdrawn by Thompson. Writing about the event fifty years later, Poe recalled:

Jackson prepared to fall back, leaving Company "A" 20th regiment as a skirmish line along the bank of Mill Creek. . . . We were directed to remain until we had orders to fall back. . . . We had to keep up a brisk firing all along our line owing to our weakness and the distance we were from the main body of our command. I thought time very long for the message to come bidding us to retire. When it did come it came to the end of the line that I had charge of. Adjutant (Robert S.) Smith, who brought the message for us to fall back, stood on a hill quite a distance from our line, and called to me loud enough to be heard by the enemy. To save further delay I arose from my cover and gave command, "Attention, company on right and left take intervals in retreat, double quick march."

*Before I got through the command company "A" was getting out of that
valley just as fast as their feet could carry them. About three regiments of
blue coats was coming after us yelling and shooting. We had to travel at
least three miles before we were safe.*[94]

Jackson still had no idea of the federal force he faced.[95] General William Averell commanded the army moving toward Jackson at Millpoint. His command included the Twenty-eighth Ohio Infantry, the Tenth West Virginia Infantry, the Second, Third and Eighth West Virginia Mounted infantries, the Fourteenth Pennsylvania Cavalry, and three artillery companies. Averell had around 3,500 men in his army.[96] Jackson had around four hundred men on hand to dispute Averell's progress. On the night of 5 November Jackson calculated that the federal force in front of him numbered around 3,500 men. His astonishingly accurate estimate was derived from counting campfires of the federal encampment on the plateau known as the Little Levels.[97]

On 5 November, Jackson sent a dispatch to General Echols advising him that if the federals continued to advance, he would establish a defensive position on Droop Mountain and fight them until he was reinforced. By nine o'clock that morning Echols had dispatched the Twenty-second Virginia Infantry Regiment, the Twenty-third and Twenty-sixth Virginia infantry battalions and the Fourteenth Virginia cavalry regiment to reinforce Jackson. One four gun battery and one two gun battery also joined the flow toward Droop Mountain. The four units sent to Jackson's support numbered only around one thousand soldiers.[98]

With no reinforcements in sight, William Jackson and his desperately outmanned companies dug in near the top of Droop Mountain. Jackson was forced to stretch his thin line in a fishhook shape around the mountain's summit. He had to block the main road leading over the mountain to Lewisburg, and he had to block the Lobelia road to his north to prevent the federals from flanking the left side of his line. He had nearly three-fourths of a mile of front line to man with four hundred men. Jackson's artillery consisted of two twelve pound howitzers commanded by Warren Lurty. On the morning of 5 November, federal sharpshooters and skirmishers began to advance on Jackson's position, but Lurty's artillery worked to better effect than the guns he had lost at Bulltown. During the morning Lurty's guns kept the Union skirmishers at a distance. Blockades thrown across the Lewisburg road by Arnett and the Beaver Creek road by Thompson delayed the arrival and placement of Union artillery. Around two o'clock in the afternoon the main federal force appeared in the fields below Droop Mountain. To Jackson's relief, the federals halted their advance and went into camp near Hillsboro.[99]

Jackson's troops spent the evening and night of 5 November strengthening their positions on Droop Mountain. Jackson received a communication from Echols advising him that help was on the way, and early in the evening Colonel James Cochran arrived with the Fourteenth Virginia Cavalry. The precipitous slope and steeply graded main road over Droop Mountain was nearly impregnable. Jackson placed his artillery on an embankment overlooking the road at the summit. He decided that a couple of infantry companies would be sufficient to protect the battery and stop any attack from that direction. On the summit of Droop Mountain at the center of Jackson's position, he placed Colonel William Arnett and several companies of the Twentieth Virginia Cavalry. During the night Arnett's men hastily cut trees and formed breastworks. The steepness of the mountain and the fact that several cleared fields reached nearly to the summit, led Jackson to believe that the federals would not risk a major assault at that point.[100]

The back side of Droop Mountain was more problematical. The Lobelia road cut through low hills on the western slope of Droop Mountain, and rejoined the Lewisburg road about two miles south of Jackson's position. The terrain along the Lobelia road, although heavily wooded and irregular, sloped gradually to the mountain's summit. Jackson concluded that the main federal assault on the mountain would come from that direction. During the night Jackson positioned two companies of the Fourteenth Cavalry across the Lobelia road. At dawn on 6 November, as federal skirmishers began probing Jackson's defenses, Jackson sent William Thompson and several companies of the Nineteenth Cavalry to strengthen the line on the left, which Jackson perceived as the key to defense of the mountain.[101]

Around nine o'clock on the morning of 6 November, General Echols arrived from Lewisburg and assumed command of the defense of Droop Mountain. Jackson led Echols on a hurried tour of the defensive line he had established, and Echols endorsed Jackson's arrangements to meet the anticipated assault. Colonel George Patton arrived with the Twenty-second Virginia Infantry and Colonel Clarence Derrick appeared shortly afterwards with the Twenty-third Virginia Battalion of Infantry. Echols placed Patton behind the center of Jackson's line, where he could be moved to reinforce any point which might weaken during the assault. Derrick was sent to support the artillery on the right of the line.[102]

Averell launched his assault on Droop Mountain at eleven o'clock on the morning of 6 November. He ordered James Schoonmaker and the Fourteenth Pennsylvania Cavalry to demonstrate along the main Lewisburg road to divert Confederate attention from the main attacks he planned to wage on the center and left of the Confederate position. To support Schoonmaker and lend credence to his feint, Averell placed all of his artillery on the right and ordered a constant bombardment of the Confederate artillery position

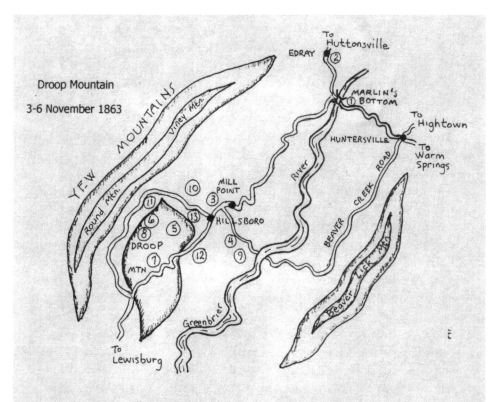

Droop Mountain

3-6 November 1863

Troop Movements Around Droop Mountain, 3 – 6 November 1863

1 – Arnett, 3 November
2 -- Marshall, 3 November
3 -- Jackson, 3-4 November
4 – Thompson, 4 November
5 – Arnett, 5-6 November
6 – Cochran, 5-6 November
7 – Lurty, 5-6 November
8 – Thompson, 6 November
9 – Averell, 4 November
10 – Averell, 5 November
11 – Moor and Harris, 6 November
12 – Schoonmaker, 6 November
13 – Averell, 6 November

at the summit of the mountain. Colonel Augustus Moor and the Twenty-eighth Ohio Infantry assaulted the Confederate left along the Lobelia road. Colonel Thomas Harris and the Tenth West Virginia Infantry supported Moor. The Second, Third and Eighth West Virginia Infantry regiments were positioned in the center of Averell's line at the foot of Droop Mountain. They would not attack until Moor turned the Confederate flank on the left.[103]

When the attack by Moor began at eleven o'clock, less than four hundred men of the Nineteenth Cavalry were in position to meet the assault of Moor's nearly two thousand federal infantry. The companies of John Sprigg, James Boggs, Jacob Marshall and Marcus Jarrett, commanded by Major Joseph Kessler, held the federal attack for a short time. Jackson recognized that despite the noise being made on the right and occasional firing from the center, the main federal assault was concentrated on the left. He sent Colonel Thompson and one hundred seventy-five men to support the hard-pressed companies of the Nineteenth Cavalry. Thompson barely arrived when he sent a courier to Echols and Jackson demanding more reinforcements. Echols directed two companies of the Fourteenth Cavalry and the Twenty-third Battalion to Thompson's assistance. As an afterthought, he ordered Company A of the Twentieth Cavalry under Lieutenant David Burns to abandon its position in the center of the line and move to the left.[104] From his position opposite the Confederate center, General Averell observed Company A's movement. He concluded that the Confederate left was weakening, and he ordered a direct assault on Arnett's position in the center of the Confederate line at the top of Droop Mountain.[105] To attack Arnett's position the federal troops had to cross an area of open ground on a steep hillside. From behind their improvised breastworks, Arnett's men poured a destructive fire into the advancing blue coats, forcing them to retreat and regroup several times.[106]

On the Confederate left the superior numbers of the federal attackers began to push back the Confederate defenders. Echols ordered George Patton and three companies of the Twenty-second Infantry to reinforce the left. When Patton arrived he discovered that the entire Confederate line was withdrawing and in danger of collapse. William Thompson was attempting to rally his troops, but with little success. Patton ordered his three companies to charge the advancing federals with bayonets, and this daring and dangerous move actually began pushing back Moor's advance. Inspired by Patton's success, Thompson was able to form a sizable detachment from among his Nineteenth Cavalry companies. They were preparing to advance in support of Patton's companies when Patton received a communication from Echols stating that the right side of the Confederate line at the summit had given way and that the left wing should pull back to the top of the mountain immediately.[107] Patton ordered the troops to withdraw slowly, but at that moment the Tenth West Virginia Infantry, held in reserve during most of the fighting

William Lowther Jackson.

William Lowther Jackson.

Uniform of William Lowther Jackson. *Courtesy John M. Ashcraft*

Brigadier General William Woods Averell - he commanded his 4th Separate Brigade, U.S. Army, in the Droop Mountain battle and campaign. *Courtesy National Archives*

Johnson N. Camden. *Courtesy West Virginia State Archives*

Brigadier General John Echols - he commanded the 1ˢᵗ Brigade, Army of Southwest Virginia, C.S.A., and was field commander of all Confederate forces at Droop Mountain. *Courtesy U.S. Army Military History Institute (MOLLUS Collection).*

Col. Thomas Maley Harris - of the 10th West Virginia Volunteer Infantry. Gallantly led his regiment against the Confederate left flank at Droop Mountain, contributing to the subsequent Federal breakthrough. *Courtesy U. S. Army Military History Institute (MOLLUS Collection)*

Brigadier General John Daniel Imboden – he commanded the (Shenandoah) Valley District, C.S.A., during the Droop Mountain campaign and made an unsuccessful pursuit of Averell. *Courtesy U.S. Army Military History Institute (MOLLUS Collection)*

General Thomas Jonathan "Stonewall" Jackson. *Courtesy WV State Archives*

General Albert G. Jenkins. *Courtesy Library of Congress*

General William E. Jones. *Courtesy West Virginia State Archives*

Capt. Jacob Williamson Marshall - Co. I, 19th Virginia Cavalry. A pre-war resident of Randolph County, Marshall was appointed Captain on March 19, 1863 and temporarily kept the Federal attack on the Confederate left at Droop Mountain in check. His commanding officer said that during the affair he "distinguished himself for his coolness and calm disregard of danger." He survived the war, became a merchant, hotel operator, farmer, and Census Deputy Collector for the Internal Revenue Service. He passed away in 1899. *Courtesy Pocahontas County Historical Society*

General John W. McCausland. *Courtesy West Virginia State Archives*

Lt. Col. William P. Thompson - of the 19ᵗʰ Virginia Cavalry. He commanded the Confederate left flank at Droop Mountain. *Courtesy Author's Collection*

General Jubal Early, 1816-1894. *Courtesy Tim McKinney*

General Lunsford Lomax, 1835-1913. *Courtesy Tim McKinney*

W.L. Jackson's grave. *Courtesy Joe Ferrell*

W.L. Jackson's grave (detail). *Courtesy Joe Ferrell*

on the left, asserted itself on the extreme right of the federal line. The new attack with fresh troops turned the tide, and the Confederate withdrawal became a rout.[108]

By four o'clock in the afternoon the scene at the top of Droop Mountain was chaotic. When George Patton arrived at the summit, Echols ordered him to move to the front and rally the troops. Patton noted in his report that he could not execute Echols' order because "the whole road was blocked with artillery, caissons, wagons, and horses, which forced many of the men to take to the woods to escape capture."[109] Captain John K. Thompson of the Twenty-second Virginia Infantry, who had led the charge on the left of the line which momentarily stopped the federal advance, also was caught in the disarray on top of the mountain. "Artillery, baggage wagons, and fleeing cavalry," Thompson wrote, "blocked up the road for some distance to our rear. Several efforts were made to rally the troops, but without effect, so that nothing was left but to draw off, which was done amid much confusion."[110]

David Poe, captain of Company A, Twentieth Virginia Cavalry, recalled that Company A was the last unit to abandon its position in the center of the Confederate line at Droop Mountain. Poe's eyewitness account of the withdrawal clearly detailed the panic and confusion of the retreat: *At the end of the mountain where Company "A" was stationed there was some very hard fighting and we lost a few men. I saw Lieut. Ulysses Morgan killed. . . . The life of Capt. Downs' men Sergt. Wm. Straight, was wounded; Capt. (David) Camp's blanket was nearly shot off of him, and had as many as eight or ten holes in it. Milton Lake had a port hole in his breastworks. A blue coat crawled up to a tree to Lake, peeped over a root and shot at Lake through the hole, filling his mouth and eyes with rotten wood and trash from his temporary works. Lake could see a small part of him above the root and arose from his hiding place, standing erect and fired. The ball passed through the bark of the root and the soldier rolled down the hill, while a dozen or more bullets whizzed around Lake's head. Gen. Jackson was near by and told Lake to lie down or he would get his head shot off. When we fell back to the road we found that our retreat by that route was cut off. Then we filed to our left leaving the road . . . to escape capture. . . . It was some time before we all got together in good shape again.[111]*

The first reports from Droop Mountain produced panic among the Confederate high command. General Samuel Jones at Dublin rushed communications to Richmond the day after the battle lamenting that "General Echols was badly defeated, with heavy loss in killed, wounded, and prisoners,

yesterday. . . . I fear he cannot escape the enemy's cavalry."[112] The next day
Jones wrote to James Seddon, Confederate Secretary of War, that "Echols'
brigade is nearly destroyed. . . . Send reinforcements if possible."[113] Jefferson
Davis replied tersely to Jones' lament: "Unless local defense men and militia
can be had, there is no reinforcement possible, and it only remains to con-
centrate on the best position and make entrenchments, if they will avail."[114]
William Jackson contributed to the general sense of foreboding in his report
to Echols on 9 November. "I fear my loss is about 150 in killed and wounded,"
Jackson wrote, "including a number of gallant officers. You will appreciate
the difficulty in estimating the loss at this time."[115] Jackson's losses were not
as severe as he first feared. After collecting numerous stragglers who fled
from the battle scene at Droop Mountain, Jackson tabulated his official losses
for the Nineteenth and Twentieth cavalries in the action on 6 November as
eleven killed, thirteen wounded, and twenty-eight captured.[116]

The Confederate leadership in Richmond perceived the defeat at Droop
Mountain as a significant setback for the struggling nation. Someone had to
be held accountable for the disaster, and William L. Jackson and his command became the objects of official criticism. John Imboden started focus-
ing criticism on Jackson and his men in a report he filed on 14 November.
Imboden, whose brigade was not at Droop Mountain but made an unsuccessful attempt at Covington to cut off Averell's withdrawal from Lewisburg
on 9 November, concluded the report on his campaign with a critical reference to some of Jackson's soldiers:

> I regret to have to add that of nearly 200 stragglers from Colonel Jackson's
> – whom I found at Covington and supplied with funds to subsist them-
> selves, and supplied with arms, where they had lost their own, out of
> some Virginia State arms I found at Covington – a large number ran off
> to the woods and mountains as soon as my artillery opened on the enemy,
> although I had organized them into two companies and ordered them to
> take part in the fight I then expected would occur. A part remained and
> were willing to fight, but a large number fled most shamefully before the
> enemy was nearer than 2 miles of where I left them to await orders.[117]

Secretary of War James Seddon accepted Imboden's criticism of Jackson's
men and forwarded instructions to Samuel Jones on 1 December that "Colonel Jackson's attention should be called to the conduct of part of his men
who had straggled."[118] Imboden did not identify the regiments or companies of the stragglers he encountered. In his report of the Droop Mountain
battle, written the day after Imboden claimed to have encountered the two
hundred stragglers, Jackson admitted that many of his command were unac-
counted for and that he could only estimate casualties. Jackson took no offi-

cial notice of Imboden's complaint. By 1 December Jackson had reassembled his two cavalry regiments and established his winter headquarters at Warm Springs, Bath County. All of the company officers were available when Averell struck again on 12 December 1863.

SALEM DEPOT

The purpose of William Averell's raid into the Greenbrier Valley in November 1863 was to attack the Virginia and Tennessee Railroad at Dublin Station, Pulaski County. The New River bridge at Dublin was critical to continued operation of the railroad, the only transportation link between Robert E. Lee's Army of Northern Virginia and Braxton Bragg's Army of Tennessee. Averell's attempt to reach the New River bridge in November fell apart when a Union force sent from Charleston to meet him at Lewisburg arrived in an exhausted condition and could not continue. Retreating Confederates blocked the road from Lewisburg to Union by cutting trees across the road, and reports that a large Confederate force had gathered near Dublin Station to oppose his advance forced Averell to conclude that an attack on the railroad was impractical. He returned to Beverly with his army intact to await another opportunity.[119] On 6 December 1863 Averell received an order from Brigadier General Benjamin Kelley, instructing him to take all of his available force and proceed by the most practicable route to the line of the Virginia and Tennessee Railroad, either at Bonsack's Station in Botetourt County, or at Salem in Roanoke County. Once he reached the railroad he was to destroy all bridges, water stations and depots along the line and tear up the rails "as far as possible."[120]

Averell left his headquarters at New Creek, Hampshire County, on 8 December 1863 with most of the same regiments that had fought at Droop Mountain a month earlier. Four different Union commands were ordered to support Averell's invasion by creating diversionary movements. General Eliakim Scammon, commander of Union forces in the Kanawha Valley, was ordered to capture Lewisburg to prevent any Confederate attempt from the north to cut off Averell on his way to Salem. Augustus Moor, who had led the Twenty-eighth Ohio Infantry on its successful turning of the Confederate left at Droop Mountain, was ordered to patrol the Lewisburg road from Marlin's Bottom to Frankford to secure Averell's line of retreat. Brigadier General Jeremiah C. Sullivan in the lower Shenandoah Valley was ordered to send parts of his brigade along the Valley Pike and feint an attack on Staunton to draw Confederate attention away from Averell's progress through the upper Jackson's River valley. Finally, Colonel Joseph Thoburn was ordered to meet Averell at Monterey with the First West Virginia Infantry. Thoburn would take his force eastward along the Parkersburg and Staunton Turnpike toward Staunton as a diversion while Averell moved with his main force down the Back Creek road in Bath County.[121]

Before William Jackson learned of Averell's latest invasion of Bath County, he lost nearly half of his available force. Augustus Moor and the Twenty-eighth Ohio Infantry arrived at the Greenbrier River bridge at Marlin's Bottom on the evening of 11 December. The federal troops drove back Jackson's pickets at the bridge, but during the night moved on south on the Lewisburg road. Jackson sent Colonel William Thompson and one hundred and twenty-five men to scout the federal movement. Not content to merely watch the federals moving along the road, Thompson launched an attack on the column's rear guard. Moor's Ohioans reversed their course and counterattacked. Thompson's men, outnumbered ten to one, fled into the mountains. When Thompson reported to Jackson at Hot Springs at one o'clock in the morning on 14 December he had only twenty-five men with him. Another one hundred and fifty men were lost on the afternoon of 13 December, when Jacob Marshall's command was attacked and dispersed at Gatewood's by Averell's main force. Marshall faced odds of twenty-five against one, and his men barely paused to return fire before disappearing back up the Warm Springs road toward Huntersville. The men lost by Thompson and Marshall's command did not reappear in Jackson's camp until Averell's army returned from Salem in late December.[122]

During the afternoon of 13 December, Jackson received a dispatch advising him of Thoburn's movement toward Staunton from Monterey. Jackson concluded that his tiny command was the object of the federal offensive. He suspected that Thoburn's troops would turn south from McDowell and trap Jackson's regiments between him and the federal force on the Back Creek road. To avoid the trap, Jackson began moving his entire regiment south from Hot Springs during a heavy rainstorm, hoping to meet reinforcements along the way.[123] In the process Jackson became embroiled in one of the most confusing campaigns of the Civil War. William Averell's raid on the Salem Depot of the Virginia and Tennessee Railroad on 16 December 1863 sliced through six Confederate brigades sent to stop him. Despite traveling through two hundred miles of Confederate territory in torrential rains, Averell managed to attack Salem completely by surprise. With nearly 12,000 Confederate troops converging on the area, Averell engineered an escape without parallel in the war's annals. During the six days of his retreat from Salem to Beverly, Averell's men essentially were unarmed. Freezing rains during the first two days of their retreat had soaked most of their powder, and their horses were shod inadequately. Nevertheless, Averell raided Salem and escaped virtually unscathed. Six deaths, all by accidental drowning, five men wounded, and one hundred and nineteen men captured comprised Averell's casualty list.[124] William L. Jackson and the Nineteenth and Twentieth

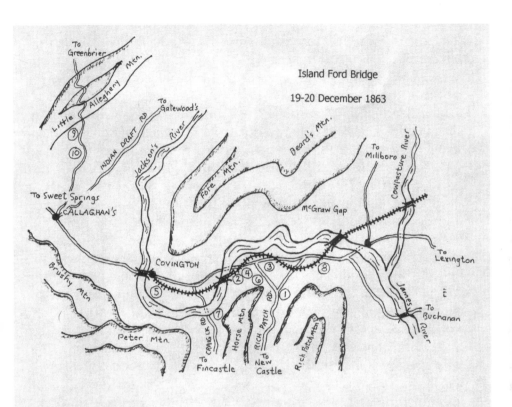

Island Ford Bridge

19-20 December 1863

Troop Movements Around Island Ford Bridge, 19 – 20 December 1863

1 – Sprigg and Lady, 19 December
2 – McCallister, 19 December
3 – Jackson, 19 December
4 – Downs and Poe, 19 December
5 – Averell, 19 December
6 – Fourteenth Pennsylvania Cavalry, 19 December
7 – Fourteenth Pennsylvania Cavalry, 20 December
8 – Arnett, 20 December
9 – Averell, 20 Decembe
10 – Sprigg, 20 December

Virginia cavalries played a major role in allowing Averell to escape punishment for his raid.

When Jacob Marshall's company was attacked and dispersed at Gatewood's by Averell's raiders on 13 December, Jackson believed that the federal force was part of the detachment that had appeared at Marlin's Bottom a few days earlier. He expected the federals at Gatewood's to continue along the Warm Springs road and try to trap his small force between them and the federal army that had been reported at McDowell. He withdrew his entire command to Hot Springs, thinking that he was out of harm's way.[125] Jackson had only one hundred and fifty mounted men. The remainder of the horses belonging to the Nineteenth and Twentieth had been taken to Crab Bottom, Highland County, to forage for the winter. The four hundred men remaining under Jackson's command at the time of Averell's raid were dismounted cavalrymen.[126] While at Hot Springs, Jackson received an urgent dispatch from John D. Imboden on Shenandoah Mountain urging Jackson to come to his assistance. Sullivan had launched his diversionary movement against Imboden, who feared that he could not protect Staunton without reinforcements. Jackson believed at the time that the federal movements in the area were aimed at destroying his command and that the attack against Imboden was a feint. He replied to Imboden that he was also under attack and had been driven from Warm Springs. He advised Imboden that he thought the federals at Staunton were decoys.[127]

Jackson had just sent his dispatch to Imboden when couriers brought him information that a large force of federal cavalry was approaching Callaghan's Station on the Back Creek road. Jackson, not realizing that this was the force that had scattered Marshall's company at Gatewood's, could scarcely believe that federal cavalry estimated at more than two thousand mounted men had appeared on the Back Creek road without his knowledge. With no orders to address this unexpected problem, Jackson decided on his own initiative to head for Callaghan's in an attempt to block the federal advance. Scouts reported that Jackson's River was flooded and could not be crossed. Jackson altered his line of march to take him through McGraw's Gap at Clifton Forge and across the river on the railroad bridges at Clifton Forge and Covington. He sent Colonel Thompson ahead of the dismounted cavalry, reluctantly serving as infantry, to scout the road to Callaghan's. Thompson soon returned to report that General Averell had passed through Callaghan's earlier in the day in the direction of Sweet Springs, Monroe County. Jackson had been advised that John Echols and his brigade had been rushed to Sweet Springs to block any federal movement in that area, and he concluded that the federal raiding party was trapped between Echols at Sweet Springs and his own command at Callaghan's. Jackson began placing his four hundred men in positions to intercept the federals if Echols forced them back from Sweet Springs. However, around two o'clock in the afternoon of 17 December Jackson received orders from General Samuel Jones to retire to Clifton Forge and establish defensive positions around the intersection of the Rich Patch road and the Covington road. Before he had all of his men in position, Jackson received another communication from Jones advising him to return to Callaghan's and establish a defensive position there. At the same time a courier handed Jackson a dispatch from General Jubal Early, who had brought a large force from Staunton as far as Millboro Station to help trap Averell. Early ordered Jackson to fall back to the Lick Run bridge five miles east of Clifton Forge to block Averell's possible escape over the Lynchburg and Dribell Springs road. Since none of the flurry of dispatches Jackson received during 17-18 December mentioned the exact location of Averell's force, Jackson decided to remain where he was until someone actually sighted the enemy.[128] At the time Jackson received the dispatch from Early, Averell had already destroyed the supply depot at Salem, and had selected the Rich Patch road as the most favorable route to bring him back to Jackson's River. By the time Jackson made the decision to ignore orders from both Samuel Jones and Jubal Early, Averell was fifteen miles away with twenty-five hundred cavalrymen heading straight for Jackson's position at Clifton Forge.[129]

On the afternoon of 19 December, a scout reported to Jackson that he had seen three federal cavalrymen along the Craig Creek road south of Rich Patch Mountain. Jackson sent John Sprigg and fifty mounted men to investigate. Shortly after Sprigg left, Major John Lady reported that the Fincastle road was empty of federals. Lady's report convinced Jackson that Averell's main force was on the Rich Patch road. He sent Lady after Sprigg with reinforcements and orders to skirmish with the advancing federals, while Jackson made arrangements to stop their retreat at Clifton Forge.[130]

Two Central Virginia Railroad bridges spanned Jackson's River in the immediate vicinity of Jackson's position. Since the river could not be crossed because of high water, Jackson believed that destruction of the bridges would block Averell's retreat. Jackson had received dispatches advising him that Jubal Early and Fitzhugh Lee were converging on Clifton Forge with large contingents of infantry and cavalry. If Jackson could hold Averell between Clifton Forge and Covington until Early and Lee arrived, Averell's entire command could be captured. However, Jackson faced an immediate challenge; he was out of available men. Jackson located Captain Thompson McCallister and the Alleghany County Home Guards and gave McAllister and his men the critical task of destroying the Island Ford Bridge east of Covington. McAllister was sent off with instructions to guard the bridge, and to burn it if federal troops appeared on the road. Later in the afternoon Jackson realized that this most crucial assignment had been given to poorly armed, untrained civilians. He sent Lieutenant Boyd, a member of an engineer corps who happened to be in the area, to the Island Ford Bridge to supervise its destruction. Still apprehensive over the bridge's destruction, Jackson sent George Downs and Company A of the Nineteenth Cavalry to establish a defensive position in front of the bridge.[131]

While Jackson focused on destruction of the Island Ford Bridge, Major Lady and Captain Sprigg had encountered Averell's entire force on the Rich Patch road. Averell had little ammunition available because most of his troops' powder had been soaked during the incessant rainfall which had followed them ever since the raid began. Nevertheless, with his small supply of dry powder and a numerical superiority of twenty to one Averell easily brushed aside the attempt by Lady and Sprigg to delay his progress. Jackson's report of his activities on the evening of 19 December described what happened next:

> *In the meantime (it had become dark), I moved my whole command to the point of intersection of the Rich Patch and Covington roads. I also dispatched several different couriers and aides to the bridge to order its destruction. A considerable force of the enemy, by some route that had never been explained to me – although I sought information from every source, and was assured that I was guarding every possible approach – threw themselves between me and the bridge, cut off Lieutenant Boyd, fired into or captured my messengers, and, as it now appears, rushed upon the bridge, surprising and scattering the home guards before they set fire to the bridge.*[132]

The "considerable force of the enemy" which had successfully rushed and seized control of the Island Ford Bridge was Averell's entire force, with the exception of his rear guard, the Fourteenth Pennsylvania Cavalry. Jackson's attempt to cut off Averell's retreat failed in spectacular fashion, but he still had an opportunity to inflict some damage on Averell's brigade. Informed that Averell's rear guard was still on the east side of the Island Ford Bridge, Jackson ordered Colonel Arnett and the Twentieth Cavalry, all of it dismounted, to prevent the federals from reaching the bridge.[133]

Having heard nothing from his couriers sent to give the order to burn the Island Ford Bridge, Jackson decided to ride to the bridge and personally supervise the operation. When he arrived at the bridge some of the men from George Downs' company were milling about in confusion. They informed Jackson that a large number of federal troops had crossed the bridge and had mounted a guard at the east end of the structure. Jackson did not find their report credible. He rode toward the bridge intending to ignite the bridge himself, when a volley of rifle fire whistled over his head. Jackson prudently retired to the hillside overlooking the bridge to determine what to do next. Other officers attempting to deal with the situation were unable to locate Jackson for the next couple of hours, and rumors circulated that he had been captured.[134] Left to operate on their own initiative, Jackson's subordinates failed to react competently or efficiently.

Sprigg and Lady had already abandoned their attack on Averell's main force, and tried to regroup their men in the dark and rain-soaked forest along the Rich Patch road. George Downs and his company arrived at the Island Ford Bridge after Averell had crossed and prepared to prevent the federal rear guard from crossing. Arnett sent a company of less than twenty men under the command of Captain David Poe to reinforce Downs. Taking advantage of the darkness and rain, this small group attacked federal sentinels stationed at a railroad underpass. The sentinels fled from the small group of screaming rebels, and the Confederates chased them for nearly half a mile before they stumbled into a group of wagons, ambulances, blacks, and stragglers. The stragglers were disarmed and Major Lady with some mounted troops conducted the wagons and ambulances beyond Confederate lines. Poe and Downs turned their men around and hurried back to the Island Ford Bridge to await the main force of the Fourteenth Cavalry. Poe stationed men at an embankment a short distance in front of the entrance onto the Island Ford Bridge. Downs took a position a few hundred yards in advance of Poe. In his memoirs, published in 1911, Poe recalled the circumstances surrounding the fight for the bridge:

> *When Capt. Downs found that the 14ᵗʰ Pennsylvania cavalry was in his rear he took his men into the mountains and remained there all night. . . . That left the road clear for the 14ᵗʰ Pennsylvania cavalry until they came up to where my men were. . . . The first I knew of the situation the officers of the 14ᵗʰ Pennsylvania came up and demanded of us who we were. Their dialect gave them away. We were near a cut in the railroad, and I ordered my men, twenty-two in number, to get in the cut and a fight took place. We drove them back three times and they then settled down until morning.[135]*

Jackson's report on the episode at the entrance to the Island Ford Bridge agreed with Poe's account in events but differed in personnel. According to Jackson,

> *Finding Major Lady, with 50 men, I moved with him to a position near the bridge, and directed him to resist all efforts of the enemy on the same side to get to the bridge. Three times during the night did this little band successfully repel attempts to reach the bridge by the enemy on the same side, and they held this position until 8 a. m. of the 20ᵗʰ instant.[136]*

Regardless of who defended the bridge, the Fourteenth Cavalry was prevented from crossing it during the night of 19 December to join the rest of Averell's command on the west side of Jackson's River. During the night and early morning of 19-20 December, Averell sent most of his command up the Lewisburg road to Callaghan's. They blockaded roads leading into Callaghan's from Lewisburg and Sweet Springs, but Averell knew that the Confederate pursuit he had to fear, Early and Fitzhugh Lee, was still on the eastern side of the Island Ford Bridge. Despite the fact that the Fourteenth Cavalry had not yet crossed to safety, Averell ordered the bridge burned. At eight o'clock in the morning while Confederate sharpshooters fired at them, a squadron of federal soldiers poured oil onto the bridge and set it on fire. In a short time the bridge's support timbers burned through and the structure collapsed into Jackson's River. Averell was safe from Early and Lee, but the Fourteenth Pennsylvania was marooned in enemy territory.[137]

When Jackson realized that he had the Fourteenth Cavalry at his mercy, he ordered Colonel Arnett to attack them with everything he had. Arnett, with only two hundred men under his command, had a better idea. He was convinced that the Pennsylvanians could not ford flood-swollen Jackson's River. He believed that the federals would make for the intact railroad bridge at Clifton Forge and try to rejoin Averell through the McGraw Gap pass, the same route Jackson had taken into Covington. Arnett withdrew his small force to Clifton Forge and waited for the Pennsylvanians to show up. Arnett did not know that the federal troops had found a ford through Jackson's River that they were willing to risk crossing to avoid capture. Colonel James Schoonmaker unhitched his teams and set fire to his supply wagons. Then he led his men into the freezing water of Jackson's River. Six men and several horses were drowned during the hazardous crossing, but Schoonmaker emerged on the west bank mostly intact. Arnett waited for him in vain five miles to the east. When the Pennsylvanians caught up with Averell at Callaghan's, an amused Schoonmaker handed Averell a note from Jubal Early advising Averell that he was "completely surrounded, and any attempt to escape would be useless, and that he desired to avoid further effusion of blood." Averell, who had not lost a man to enemy bullets, did not bother to reply. In his preliminary report on the expedition, Averell remarked, "Not less than 12,000 men were maneuvered to effect my capture, but when they thought it most certain, it was found Early was late."[138] With thousands of Confederate troops converging on Covington, Averell confidently directed his brigade onto a seldom-used road across Little Allegheny Mountain to Anthony's Creek, Greenbrier County. By 24 December he and his entire command were back in Beverly.[139]

When Jackson realized that Averell was getting away, he sent John Sprigg and some mounted soldiers after them. Sprigg got close enough to exchange shots with Averell's rear guard, but he realized that even if he caught up with the federals he did not have sufficient troops to fight them. Sprigg halted his pursuit a few miles out of Callaghan's.[140] While Sprigg was shooting at Averell's retreating rear guard, Jackson received a sarcastic dispatch from Jubal Early. "There is no use," Early wrote, "in pursuing the enemy with infantry, unless for some special purpose, of which you must judge."[141]

UNDER FIRE

William Averell's raid on Salem in December 1863 was a disaster for the Confederate commands stationed to protect the region. Averell had destroyed tons of irreplaceable supplies at Salem Depot. The Virginia and Tennessee Railroad had been rendered useless at a critical time — when Bragg and Longstreet's forces in eastern Tennessee were depending on the railroad to keep their forces supplied with men and materiel. That Averell and nearly three thousand cavalrymen were able to travel four hundred miles through Confederate-held territory without once encountering serious opposition alarmed private citizens, the government in Richmond, and the Confederate news media. Richmond newspapers were sharply critical of the conduct of Jubal Early and Fitzhugh Lee, among others.[142]

The Confederate commanders involved in the fiasco immediately began making excuses and shifting blame. Responsibility for protecting the Salem Depot fell under the jurisdiction of Major General Samuel Jones. When Averell arrived at Salem on the morning of 16 December, he found no Confederate troops there to guard the valuable collection of supplies. Jones explained the lack of a protective force by pointing out that Averell had not arrived at Salem through territory under his command, and that it was Jubal Early's responsibility to stop him before he ever reached Salem. Jones complained that he was never advised that Early and Fitzhugh Lee had been ordered to pursue Averell. His assessment of the damage done to the railroad bordered on the incredible. "The damage done the railroad was repaired in three or four days. The railroad was rather improved than injured by the raid, as the few small bridges burned were in such condition that they were scarcely safe, and would have required rebuilding very soon."[143] John Echols at Lewisburg failed to engage the Union army sent from Charleston to divert him from Averell's passing cavalry, and sat by quietly while Averell escaped through Greenbrier County. He wrote a carefully worded report in which he placed responsibility for every move he made on General Jones. Several times in his report Echols mentioned that he expected General Early and Colonel Jackson to drive Averell toward his waiting brigade, but that they failed to do so.[144] Jubal Early, Fitzhugh Lee and John Imboden did not bother to file reports on their parts in the fiasco.

The most serious criticism of any officer involved in the pursuit of Averell was reserved for William L. Jackson. On 26 December Major Edward McMahon, a Confederate quartermaster attached to Jones' command, sent a communication to Jones. McMahon was not present during any of the action around Covington and the Island Ford Bridge, but he was acquainted with Thompson McCallister, captain of the Alleghany County Home Guards, who had failed to burn the bridge after Jackson ordered him to do so. McCallister condemned Jackson and his men in conversations with McMahon, and McMahon wrote down his comments and forwarded them to Jones. McMahon's letter to Jones included the following observations:

Jackson . . . made no preparation to meet the enemy, either by permanent or temporary works, or to prevent his passage west; that all done by the colonel was to build a fence across the road at the lower end of the Alum Rock. Scouts were not sent over 4 miles from camp until one of the provost guard ran into camp and reported the advance of the enemy through the Rich Patch; that no plan of battle was prepared; that no speedy arrangements were made after notice to meet the enemy; that the whereabouts of the commanding officer was not known during the period that it was necessary; that his orders to Colonel Arnett were not obeyed; that he (the colonel) ordered Captain McAllister to make ready to burn the Island Ford Bridge, but not to burn it until he received orders to do so; that no arrangements were made to insure the certainty of orders to do so; that no arrangements were made to insure the certainty of orders reaching McAllister, and that the enemy were on McAllister before he knew of them; . . . that the enemy crossed the bridge and burned it, leaving Fourteenth Pennsylvania and the wagon train behind; that that regiment hoisted a white flag three times and yet escaped; that instead of gathering up stragglers the soldiers were running about plundering and gathering up property abandoned by the enemy, and that almost every crime has been perpetrated by the command from burglary down to rape.[145]

Although the allegations by McMahon against Jackson were serious, no charges of misconduct were brought against him. General Jones forwarded McMahon's letter without comment to Samuel Cooper, Inspector General of the Confederate States Army, in Richmond. Cooper did not investigate the substance of McMahon's complaints. Evidently Jones discussed the allegations with Jackson. On 18 January 1864, Jackson issued a circular to his command at Warm Springs informing the men that a petition had been drawn up in Alleghany County alleging that the soldiers of the Nineteenth and Twentieth cavalries had committed crimes against the civilian population during the recent campaign. He cautioned his officers to consider the reputation of the regiments and to exercise better discipline.[146]

Some citizens of Pocahontas County also wrote a letter of complaint to Richmond about Jackson and the efficiency of his men in the aftermath of Averell's raid. The letter alleged that Jackson was tyrannical and oppressive, and that his soldiers wandered about the countryside committing outrages and thefts against private citizens. Worse, the letter continued, was that Jackson's men never seemed to be around when it was time to fight the Yankees. While the perpetrators of the crimes alleged against Jackson's men in Alleghany County were never identified, in this instance the Pocahontas citizens' complaint almost certainly referred to the men of Jacob Marshall's command. After being cut off from Jackson's main force at Gatewood's on 13 December, Marshall remained in Pocahontas County harassing Augustus Moor's Ohio infantry until Averell returned to the area in late December. Marshall's troops were the only soldiers belonging to the Nineteenth Cavalry in the area between 13-24 December. William Price, a Pocahontas County historian, revealed some substance to the citizens' complaints. Averell's men, Price wrote,

were in perfect agony as they approached the Marlinton Bridge. . . . At Edray they camped, and so worn were they that the sentinels could not keep awake. It is said that a hundred men could have taken the whole army. They were ready to drop with fatigue, and their powder was wet. The government (United States) recognized this (Averell's raid) as a brilliant achievement, though their escape was due to pure luck, the Confederates taking the wrong roads.[147]

Rumors of Jackson's disgrace in Alleghany County also received some attention from federal officers. Writing to Brigadier General Benjamin Kelley at Cumberland on 30 January 1864, Moses S. Hall, Lieutenant Colonel of the Tenth West Virginia Infantry at Beverly, commented that deserters had informed him that "Bill Jackson . . . is under arrest for cowardice at or near Covington, during the last raid of General Averell."[148] Hall continued his letter with an overview of the situation in Pocahontas and Bath counties:

One of them (deserters) remarked that he heard some officers talking in Jackson's camp, near Warm Springs, that if we succeeded in capturing their party out now that we would make a good haul. I learn this evening that this must have referred to Captain Spriggs, of Braxton. He is there, I learn, stealing horses. Colonel Arnett, of the Twentieth Virginia Cavalry, formerly from Marion County, wrote an article, which was published in the Richmond papers, that "they must and would retake and

hold all of the country to the banks of the blue Ohio" the next season.
This article was read at dress-parade. . . . I am assured by these poor
creatures that Jackson will not have 200 men in his command by the 1ˢᵗ
of May if something is not done for the good of the Confederacy. The rolls
are called four times a day to keep their men from deserting.[149]

Kelley received Hall's letter during the first week of February. A few days later he must have wondered if Hall was the victim of a campaign of disinformation. On 10 February, Kelley received a copy of a letter from Colonel Nathan Wilkinson at Grafton written to Lieutenant M. J. Russell at New Creek. Wilkinson warned Russell that Jackson had under his command his largest force yet, some four thousand men, and that a spring campaign against western Virginia was planned.[150]

DISSENSION

In March 1864, an incident occurred in Jackson's camp at Warm Springs that seriously affected the morale of his command and created dissension among some of his company officers. The episode centered on the unfortunate military career of Jasper Johnson, a private in John Sprigg's company of the Nineteenth Cavalry. Johnson, a native of Ravenswood, Jackson County, Virginia, enlisted in John Sprigg's company of the Nineteenth Cavalry at Frankford, Greenbrier County, 9 March 1863. Records did not indicate that Johnson served with any military unit prior to his enlistment in the Nineteenth Cavalry, but he probably had served with Sprigg's company during 1862 when the company was part of the Third Virginia State Line. Sometime during the summer of 1863, while on a scouting mission, Johnson was captured by a federal patrol. Given an option of going to prison or joining the Union army, Johnson chose enlistment.[151]

During his first field operation as a Union soldier, Johnson deserted his command and returned to the Nineteenth Cavalry in Bath County. He was welcomed back to Company B, and he resumed his previous duties as one of Sprigg's raiders. During Sprigg's extended scouting trip into Braxton and Webster counties in July and August 1863, most of his men spent some time at their homes. The men were ordered to rendezvous for the return to their base camp around 1 September. When the troops gathered to return to Bath County, Jasper Johnson was not present. Sprigg reported Johnson as a deserter when he returned to Camp Northwest. Johnson's attempt to stay home and avoid further involvement in the war was short-lived. A federal patrol in Jackson County captured Johnson at his home and escorted him back to Beverly for trial as a federal deserter. A court martial convicted him of desertion and sentenced him to be shot.

Before the sentence could be carried out, William Averell learned of Johnson's background as a former member of the Nineteenth Cavalry. He offered Johnson yet another opportunity to escape punishment for desertion. Averell was planning his Salem raid and he needed guides to direct him through the back country of Bath and Alleghany counties. He offered Johnson a job as a guide, and Johnson accepted. Johnson rode with Averell's cavalry to Salem, but on the return trip his luck turned from bad to worse. During the frantic confusion at Island Ford Bridge, Johnson was captured by some members of the Nineteenth Cavalry who recognized him. When the Nineteenth Cavalry returned to their camp at Warm Springs, Johnson was taken along as a prisoner of war. A court martial convened in early March, and Johnson was convicted of desertion and aiding the enemy. He was sentenced to be shot on 15 March by a squad of volunteers drawn from the Nineteenth and Twentieth cavalries. William Jackson approved the conviction and the sentence. John Sprigg, however, came to Johnson's defense. Sprigg claimed that Johnson was a victim of circumstances and that a death sentence was inappropriate. Jackson, perhaps stung by recent criticism that he was a lax disciplinarian, refused to listen to Sprigg's argument. When Jackson's intransigence on the matter became known, several members of Sprigg's company arranged for Johnson to escape. However, the demoralized victim refused to cooperate with their plans. Since he was under a death sentence from both armies, Johnson reasoned that if he were captured again he would be shot anyway. With nowhere to hide, Johnson decided to stay where he was. On 15 March 1864, Jasper Johnson was executed by a firing squad made up of members of his former regiment.[152]

Jackson's inflexible stand in the Jasper Johnson case probably was intended as an object lesson for his command. By the winter of 1863-64, desertion had become a serious problem for many Confederate units, but especially for those stationed on the West Virginia-Virginia line. Most of the troops in those commands were natives of the western Virginia region, and were seldom more than a couple of days distance from their homes. Opportunity to desert occurred every time a federal force was encountered. An important part of the strategy of warfare practiced by regiments such as the Nineteenth and Twentieth cavalries was the ability of the men to flee into the woods and continue fighting as guerrillas without relying on a central command to give them orders. No noticeable changes appeared in the desertion rate of the Nineteenth and Twentieth cavalries following the Jasper Johnson incident. A few men left without leave every month, just as they had been doing since the regiments were organized in the spring of 1863. There was, however, one notable desertion.

The dispute between Jackson and John Sprigg over the dispensation of the Jasper Johnson case continued after Johnson's execution. Sprigg, whom

Jackson had cited for gallantry during the pursuit of Averell at Covington in December,[153] was perhaps the most active and daring of Jackson's company commanders. Sprigg was assigned by Jackson to supervise the Nineteenth and Twentieth cavalries' horses during their winter forage at Doe Hill, Highland County. Although protecting the cavalry mounts during their winter forage was vital for maintaining the fighting capacity of the Nineteenth and Twentieth cavalries, Jackson's assignment of the task to John Sprigg was a misuse of sorely needed leadership in the field. Clearly Sprigg's assignment as a herdsman was a subtle reprimand by Jackson. During April, the election of Major Joseph Kessler as lieutenant colonel of the Forty-sixth Battalion of Virginia Cavalry created a vacancy on Jackson's staff. Jackson wanted William McNeel to fill the position, but McNeel had been elected to the Virginia Assembly the previous November and was in Richmond. McNeel declined the appointment and Jackson appointed George Downs in his stead, despite Downs' inexcusable conduct at Island Ford Bridge. Apparently Jackson did not consider offering the appointment to Sprigg, although Sprigg's battlefield performance greatly exceeded Downs' record.[154] In June 1864, Sprigg resigned his command and returned to Braxton County where he attempted to raise an independent company of scouts. Jackson refused to accept his resignation and reported him as absent without leave in August. Sprigg was listed on regimental muster rolls as a deserter throughout the fall of 1864. Grudgingly accepting the loss, Jackson finally appointed Jack Chewning as captain of Company B in February 1865.[155]

6

CROOK AND AVERELL

The aftermath of William Averell's raid on Salem Depot and his subsequent escape from pursuit plagued the Confederate officers involved during the winter months of 1864. Concern for the complete breakdown of communications and cooperation among western commanders even reached the attention of Robert E. Lee. Writing to Samuel Cooper on 13 January 1864, Lee noted that the performance of western brigades had disappointed him during the recent campaign against Averell. "I refer particularly," Lee wrote, "to the commands of General Imboden, Col. W. L. Jackson, and Maj. Gen. Sam. Jones. My own opportunities of observation have not impressed me favorably with regard to the discipline and efficiency of General Imboden's troops, and the accounts I receive represent the others, with few exceptions, to be no better."[1] Lee recommended a reorganization of the western department of Virginia and a change of command. During the first week of March, John C. Breckinridge, a former Vice-President of the United States and the Southern Democratic candidate for president in 1860, replaced Samuel Jones as commander of the Department of Western Virginia.

Breckinridge hoped to prevent another incursion against the Virginia and Tennessee Railroad by constructing a series of fortifications across major routes of access to the Shenandoah Valley. Millboro Springs, a Confederate supply depot within the confines of the territory patrolled by William L. Jackson's regiments, was one site selected by Breckinridge for fortification. Robert E. Lee suggested to Breckinridge that Jackson should take charge of constructing fortifications at Millboro Springs. Jackson was a logical choice to direct the construction, according to Lee, since "in more than one instance Col. W. L. Jackson has been obliged to retire before the approach of the enemy east of the Warm Springs Mountain, and as he is now located in that region I thought it would be advantageous for him to construct the works, if practicable, intended to intercept the advance of the enemy after crossing the ridge."[2]

Jackson had no time to build fortifications anywhere. Scouts constantly reported a massive federal build-up at Beverly, and Jackson feared that an invasion of the Greenbrier Valley was imminent. On 29 March he sent an

alarming dispatch to John Echols. Friends in Beverly, Jackson revealed, had
warned him that another raid from Averell was expected. Perhaps to establish grounds for his own defense in case Averell drove him out of Bath County
again, Jackson lamented that, "My horses are not secure where I am feeding
them hay; they will not be able for service until late in the spring, but I have
no safe place to take them. Rockbridge and other counties seem to be in this
department when the enemy advances, but entirely out side of it when forage and supplies are needed."[3]

In mid-April 1864, a federal infantry detachment from Beverly attacked
Jacob Marshall's company at the Greenbrier River bridge at Marlin's Bottom. Marshall succeeded in preventing the federals from seizing the bridge,
and forced them to withdraw hastily and in disorder. Some of Marshall's
men pursued the retreating federals as far as Edray, six miles from Marlin's
Bottom, but allowed them to escape without further damage. Two weeks
later the same federals were back at the bridge, and this time they overran it.
Jackson's scouts reported that the federal troop build-up at Beverly was continuing. Jackson was concerned. On 20 April he wrote to Echols expressing
fears that "the enemy at Beverly are preparing for a move. . . . I am of the
opinion, from all I can learn, that the enemy either intend a raid or are
preparing to resist one. If they come I do not think they will move for eight
or ten days, on account of the unsettled state of the weather." [4]

Jackson's estimate of the timetable of Union movements was on target,
but his fear that a major assault would be launched against him proved incorrect. Instead of attacking Jackson, federal forces launched assaults at New
Market, Shenandoah County, nearly one hundred miles north of Jackson's
position, and at Dublin Station, Pulaski County, nearly one hundred miles
south. Confederate commanders at both points of attack wanted Jackson's
brigade to assist with their defense. Jackson received orders from Albert G.
Jenkins at Dublin before he received similar orders from John Breckinridge
at New Market. Jenkins was uncertain about the federal army's destination,
and on 3 May he directed Jackson to establish a defensive position at
Callaghan's Station in case the target was Salem Depot. Jackson's horses were
not ready to conduct a lengthy and strenuous campaign, and on the evening
of 3 May he led around eight hundred dismounted cavalrymen on a forced
march to Jackson's River Depot. The forty-mile march severely tried the
stamina of soldiers accustomed to riding, but despite such conditions, William Jackson's version of "foot cavalry" found humor in the situation. Captain David Poe later recalled:

> The most of our brigade was dismounted and were soon on a forced
> march. Road were bad, occasionally snow and rain were falling. Our
> old shoes and boots were fast giving out; many were barefooted long

*before we got in front of the enemy. I myself, marched two or three days
with my bare feet in snow and rain. We secured a small supply of shoes
on the way; they were red leather, and the boys would guy each other by
asking when they were going to take their footgear to the shop to have
them painted.*[5]

Jackson's foot weary soldiers arrived at Callaghan's Station on 6 May, but
the next day Jenkins ordered him to advance to Union, Monroe County.
While en route to Union, Jackson received another order from Jenkins directing him to report to Narrows, Virginia, and place himself and his men
under the command of Colonel William H. French. Jackson reported to
French on the evening of 9 May, and his brigade arrived at Narrows the
following afternoon.[6]

Neither French nor Jackson was aware that General Jenkins had been
wounded and captured at the Battle of Cloyd's Mountain near Dublin on 9
May.[7] Both colonels were surprised on the morning of 11 May to receive an
order from Colonel John McCausland, "commanding Department of Western Virginia." McCausland gave a few sketchy details of the Confederate
disaster at Cloyd's Mountain, including the facts that he had been driven out
of Dublin and that federal forces numbered some nine thousand men commanded by General George Crook. McCausland wanted French and Jackson to meet him at Christiansburg, where they could combine for an attack
on Crook's army which had moved on to Blacksburg.[8]

Between them French and Jackson were able to muster fifteen hundred
troops, only eighty of whom were mounted. Their march toward
Christiansburg got off to a slow start because New River had to be forded
twice in the first fifteen miles. French and Jackson attempted to reach Gap
Mountain above Blacksburg before Crook could get there. If they could seize
the pass across the mountain, Crook's force would be trapped between French
and Jackson and the army of McCausland following Crook from Blacksburg.
Because of the delay caused by the crossings of New River, Crook's men were
able to seize the high ground at Gap Mountain before French and Jackson
arrived. The Confederate officers formed a defensive position at Newport at
the foot of Gap Mountain, but Crook's nine thousand men pushed the fifteen hundred Confederates out of the way after brief skirmishing. Jackson
and French pulled back to Brown's Ferry on Sinking Creek, expecting Crook
to move toward them. Instead, Crook slipped away to the northeast and
crossed Salt Pond Mountain into Monroe County. Jackson and French quickly
organized a group of three hundred and twenty-five men to pursue and harass him.[9]

Jackson and French would have pursued Crook with their entire force,
but scouts brought them news that yet another federal column was

approaching their position from Christiansburg. This force turned out to be two cavalry brigades commanded by William Averell. While Crook had been engaged at Dublin, Averell had led more than two thousand mounted troops on a raid to Saltville, Smyth County, in an attempt to destroy the salt works located there. Finding Saltville well-defended by John Hunt Morgan and William E. Jones, Averell hastily withdrew eastward, intending to cover Crook's flank as he retired from Dublin. Detachments from Morgan and Jones' commands pursued Averell's forces and skirmished with them at Wytheville on 10 May. Averell suffered casualties at Wytheville, but his superior numbers prevented his tormentors from interrupting his withdrawal. Averell reached Blacksburg on 11 May, only to find that Crook had left the day before. While Jackson and French raced Crook for control of the high ground at Gap Mountain, Averell spent the day ripping up railroad tracks east of Blacksburg and burning the railroad depot at Christiansburg. Averell left Christiansburg on the Gap Mountain road during the afternoon of 12 May. As he approached the top of Gap Mountain early on the morning of 13 May, he found the pass in the possession of Jackson and French. Averell sent skirmishers out to test the strength of the Confederate position, and concluded that a direct attack on the mountain pass would be imprudent. He sent a detachment to feint a flanking movement on the Confederate left, while he withdrew his main force eastward on the Catawba Road.[10] When the federal flanking party suddenly disengaged, mounted its horses, and retreated hastily back the way they had come, Jackson and French could only stand in bitter frustration alongside their barefoot infantry and watch them ride away.

McCausland arrived at Gap Mountain at seven o'clock on the evening of 13 May. Apprised of Averell's withdrawal, he ordered Jackson to take his brigade and attempt to cut off Averell's retreat as he entered Monroe County. On the following morning in a driving rainstorm, Jackson and his brigade set out for the Salt Pond road and Union, Monroe County. The cavalrymen still were dismounted, mostly barefoot, and on half rations. Jackson anticipated relieving the shoe and ration shortage by having his supply train move from Narrows and intercept him along the Salt Pond road. While en route between Narrows and the Salt Pond Mountain road, a scout met the wagon train and warned the escort that a large federal force was on the road just ahead of them. Although Jackson instructed the train's officers to withdraw the precious supply train southward into Botetourt County if the train was threatened, the men simply abandoned the wagons and fled. Several hours later, a scouting party from Crook's retreating army found the abandoned train sitting in the middle of the road. The wagons were burned along with a twelve-pound howitzer being transported in one of the wagons. Jackson was furious. On 16 May he wrote to McCausland from Gap Mills, Monroe

County, that he had caught up with the rear guard of Averell's forces but that he had to discontinue his pursuit. Jackson explained why he could go no farther:

> *My command not being mounted will be compelled to stop the pursuit on account of sore feet, want of shoes, and rations. . . . By some shameful conduct a piece of artillery and my train on the way to me to the Narrows, and turned off to connect with me on the Salt Pond road, was abandoned, and destroyed by Crook on Peter's Mountain, as he fell back. There was ample notice and time to save the whole. A strict investigation will be instituted and the guilty shall be punished. Having now no train I shall be compelled to go to the Depot (Jackson's River Depot) until I can raise one . . .*[11]

Confederate commanders during Crook's campaign against Dublin tried to be optimistic and positive when evaluating their performance. John McCausland reported that he believed the federals had failed completely in their objective and that they had "accomplished nothing commensurate with their preparations."[12] Colonel French stated that he could not "speak too highly of the conduct of the officers and men when facing General Crook on the 12th, and General Averell on the 13th. I derived much aid from the counsels of Col. William L. Jackson, and take pleasure in expressing my confidence in his courage and ability."[13] Jackson noted that, "They (Crook and Averell) have utterly failed to accomplish their object, which was a movement via Lynchburg to the south side of James River."[14] Jackson, however, had misinterpreted the federal objective. Crook's orders were to destroy the Dublin station on the Virginia and Tennessee Railroad, then to move northeast and effect a junction with General Franz Sigel's corps at Staunton. If successful, such a movement would have cleared Confederate threats from the rear of Ulysses S. Grant's army that had just opened the Wilderness Campaign north of Richmond. Crook received word of Sigel's defeat at New Market and his withdrawal down the Shenandoah Valley on 16 May. Since Crook's rendezvous with Sigel was rendered meaningless by the defeat at New Market, Crook returned to Charleston while Averell led his cavalry brigade back to Beverly. However, had Sigel not been defeated by Breckinridge at New Market, there would have been no Confederate force in the field to prevent Crook and Averell from marching unchallenged from Union to Staunton. The Confederacy narrowly escaped disaster by allowing Crook and Averell to escape from Dublin.

William L. Jackson's role in once again permitting a federal force to escape destruction while deep inside Confederate lines was symptomatic of a malaise which had plagued his command almost since its inception. Chronic lack of basic supplies such as food and clothing left his men in poor fighting condition. Despite its designation as a cavalry unit, persistent shortages of quality horses kept the regiments mostly on foot at critical times, when their opposition was mounted. Inability or unwillingness of subordinates to follow Jackson's orders imperiled the command's ability to fight. French's praise of Jackson's courage and ability at Gap Mountain did little to dispel a general impression persistent among the Confederate high command in Richmond that Jackson and his regiments were incompetent and inefficient.[15]

LYNCHBURG

After halting his pursuit of Averell's cavalry at the Greenbrier River two miles southeast of Lewisburg, Jackson brought his exhausted command back to Jackson's River Depot near Covington. He arrived there on 20 May and stayed in camp for a week resting the men and refitting his brigade. During the week some of the regiment's horses were brought to camp from Bath County, and Jackson placed Major John Lady in command of the mounted troops. While Jackson was busy restoring his brigade's capacity to campaign, other Confederate commands in the area were unclear about preparations for future actions. Under severe pressure from Ulysses S. Grant around Richmond, Lee called John C. Breckinridge to join him there, a move that temporarily removed the commanding general from the Shenandoah Valley. William E. Jones, Jackson's colleague during the Jones-Imboden raid in western Virginia in 1863, was recalled from Tennessee and placed in charge of several patchwork brigades, including Jackson's. On 29 May 1864, Jackson sent a dispatch to Jones advising him that federal troops were in force in Greenbrier County, but that John Imboden had sent an urgent request that Jackson join him at Millboro Springs in Bath County. The following day Jackson sent a wire to Major Charles Stringfellow, Breckinridge's adjutant, asking him whether he should stay at Callaghan's or move to assist Imboden. Jones replied through Stringfellow that Jackson should go to support Imboden and that John McCausland could move his brigade into Jackson's position at Callaghan's.[16] Jackson and his brigade pulled out of Callaghan's on 1 June to join Imboden at Millboro. The next day George Crook and William Averell, commanding nearly ten thousand union infantry and cavalry, attacked McCausland at Covington.

Jackson's brigade, made up of the Nineteenth and Twentieth Cavalry Regiments and the Forty-sixth and Forty-seventh Battalions of Virginia Cavalry, included around seven hundred men during the first week of June 1864. Only about one hundred twenty-five of the men were mounted. McCausland's force at Covington was only slightly larger. McCausland realized immediately that making a stand against Crook and Averell was impractical. Instead, he withdrew before the federal advance, harassing the enemy's flanks and skirmishing with detachments in the front. Jackson, advised of events in his rear, hastened through Warm Springs and Goshen Depot to Millboro, only to find that Imboden had left to support William Jones who was under attack north of Staunton. Lacking any orders except Jones' agreement that he should join Imboden, Jackson started down the Shenandoah Valley in search of a command to join. Jackson moved to Goshen on the Shenandoah Valley pike, then headed north through Craigsville and Buffalo Gap five miles west of Staunton. At Buffalo Gap Jackson halted while he sent scouts toward Staunton in an attempt to discover what was happening. His scouts soon returned with the unsettling news that Union soldiers were in control of the town. On 6 June, while Jackson conferred with his officers about their next move, McCausland suddenly appeared with fragments of his brigade. McCausland reported to Jackson that Crook and Averell were on their way to Staunton to link with David Hunter's army. McCausland also informed Jackson of William Jones' defeat and death on 5 June at Piedmont north of Staunton. Survivors of Jones's shattered army were reported to be gathering at Waynesboro under the command of General John C. Vaughn. Vaughn had sent out desperate pleas for reinforcements, but McCausland's brigade was exhausted and scattered as a result of its five days of running skirmishes with Crook and Averell. Since Jackson's brigade was in comparatively better condition, McCausland asked Jackson to go to Waynesboro and reinforce Vaughn, despite the fact that most of Jackson's men were dismounted.[17]

Before leaving Buffalo Gap, McCausland and Jackson concluded that the combined forces of Hunter, Crook and Averell in Staunton soon would move toward Lynchburg and its vital railroad junctions. The two veteran cavalry commanders realized that they could not stop Hunter's eighteen thousand federal troops with their fifteen hundred men, but they believed that they could slow the Union advance until Lynchburg could be fortified to defend itself. After agreeing to destroy every bridge in the path of the federal army between Staunton and Lynchburg and to constantly harass the federals with hit and run raids, Jackson moved south around Staunton to join Vaughn at Waynesboro. On 8 June Jackson added his seven hundred soldiers to Vaughn's depleted brigade. When David Hunter led his federal army out of Staunton onto the Lynchburg road on the morning of 10 June, nothing stood in his way except the undermanned and mostly dismounted brigades of Jackson, McCausland and Vaughn.[18]

None of the Confederate officers who assumed the task of delaying Hunter's attack on Lynchburg reported their actions between 10 – 17 June. The only information on skirmishes between Staunton and Lynchburg came from reports filed by Hunter, Crook and Averell. Their reports discounted the Confederate effort to retard their progress toward Lynchburg, yet it took

Hunter seven days to negotiate seventy miles. Hunter separated his eighteen thousand men into four columns, each of which took a different road to Lexington. Hunter intended to clear all Confederate resistance from the valley, unite his forces in Lexington, then advance the remaining thirty miles to Lynchburg as a single, overwhelming force. Jackson, McCausland and Vaughn rushed their men from one point to another in front of the federal forces frequently forcing them to halt and form battle lines. Although the Confederates did little damage to Hunter's army, their delaying tactics allowed Robert E. Lee to rush reinforcements under General Jubal Early to Lynchburg in time to prepare a defense for the city.[19]

Jackson and Vaughn arrived in Lynchburg on 16 June. Their cavalry brigades, mostly dismounted, were placed under the command of Brigadier General Robert Ransom, newly appointed at Breckinridge's insistence to lead the cavalry division.[20] Since few of Jackson's men had horses, Ransom placed Jackson's regiments on the right of the Confederate line of defense organized by Breckinridge and Early. The men frantically dug rifle pits to prepare for the federal assault, but on the afternoon of 17 June, John Imboden impressed Jackson and his brigade to go with him to the relief of John McCausland. McCausland's brigade had resisted Hunter's advance from Lexington, skirmishing and withdrawing daily in the face of overwhelming odds. McCausland had taken a stand at New London, ten miles southwest of Lynchburg, but was being driven back toward the city by George Crook's infantry. When Imboden and Jackson arrived at New London they met McCausland's men rapidly retreating. Skirmishing with advance elements of Crook's army, Imboden and Jackson erected breastworks near the Quaker Meeting House on the Salem road. The federal troops immediately assaulted Imboden's and Jackson's positions and began pushing the embattled Confederates back.[21] Fearing an attack on his flank, Jackson ordered his men to retreat, but only the men at the rear of the line heard the command. When the riflemen manning the front of the position noticed their support withdrawing, they abandoned their posts in panic and disorder. Jackson halted the stampede and ordered everyone to return to the improvised breastworks. Once the men had returned to their previous positions, Jackson again gave the order to retreat. This time the men withdrew in an orderly fashion.[22] Crook's forces continued to press Jackson's and Imboden's men until they reached the Confederate line established by Early two miles southwest of Lynchburg. Jackson's brigade retired to the rifle pits they had dug on 16 June and spent an uneasy night awaiting Hunter's attack the following day.

Early on Saturday, 18 June, Hunter cautiously probed at Lynchburg's defenses. Captured Confederates told Hunter that Early had twenty thousand fresh troops ringing Lynchburg, and he lost his nerve. During the evening of 18 June, Hunter met with his officers and discussed the Union army's options. Most of the officers recommended an immediate withdrawal. The federal force was hundreds of miles from reinforcements, supplies did not exist beyond what the army carried with it, and the Confederate army facing it had gathered strength. Hunter ordered a withdrawal and during the night his army began to retire over the road toward Liberty.[23] Early decided to attack the federals the following morning, but when his advance skirmishers moved toward the Union lines they discovered that Hunter's army was gone. Early ordered Ransom to pursue Hunter with the cavalry. Imboden and McCausland led the pursuit, but Imboden quickly fell behind the aggressive McCausland. Although McCausland managed to get ahead of Hunter's army at Hanging Rock north of Salem, Ransom declined to order an attack until most of the federal army had passed out of danger. McCausland finally was allowed to attack Hunter's wagon train and his frustrated men nearly destroyed the entire train. Hunter was left to return to the Kanawha Valley without rations through hostile territory.[24]

WASHINGTON, D. C.

Jackson's mounted men under Major Lady joined McCausland in the pursuit of Hunter, but Jackson and most of his men remained in Lynchburg. When it became clear that Hunter's army was retreating into West Virginia instead of back into the Shenandoah Valley, Jubal Early conceived a plan to create a disturbance in the valley that would relieve some of the pressure against Lee at Richmond. With Lee's endorsement, Early proposed to move his entire corps into the Shenandoah Valley, recover territory lost in Hunter's advance in early June, and threaten Union positions north of the Potomac River. Early and Lee believed that a demonstration in force so close to Washington, D. C., would force Grant to send some of his troops from the Petersburg front reducing the staggering odds with which Lee was trying to contend.[25] Early began his Valley campaign on the morning of 20 June 1864. Jackson's weary brigade joined the march and by 27 June the men were camped near Staunton. During the next week Jackson's brigade slowly advanced down the Shenandoah Valley and crossed into Maryland around 4 July. John Lady and the mounted men of the brigade joined Jackson near Sharpsburg, Maryland on 5 July. Over the next two days Jackson's men scoured the Maryland countryside for horses, and by 7 July the entire brigade was again mounted cavalry.[26] Although Jackson clearly was subordinate to most officers accompanying Early's army, federal authorities evidently believed he was a key member of the campaign. On 3 July 1864, Henry Halleck, Chief of Staff in Washington, telegraphed to Ulysses S. Grant at City Point that he had received "reports that Early, Breckinridge, and Jackson, with Mosby's guerrillas are said to be moving from Staunton down the Shenandoah Valley."[27]

Halleck's wire did not mention John Gordon, Robert Rodes, Bradley Johnson, Robert Ransom or John McCausland, all of whom were with Early and outranked William Jackson.

During Jubal Early's Valley Campaign, William Jackson's brigade seldom fought as a unit. With less than four thousand cavalrymen to scout and guard his flanks, Early spread his cavalry thinly between Winchester and the Potomac River. One group of Jackson's cavalry fought with John McCausland at the battle of Monocacy, Maryland on 9 July 1864. At the same time, another detachment was sent to Point of Rocks, a few miles west of Monocacy, to destroy tracks on the Baltimore and Ohio Railroad. Other companies were scattered throughout the Maryland countryside rounding up horses and forage and scouting federal troop movements.[28] At least three of Jackson's companies were not with the brigade in the Shenandoah Valley. Jacob Marshall and William McNeel remained in Pocahontas County harassing federal patrols sent into Pocahontas and Randolph counties from Beverly. John Sprigg, who had been guarding the brigade's horses in Highland County, resigned his captain's commission and returned to Braxton County to form an independent partisan company. Many of the members of Company B accompanied their former captain back to central West Virginia.[29]

On 11 July 1864, Jackson's brigade penetrated the defenses of Washington, D. C. as far as the Seventh Street fort near Silver Spring, Maryland. Early joined Jackson's command on the evening of 11 July to survey Washington's defenses.[30] Early was inclined to attack the city the following day, and his officers, including Jackson, endorsed the battle plan. However, during the night two divisions from the federal Sixth Corps arrived to man Washington's defensive perimeter. Early concluded that he did not have sufficient manpower to successfully carry the federal positions. He ordered his army to retire quietly from the Washington area during the night of 12 July. Jackson's brigade had the assignment of guarding the rear of the army's withdrawal.[31]

THE LOWER VALLEY

Between 13 – 23 July Jackson's brigade skirmished daily with federal detachments in pursuit of Early's army. Skirmishes were fought at Rockville, Darkestown, Waterford, Charles Town and Bunker Hill. One incident during Early's retreat from Washington demonstrated Jackson's capacity to adjust to battlefield conditions, and showed a sense of humor despite the desperateness of the situation. Company A of the Twentieth Cavalry, under the command of Lieutenant David Poe, found itself as a rear guard for the rear guard near Darkesville, Jefferson County, on 16 July. From the protection of an apple orchard, Poe watched a group of federal skirmishers he estimated at

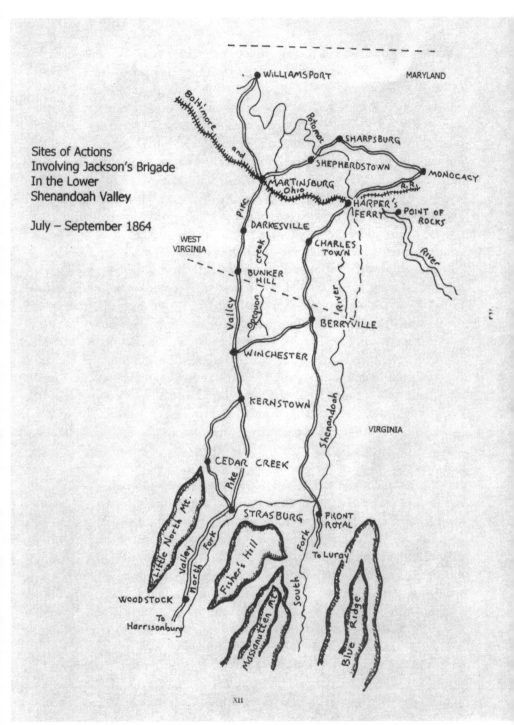

Sites of Actions
Involving Jackson's Brigade
In the Lower
Shenandoah Valley

July – September 1864

MARYLAND

WILLIAMSPORT

Baltimore and

Potomac

SHARPSBURG

SHEPHERDSTOWN

MONOCACY

MARTINSBURG
Ohio

R.R.

HARPER'S
FERRY

POINT OF
ROCKS

Pike

DARKESVILLE

WEST
VIRGINIA

Creek

CHARLES
TOWN

River

BUNKER
HILL

Opequon

River

Valley

BERRYVILLE

WINCHESTER

KERNSTOWN

Shenandoah

VIRGINIA

CEDAR CREEK

Pike

Little North Mt.

STRASBURG

FRONT
ROYAL

Valley

North Fork

Fisher's Hill

South Fork

To Luray

WOODSTOCK

To
Harrisonburg

Massanutten Mt.

Blue Ridge

XII

around one hundred and fifty men take positions around a house and a barn from which they could snipe at retreating Confederates. Colonel William Arnett observed the federals in their defensive position and ordered Poe with his company to charge them. Poe, realizing that his mounted men could not take the house and barn without suffering unacceptable casualties, refused to execute the command. Arnett, on a low hill to the right of Poe's position, with a company of the Eighth Virginia Infantry shouted at Poe to charge the house and barn. Poe ordered his men to remain as they were. Arnett, enraged that Poe was not obeying orders, left the security of his hilltop and rode toward Poe's line. Federal sharpshooters in the barn immediately opened fire on Arnett and his aide, Lieutenant David Lilly. Lilly was wounded in the hand before he and his colonel reached Poe's position. Finally realizing why Poe had not charged, Arnett ordered Poe to dismount his men and sent orders to the Eighth Infantry to join him in the orchard. Placing Poe in command, Arnett ordered him to drive the federals out of their position. Poe sent the Eighth Infantry men forward to skirmish with the bluecoats while he took his company of dismounted cavalrymen through a hollow shielded from view of the soldiers in the house and barn. Poe's men got in the rear of the federals and opened fire on them, forcing the federals to abandon their position and fall back. After Poe rejoined his regiment, Colonel Arnett and William Jackson rode up to him. Arnett raised his hat and complimented Poe for disobeying his orders to charge the house and barn. Jackson remarked that that was the first time he had ever heard a soldier complimented for disobeying orders. Arnett explained to his brigade commander that if Poe had followed his original orders, he might have lost all of his men and horses. Jackson replied that it was right for an officer to exercise his judgment in cases of emergency.[32]

Near Winchester, Jackson was confronted by his old nemesis, William Averell. On the evening of 19 July, Averell's cavalry brigade caught Jackson's force four miles northeast of Winchester. With both cavalry brigades dismounted, Averell's superior numbers drove Jackson's men back until they were able to establish a defensive line at Rutherford's farm at dusk. During the night Dodson Ramseur brought up his infantry brigade to reinforce Jackson. When Averell attacked the following morning, Ramseur's men recoiled under the fury of the attack. Jackson's cavalry waited patiently in the woods alongside Rutherford's fields until Averell's men appeared opposite them, confident that they had the Confederates on the run. Jackson ordered a full-scale cavalry charge by his brigade. In one of the most satisfying moments of the war for William Jackson and his frustrated cavalrymen, the shocked Union soldiers who had hung the nickname "Mudwall" on William Jackson because he would not stand and fight, withdrew in disorder to the rear. Averell had a strong line of both mounted and dismounted cavalrymen in reserve and Jackson could not pursue the fleeing federals, but his action did give Ramseur's panicked infantrymen time to regroup.[33] A cautious Averell decided not to reengage Ramseur's men, and for the first time in its career, Jackson's brigade possessed a battlefield fairly won from Averell, if only for a few minutes. Matthias Potts, a private in Company C of the Twentieth Cavalry, recalled the aftermath of the battle in a memoir written sixty years after the event:

> *Wm. L. Jackson had been by some branded a coward but he was a very brave man, a man that old Kentucky will always be proud of. Ramshur's (sic.) men always respected our brigade. When we would ride by, they would take off their caps and say, "That is Jackson's brigade. They saved us at Winchester."*[34]

Jackson's brigade continued skirmishing with federal forces between Winchester and Strasburg until 24 July, when Early suddenly turned on his pursuers at Kernstown on the same field where Stonewall Jackson had fought an indecisive battle in the spring of 1862. Led by John Breckinridge and John Echols, Early's army shattered a cavalry brigade in advance of George Crook's infantry division, then routed Crook's infantry. Jackson's brigade was stationed on the right wing of Early's army at Kernstown and participated in the pursuit of Crook's panicked division.

With Crook's army forced north of the Potomac River, Early sent John McCausland and Bradley Johnson on a raid into Pennsylvania. Jackson's assignment during McCausland's raid was to create a diversion in the vicinity of Shepherdstown. William Averell, in charge of the cavalry brigade responsible for preventing an incursion into Pennsylvania, was uncertain whether Jackson or McCausland was leading a raid into his territory.[35] While he waited at Greencastle, Pennsylvania, trying to figure out which invasion was the real one, McCausland descended on Chambersburg on the morning of 30 July 1864. McCausland routed the small federal force defending the city and issued a demand for ransom in the amount of one hundred thousand dollars in gold. When the civic leaders of Chambersburg failed to produce the ransom, McCausland ordered the town burned. When Colonel William Peters refused to execute McCausland's order, Colonel Ambrose Dunn of the Thirty-seventh Virginia Battalion agreed to execute the direct destruction of the city. Dunn, cashiered from the army for his failure to follow William Jackson's orders at Beverly in July 1863, had been reinstated to command of the Thirty-seventh Battalion by Jefferson Davis only four weeks earlier.[36]

While Averell pressed McCausland's brigade as it withdrew from Chambersburg, Jackson and his brigade continued daily skirmishing with federal troops throughout West Virginia's Potomac counties and across the river in Maryland. Between 29 July and 22 August, Jackson's brigade was involved in skirmishes at Shepherdstown, Martinsburg, Sharpsburg, Boonsboro, Williamsport, Leetown, Charles Town and Winchester. Jackson's role with Early's army changed on 12 August, when Major General Lunsford Lomax replaced Robert Ransom as division commander of cavalry.[37] Lomax, a Rhode Islander and a classmate of Fitzhugh Lee at West Point, was new to the Shenandoah Valley theater. Although Lomax had been with the Army of Northern Virginia since the Gettysburg campaign, he had spent his service in Virginia with Fitzhugh Lee around Richmond and Petersburg. He was not personally acquainted with any of the officers in his new command, but he soon came to rely on William Jackson's opinion and judgment. For a few days in late August, Jackson's brigade was temporarily commanded by Major Harry W. Gilmor of the Second Maryland Cavalry Battalion. On 24 August Gilmor led Jackson's brigade along with his own Maryland battalion to a position on the Leetown road. Jackson's dismounted brigade anchored a line, which was charged three times during the day by federal cavalry under General Alfred Duffie. The line held during the night, but the following morning Gilmor withdrew his men and Jackson's brigade to Shepherdstown, where Jackson reappeared to take command of his troops.[38]

The available records do not suggest a reason for Jackson's absence from his command on 23-24 August. Perhaps he spent time in consultation with Lomax discussing strategy and reorganization of cavalry brigades in the Shenandoah Valley. Jubal Early had a low opinion of the cavalry brigades assigned to his army. Early distrusted and disliked John McCausland, although McCausland was the most aggressive cavalry commander in Early's improvised Army of the Valley. McCausland was outspoken in his criticism of superior officers, and Early had a thin skin for criticism.[39] Bradley Johnson, although favored by Lee to command Early's cavalry division, did not have Early's confidence. Early believed that John Imboden was incompetent and that his brigade was useless as a fighting force.[40] John Vaughn's lack of discipline among his troops caused Early to lobby Richmond for his replacement.[41] Early was uncertain about the abilities of William Jackson. Within limitations of manpower and equipment, Jackson had performed well during the Valley Campaign. He had the advantage of being a cousin and confidante of the immortal Stonewall Jackson, whom Jubal Early attempted to emulate in the Valley. Early never recorded his personal opinion of William Jackson, but when Early rode to the outskirts of Washington, D. C., on 11 July to view the city's defenses, William Jackson was the only brigade commander who accompanied him.[42] Lomax reported to Early on 12 August fully briefed on Early's objectives in the Valley, but with little knowledge of the personalities of his division's officers or the character of the men under his command. William L. Jackson may have been assigned by Early to provide Lomax with insight into the nature of the officers and men he would order into battle.

On 26 August Jackson returned to command in the field. He rejoined his brigade near Shepherdstown, where his troops engaged in a sharp skirmish with part of William Averell's cavalry. The skirmish had no bearing on troop movements in the area, and the Confederates involved withdrew after exchanging shots with cautious federals throughout the day. The Union commander during the action, Lieutenant Colonel James Forsyth, reported to Averell that "Mudwall Jackson's command was crushed at Shepherdstown to-day."[43] Forsyth overstated his victory. Jackson's brigade, after skirmishing most of the day with Forsyth's detachment, simply retired from the field as usual. No advance by the Confederates was intended. However, during the withdrawal toward Leetown, Jackson's brigade suffered a demoralizing incident. While mounting his horse, William Jackson's revolver accidentally discharged and wounded him in the thigh. The wound was not serious, but it was painful. Jackson would be unable to command his brigade in the field for nearly a month.[44]

Jackson's brigade had no commander during his recovery. The senior officers of the two regiments, William Thompson and William Arnett, and battalion commanders Joseph Kessler and Henry Ruffner, led the brigade in the field. The pattern of skirmishing, withdrawing, and skirmishing again continued between Martinsburg and Winchester. Perhaps because of Jackson's absence on the field, a rumor persisted among Union commanders in north central West Virginia that Jackson had disbanded his brigade and sent small companies of men into Upshur, Lewis and Randolph counties to steal horses. Several skirmishes involving partisans identified only as "Jackson's command" occurred in Upshur and Randolph counties. These raiders probably were men belonging to the companies of Jacob Marshall and William McNeel, neither of which accompanied Jackson's brigade to the Shenandoah Valley. Some of the raiders may also have been members of the new partisan company formed by John Sprigg and Albert and Frederick Chewning. The federal commander at Buckhannon, Captain Harrison H. Hagans of the First West Virginia Cavalry, sent a frantic telegram to Lieutenant Colonel Robert Youart at Beverly detailing a skirmish his men had fought at Centerville, Upshur County, on 15 September. Hagans claimed that his men had killed four of the guerrillas, including one captain.[45] Urging Youart to send reinforcements, Hagans claimed that "About seventy men of Jackson's command in upper part of this county (Upshur), supposed to be making for Webster. Report to-day at 12 o'clock that between 300 and 400 rebels were en route for this place (Buckhannon) and Weston."[46] The captain Hagans claimed to have killed was Sida Campbell of Calhoun County, captain of Co. K,

Nineteenth Virginia Cavalry. Campbell, a veteran of both the Twenty-fifth and Thirty-first Virginia Infantry regiments, had transferred to the Nineteenth Cavalry in October, 1863. During the Shenandoah Valley campaign he had a disagreement with William P. Thompson, lieutenant colonel of the Nineteenth Cavalry, and evidently volunteered to lead a party to central West Virginia to steal horses as a means of getting out of Thompson's command. In the raid at Centerville, Campbell was shot in the face, the ball entering under his right eye and exiting at the back of his right ear. A Confederate raider captured during the Centerville raid reported that Campbell had been killed in the fight. However, he survived his wound and died in Calhoun County in 1910.[47]

WINCHESTER AND FISHER'S HILL

By the middle of September, Early was convinced that the federal army gathered around Charles Town under the command of the young and untested Phillip Sheridan planned no serious forward movement to drive him from the Shenandoah Valley. On 17 September Early received a report that federal soldiers were repairing the Baltimore and Ohio Railroad tracks near Martinsburg. He ordered William Jackson and his mounted men to conduct the infantry brigades of Robert Rodes and John B. Gordon to Martinsburg and put a stop to the repair work. At the last minute Early decided to accompany Jackson at the head of the expedition. At Bunker Hill, twelve miles south of Martinsburg, Early received intelligence that Ulysses S. Grant and Sheridan had met for a conference at Charles Town on 16 September. Early concluded that a major federal assault was imminent. He quickly ordered an about face and rushed back to Winchester. He left Rodes and Gordon at Stephenson's Depot five miles north of Winchester, where John Breckinridge's division already was deployed. Jackson and his cavalry remained with the infantry divisions to watch for a federal approach. Around dawn on 19 September 1864, Early received reports that a large force of federal troops had crossed Opequon Creek at Berryville and were advancing on Winchester.[48] The Battle of Opequon Creek, or Third Winchester, had begun. By the end of the long day, Jubal Early's ambitious hope of saving the Shenandoah Valley for the Confederacy lay in ruins.

Jackson and his brigade began the day of 19 September on the left wing of Early's alignment, along with the infantry brigades of Rodes, Gordon and Breckinridge. When Early realized that the main federal assault was directed at his center, manned only by Robert Ramseur's division, he ordered the three brigades on his left to move to support Ramseur. Jackson was ordered to move his cavalry brigade to the right to support Lunsford Lomax on the Senseney road. Lomax and Jackson were opposed by James Wilson's two cavalry brigades.

While Early's infantry in the center gradually bowed to superior numbers during the day, Jackson and Lomax fought Wilson to a draw. Early finally ordered a general withdrawal at dusk. While the battered Confederate infantry regiments hurried through Winchester, Jackson, Lomax and Bradley Johnson covered their retreat.[49]

Jubal Early's confidence that Sheridan could be driven from the Shenandoah Valley suffered irreparable damage from the battle at Opequon Creek. No longer anticipating offensive actions against the federals, Early developed a siege mentality. He ordered his exhausted army to withdraw to Fisher's Hill, a natural barrier to the upper Shenandoah Valley twenty miles south of Winchester. Fisher's Hill reared out of the valley floor between Little North Mountain and Massanutten Mountain. Precipitous slopes, rocky bluffs, and a bewildering latticework of ravines made the mountain nearly impregnable. On the slopes of this formidable obstacle Early arranged his thin line of defense.[50] According to Early, Fisher's Hill "was the only place where a stand could be made."[51]

Early anticipated a frontal attack by Sheridan at Fisher's Hill. His right flank was virtually unassailable due to the steep slope of Fisher's Hill and a narrow gorge. Nevertheless, Early stationed Gabriel Wharton's infantry brigade and an artillery battalion on the right, at the bottom of the mountainside. John B. Gordon and his infantry brigade occupied the road. Across the front of Fisher's Hill, Early positioned Dodson Ramseur's three infantry brigades, commanded by John Pegram. Ramseur had command of Robert Rode's brigade on Pegram's left. Rodes had been killed at Opequon Creek on 19 September, and his brigade colonels had requested that Ramseur be assigned to command them. The terrain on the left line at Fisher's Hill was most vulnerable to attack. Here the slope of Fisher's Hill descended in a series of low ridges to the valley floor, where a back road from Strasburg wound around the foot of the mountain. Early positioned Lunsford Lomax's cavalry brigade on the left of the line. The brigades of William Jackson, Bradley Johnson, and John Imboden were dismounted and ordered to build breastworks.[52] Early had little confidence in the fighting ability of Lomax's division, yet he placed them at the most critical location of his line at Fisher's Hill. Early weakened Lomax's already depleted line by detaching John McCausland's brigade and sending it far to the right, across the North Fork of the Shenandoah River, to scout roads from Strasburg.[53]

As Sheridan approached Fisher's Hill on 21 September, Early realized that he did not have sufficient forces to make a stand. Although his defenses were good, he had only ten thousand men to oppose Sheridan's thirty-five thousand. After surveying federal positions in front of Fisher's Hill during most of the next day, Early decided to order a nighttime withdrawal. Unknown to Early, Sheridan had sent George Crook's infantry and William

Averell's cavalry along the south face of Little North Mountain to a position opposite Lomax's improvised breastworks. At four o'clock in the afternoon on 22 September, Crook's more than five thousand screaming combat veterans charged into Lomax's ill-prepared line. Most historians writing about the Battle of Fisher's Hill claimed that Lomax's division panicked and fled as Crook's attack neared their lines. Lomax defended his troops in his official report of the action. He noted that Jackson's and Johnson's men engaged the charging federals and did not retire until an infantry regiment sent to reinforce them broke and ran without firing a shot.[54] As Early's left crumbled, his entire line of defense at Fisher's Hill gave way with little resistance. A severe thunderstorm erupted near the close of the battle, helping the Confederates escape. The onset of a rainy, foggy night prevented effective federal pursuit, but the defeat at Fisher's Hill was devastating to Early's army. Early suffered over one thousand casualties at Fisher's Hill, eighty percent of them prisoners, and much of his artillery and supplies were abandoned in the headlong flight to the rear.[55]

William Jackson was one of the few commanders at Fisher's Hill who kept his unit together during the disorderly retreat. Withdrawing from the battle early in the conflict, Jackson had time to regroup his men south of Fisher's Hill as the rest of Early's army streamed by in a panic. As his brigade had done at Winchester three days earlier, Jackson's men defended the rear of Early's army as it fled for Mount Jackson more than twenty miles south of Strasburg. As a rear guard, Jackson once again encountered the cavalry brigade of William Averell. Averell had accompanied Crook's division with nearly three thousand well-mounted and equipped cavalrymen. Sheridan assigned him the task of cutting off the Confederate retreat south of Fisher's Hill. A combination of rainfall, muddy roads and darkness prevented Averell from reaching his objective. Instead he ran into Jackson's regrouped cavalry brigade, who fired out of the darkness at the federal cavalry during the long and uncomfortable night. Averell suffered no casualties, but he hesitated to advance in the darkness without knowing what he faced. Sheridan castigated Averell the following morning for failing to push Jackson's men out of the way and blamed him for the escape of Early's army. Averell was given a second chance to drive the harried Confederates into Sheridan's net the following day, but he was stopped in his tracks at Mount Jackson by elements of Ramseur's and Wharton's infantries. Furious at what he perceived to be timidity by Averell, Sheridan relieved him of command and sent him back to West Virginia to chase partisans.[56]

WOODSTOCK

On 26 August 1864, Ulysses S. Grant wrote to Philip Sheridan with a suggestion for Sheridan's Valley campaign. "Do all the damage to rail-roads

& crops you can," Grant wrote. "Carry off stock of all discriptions (*sic.*) and negroes so as to prevent further planting. If the War is to last another year we want the Shenandoah Valley to remain a barren waste."[57] Grant probably reemphasized the importance of laying waste to the Valley of Virginia during his meeting with Sheridan at Charles Town on 16 September. Having shattered Jubal Early's army and driven it into the mountains around Waynesboro, Sheridan concluded that the military phase of his Shenandoah campaign was over. Between 26 September and 5 October, Sheridan's troops destroyed farmhouses, barns and crops in the area of Harrisonburg, Port Republic and Staunton. On 6 October, Sheridan put his army in motion to return to the Potomac River and join Grant at Petersburg. Between Staunton and Winchester Sheridan destroyed everything which might be used to sustain a Confederate force in the field. Jubal Early, reduced to an impotent spectator, trailed Sheridan's army down the Shenandoah Valley and watched the breadbasket of the Confederacy go up in smoke. Only Early's cavalry disputed Sheridan's passage down the valley. Jackson's brigade, along with the other cavalry brigades in Lomax's division, harried and skirmished with Sheridan's burning parties and his rear guard. However, Early recognized that his cavalry was too weak to stop Sheridan from destroying the lower Shenandoah Valley. Early asked Lee for reinforcements, and Lee responded by sending Thomas Rosser and his six hundred cavalrymen known as the "Laurel Brigade." Rosser immediately was dubbed "Saviour of the Valley," and Early placed him in command of the cavalry division led by Fitzhugh Lee at Winchester. Lomax retained his independent cavalry division, which included Jackson's brigade.[58]

Rosser held Lomax's cavalrymen in contempt, and he operated on the fringes of Sheridan's army with little coordination between he and Lomax. On 8 October Rosser occupied a position near Tom's Brook, five miles north of Woodstock, Shenandoah County. William Jackson and Bradley Johnson occupied the town of Woodstock. The cavalry divisions were more than twenty miles north of Early's infantry at Rude's Hill. Sheridan, annoyed by the ceaseless harassment by Rosser and Lomax, ordered his cavalry commander, Brigadier General Alfred Torbert, to "start out at daylight and whip the rebel cavalry or get whipped."[59] Torbert sent George A. Custer to whip Rosser, and Wesley Merritt was detailed to dispose of Jackson and Johnson. On 9 October, Custer routed Rosser's brigade after three hours of heavy fighting. Jackson and Johnson skirmished with Merritt on the outskirts of Woodstock throughout the day and held their positions. However, when Lomax received word of Rosser's defeat at Tom's Brook, he ordered Jackson and Johnson to withdraw. Once the Confederate cavalry fell back into open fields south of Woodstock, the federal cavalry charged them. Both brigades discharged an ineffective volley at the federal horsemen, then turned and raced for Early's lines twenty miles away. The federals pursued them until they reached Early's infantry at Rude Hill.[60]

One reported episode at Woodstock illustrated the demoralized condition of Lomax's cavalry division, and Jackson's brigade in particular, in the days following the debacle at Fisher's Hill. Major Harry Gilmor of the Second Maryland Battalion described events after he and Lomax were notified that Jackson's brigade was falling back from its position north of Woodstock. Gilmor and Lomax rode to the front line and discovered that Jackson's men were retiring in confusion. Lomax attempted to rally the soldiers while Gilmor noticed an isolated group on the right side of the rapidly disintegrating line. Gilmor noted:

> *I observed a squadron on the extreme right of our line going to the rear without any apparent cause, and in good order. I rode over, and found them to be one of Jackson's Western Virginia squadrons. The men were not disheartened, but the commanding officer was, and was retreating without orders. . . . I drove off the officer with very little ceremony, wheeled the squadron, and told the men I wished to lead them to the left of the skirmish line, which we could easily break through before their reserve could come up, and assured them we could sweep round their rear and capture many prisoners. They agreed to go, but I saw there was not much dependence to be placed on them. . . . So at them we went, with a right good yell. . . . The enemy stood well, but we should have turned their flank had the men stood by me; but, seeing that the enemy did not give way on our approach, they slackened their pace, and a piece of artillery opening upon them at the moment, though at long range, they wheeled and ran, leaving me still going on among the skirmishers.[61]*

Lunsford Lomax recalled events at Woodstock differently. Lomax reported that his two brigades, Jackson's and Bradley Johnson's, held the federals in check north of Woodstock until he received word that Rosser's command had been broken at Tom's Brook. Lomax ordered Jackson and Johnson to withdraw slowly, which they did until they reached open land south of Woodstock. At that point disaster struck:

> *As long as the country was broken and wooded my command retired in good order and checked the enemy from making a rapid pursuit. The enemy at this time brought a column from the Backroad, which advanced steadily on my left while I was engaged in front. On reaching the open and unbroken country at Woodstock the enemy charged Johnson's brigade, which was completely broken. I was unable to rally this command. The brigade on the right of the road (Jackson) was unbroken and*

was detached to meet the force advancing on the left, and retired in good
order. . . . The officers and men cannot be blamed for giving way when
charged in such heavy force, having no arms to resist a charge mounted,
not a saber or pistol being in the command. My command being at one
time twenty-seven miles from any infantry support, without proper arms
or discipline, will explain in a measure why the rout was so complete.[62]

Such conflicting reports of his cavalry's performance left Early in frustrated confusion. Lacking any appreciation of the capabilities and limitations of his cavalry, Early was quick to blame most of his army's reverses on
them. Receiving a report on the disasters at Tom's Brook and Woodstock,
Early vented his despair over the performance of his cavalry brigades to Robert E. Lee that same evening. Early wrote:

I have not heard definitely from Rosser, but he is, I understand, falling
back in good order, having rallied his command, which is on what is
called the Back road, which is west of the pike; but Lomax's command,
which was on the pike, came back to this place in confusion. This is very
distressing to me, and God knows I have done all in my power to avert
the disasters which have befallen this command; but the fact is that the
enemy's cavalry is so much superior to ours, both in numbers and equip-
ment, and the country is so favorable to the operations of cavalry, that it
is impossible for ours to compete with his. Lomax's cavalry are armed
entirely with rifles and have no sabers, and the consequence is that they
cannot fight on horseback, and in this open country they cannot success-
fully fight on foot against large bodies of cavalry; besides, the command
is and has been demoralized all the time. It would be better if they could
all be put into the infantry; but if that were tried I am afraid they would
all run off.[63]

CEDAR CREEK

Jubal Early trailed Philip Sheridan's withdrawing army down the
Shenandoah Valley for two weeks. Sheridan believed that Early had no resistance left in him, and he made plans to shift part of his army out of the
Valley to join Grant at Petersburg. Even a sharp skirmish with Early's infantry at Cedar Creek a short distance north of Strasburg on 13 October did
not dissuade Sheridan from his belief that Early's army did not have the
capacity to go on the offensive. As a precautionary measure, Sheridan positioned his Sixth and Nineteenth Corps across the Valley Pike on the north
side of Cedar Creek. On 15 October Sheridan placed Major General Horatio
Wright in command of the army, and he boarded a train for Washington, D.C.
United States Secretary of War Edwin Stanton had summoned Sheridan to

Washington to discuss coordinating his operations with Ulysses S. Grant at Petersburg. Sheridan met with Stanton and United States Army Chief of Staff Henry Halleck on 16 October, and by 18 October he was back in Winchester. Around six o'clock in the morning on 19 October, a picket rode to the house where Sheridan was sleeping and informed his aides that heavy artillery could be heard rumbling in the distance toward Strasburg. Sheridan immediately dressed and started for Strasburg ten miles up the Valley. Less than half a mile south of Winchester he encountered a wagon train in disarray and wild reports that Early had defeated the federal army at Cedar Creek. Sheridan's famous ride to Cedar Creek restored Union lines shattered by Early's dawn attack, and turned one of the Confederacy's most astounding victories into one of its most demoralizing defeats.[64]

In the aftermath of Early's debacle at Cedar Creek on 19 October 1864, scapegoats were plentiful. However, in this instance neither Early nor his infantry commanders could blame the devastating rout on Lunsford Lomax's cavalry division. Lomax, William Jackson and Bradley Johnson were not present at Cedar Creek. The day before the battle, Early had sent Lomax's division eastward toward Front Royal with vague orders to attack the rear of the Union army during its anticipated retreat on 19 October. Lomax encountered a federal cavalry patrol at Front Royal on the morning of 19 October and drove it to within six miles of Winchester. Sounds of the battle at Cedar Creek reached the cavalrymen, but no dispatches from Early arrived to inform Lomax of events. Lomax, Jackson and Johnson camped near Front Royal for the night still unaware of the catastrophe that had befallen Early's army. The next day scouts reported that Early had withdrawn from Cedar Creek back to Fisher's Hill. Remaining well to the east of the federal positions around Strasburg, Lomax took his horsemen south into the Luray Valley.[65] The division remained in camp at Luray for the remainder of October.[66]

BRIGADIER GENERAL JACKSON

On 28 October 1864, Lunsford Lomax recommended William L. Jackson for promotion to the rank of brigadier general. In his recommendation of Jackson, Lomax stated that Jackson's brigade numbered nearly seventeen hundred men, six hundred of whom were mounted. He also complimented Jackson on the brigade's organization and efficiency, and he stated that the soldiers were superior fighters.[67] Lomax's evaluation of Jackson and his brigade was so contrary to other contemporary estimates of the brigade's performance that it appears disingenuous. At the time of his recommendation for promotion, Jackson was not in command of his own brigade. Brigadier General Henry B. Davidson had replaced Jackson as commander of "Jackson's Brigade" during October. An organizational chart of Early's Army of the

Valley, which fought at Cedar Creek on 19 October, was submitted to Robert E. Lee on 21 October 1864. The chart showed "Jackson's Brigade" under the command of General Davidson. The brigade included the Nineteenth and Twentieth Virginia cavalries, the Forty-sixth and Forty-seventh Battalions of Virginia Cavalry, and the Second Maryland Cavalry.[68] Although available records indicated that Jackson was not with his brigade during the latter part of October and the entire month of November, no records place him anywhere else. Had Jackson been relieved of command, Lomax's recommendation that he be promoted to brigadier general made no sense. Evidently Jackson was on assignment somewhere outside the Shenandoah Valley during his six week hiatus from his brigade, but records failed to reveal where he might have been or what he was doing during that period.

Under Davidson's direction, Jackson's brigade spent the last two weeks of October and all of November camped in the Luray Valley. The brigade did no fighting during the six weeks Davidson commanded them. Davidson accompanied Thomas Rosser to Middletown near Strasburg on 12 November. Rosser skirmished during the day with Sheridan's pickets, but Davidson and Jackson's brigade did not participate in the fighting.[69] In mid-December Jackson's brigade was ordered to Madison County, southeast of the Shenandoah Valley and the Blue Ridge Mountains. As mysteriously as he disappeared in October, Jackson reappeared at Madison Court House and resumed command of his brigade around 20 December. On 22 December, Jackson and John McCausland's brigade engaged General Alfred Torbert's First Cavalry Division at Liberty Mills, Orange County. Torbert had eight thousand cavalrymen under his command, and orders from Sheridan to seize control of the Virginia Central Railroad at Gordonsville, ten miles south of Liberty Mills. Between them Jackson and McCausland were able to put around fifteen hundred men in the field to oppose Torbert. Torbert forced the Confederates out of Liberty Mills early in the afternoon of 22 December, but as Jackson's men retreated they burned the only bridge in the area across the Rapidan River. Unable to cross at Liberty Mills, Torbert split his force and scoured the terrain north and south of the crossing to find fords. By the time he got his men across the river, darkness had fallen. Jackson and McCausland withdrew to a low mountain pass two and one-half miles north of Gordonsville, where they quickly threw together a barrier of fence rails and earthworks. At dawn on 23 December Torbert directed a frontal attack against the Confederate position. Unable to force the dismounted cavalrymen out of their defensive works, Torbert decided to send part of his force to the left of Jackson's and McCausland's position and flank them. While getting in position for the flank attack, Torbert observed Confederate infantry marching rapidly up the road from Gordonsville. Unsure of the force he was facing, Torbert elected to withdraw.[70] Jackson and McCausland temporarily had preserved the railroad lifeline to Lee's embattled forces at Petersburg.

RETURN TO THE ALLEGHENIES

During the first week in January, Jubal Early ordered Lomax's cavalry division to return to the Allegheny Mountains to forage their horses. Early's order specified that the cavalry brigades were to establish quarters in Pendleton, Highland, Bath, Alleghany and Greenbrier counties. Lomax sent Jackson and McCausland with their thin brigades to the Allegheny Mountains while he reported to Robert E. Lee at Richmond.[71] Jackson established his headquarters at Warm Springs, Bath County, where he had established his first headquarters in the spring of 1863. He kept the Nineteenth Cavalry with him, while the Twentieth Cavalry was stationed at Crab Bottom on Back Creek.[72] On 20 January 1865 Jackson received his commission as Brigadier General from Robert E. Lee.[73] Early had sent Lomax's cavalrymen to the Alleghenies to find forage for their horses and food for themselves. Although the region had escaped the excesses of Sheridan's scorched earth policy, four years of warfare had left the region devoid of food for horses and men alike. One of Jackson's first orders as a brigadier general was to send his entire brigade to their West Virginia homes to resupply themselves and forage their horses. Jackson issued his unusual order on 2 February, and directed the men to reassemble at Warm Springs within forty days.[74]

The presence of Jackson's men in central West Virginia during February did not go unnoticed by unionists. On 5 February, the federal commander at Buckhannon sent a dispatch to Clarksburg alerting the commander there to a rumor that one hundred and fifty rebels were said to be concentrating near Addison, Webster County. This group was reported to be part of a force being gathered by Thomas Rosser for an attack on Bulltown.[75] The report had credibility because only a month earlier Rosser had attacked the federal camp at Beverly, Randolph County, and captured more than half of the garrison stationed there, along with more than one hundred horses and nearly seven hundred rifles.[76] A detachment of Ohio infantry was sent into Webster County to investigate the report, and on 4 March 1865 the Ohioans surprised a partisan gathering at the farm of James Dyer on Gauley River. Albert and Frederick Chewning, former members of Company B, Nineteenth Virginia Cavalry, were killed. John Sprigg, the disaffected captain of Company B, was wounded and captured. Several other members of the Nineteenth Cavalry were taken prisoner.[77]

Colonel James P. Wilkinson, post commander at Parkersburg, telegraphed Charles H. Day, commander at Bulltown, Braxton County, on 16 February 1865 that he had reliable information that about two hundred members of "Bill Jackson's command have taken possession of Ripley and Ravenswood."[78] The report proved false. On 1 March 1865, Charles H. Morgan, General

Winfield S. Hancock's chief of staff, wrote to General Samuel S. Carroll at Cumberland, Maryland, concerning a letter he had received from the governor of West Virginia. The governor claimed that there were two thousand rebels from Jackson's, Imboden's and Rosser's commands in Hardy, Randolph, Pendleton and Pocahontas counties. Morgan asked Carroll to investigate the report and move against the rebels if the report proved valid.[79] Although the numbers reported by Morgan were exaggerated, several hundred members of those commands were in the area foraging for supplies. Federal patrols into central West Virginia counties were increased. During January, February and March, 1865, dozens of soldiers from the Nineteenth and Twentieth cavalries were captured at or near their homes. At least eight members of Company B were captured in Webster and Braxton counties during February and March.

A controversy arose within Early's cavalry command in mid-February. Writing to Early from Richmond on 15 February 1865, Lomax complained that his division was being dismantled without his knowledge and that officers were being assigned to his command without his approval. Lomax wrote that Ambrose Dunn, William Jackson's old enemy, had assumed command of the Thirty-seventh Virginia Battalion, part of McCausland's brigade, and that Dunn on his own authority had detached his battalion from McCausland's command and departed for Richmond. Dunn, according to Lomax, was under grave charges and had been ordered to Staunton to stand trial. Both Jackson and Major James Claiborne, whom Jackson had appointed to command the Thirty-seventh Battalion when he placed Dunn under arrest in July 1863, had written letters to Lomax about Dunn. Lomax noted that he had enclosed their letters in his communication to Early, but the letters were not found in Confederate files after the war. Lomax did not explain the nature of the latest charges against Dunn. His main concern, however, was the disposition of Jackson's brigade. According to Lomax:

> *Rosser states that Jackson's brigade has been ordered to report to him to form a part of his division. This is my best brigade, and I hope if I am to lose a portion of my command that I be allowed to select the brigade. . . . If my command is to be broken up without consulting me, I had better leave it. As soon as I can I will see General Lee on the subject. I feel confident that it is not your wish to deprive me of my command. I do not believe it will be for the interests of the service to take Jackson's brigade and the Thirty-seventh from my division.*[80]

Confederate records contained no reply from Early to Lomax. However, Jackson was not detached from Lomax's command and the Thirty-seventh Battalion remained with McCausland. Lee relieved Early of his command on 30 March 1865 and appointed Lomax to replace him.[81] On 31 March Ambrose Dunn resigned his commission.[82]

WAYNESBORO

Jubal Early maintained a winter camp at Staunton during January and February, 1865. The severity of the winter weather kept Sheridan from driving Early out of the Shenandoah Valley permanently, but in late February the weather moderated sufficiently for Sheridan to order an attack. On 27 February 1865, Sheridan left Winchester with ten thousand cavalrymen under the command of Wesley Merritt and George A. Custer. Gabriel Wharton's fifteen hundred frozen and starving infantrymen protected Early's camp.[83] Thomas Rosser was in Staunton with around one hundred cavalrymen. On 1 March Rosser's men attempted to fight Sheridan's force, but after exchanging a few shots Rosser withdrew toward Buffalo Gap. Early and Wharton's infantry fled in the direction of Charlottesville. In a driving sleet storm, Custer caught up with Wharton's men a few miles west of Waynesboro. Custer's five thousand cavalrymen charged the hopelessly outnumbered Confederate infantry. After firing a couple of rounds at the onrushing federal horsemen, most of the men tried to escape into the mountains. The Union cavalrymen easily ran them down, and nearly all of Wharton's force was captured. Early, Wharton, and a few staff members escaped Custer's net by riding through the woods and escaping through Rockfish Gap.[84]

Shortly before Sheridan had driven Early out of Staunton, Lomax had returned to the Valley from Richmond and established his headquarters at Millboro Springs in Bath County. When Rosser realized that Sheridan was moving against Early's camp in late February, he sent a dispatch to Lomax asking him to bring all available cavalrymen and come to his assistance at Staunton. Early countermanded Rosser's request and ordered Lomax to station his troops at Pond Gap on the Lynchburg road in case Sheridan broke through at Staunton. Lomax would be responsible for preventing Sheridan from reaching Lynchburg and the critical railroad junctions at that city.[85] Lomax obeyed Early's orders to move to Pond Gap, but he sent William Jackson toward Staunton to support Rosser. Lomax was unaware that Rosser and Early had been driven out of Staunton on 1 March. Jackson had only a few troops with him, but he established a camp at Buffalo Gap six miles west of Staunton on 4 March, unaware that Early's army had been captured at Waynesboro two days earlier. On the day Jackson arrived at Buffalo Gap, he received a dispatch from Rosser asking him to send troops to help him recapture the prisoners taken by Custer at Waynesboro on 2 March. Jackson returned a message explaining that he had no troops at the moment, but that he was expecting around one hundred and fifty men to arrive at Buffalo Gap that night. Jackson promised to bring them to Rosser's aid if the men appeared. The next day Jedekiah Hotchkiss, a friend of William Jackson's since their days together on Stonewall Jackson's staff in 1862, arrived at Buffalo Gap with a personal plea to send assistance to Rosser. Some companies of the Twentieth Cavalry had arrived at Buffalo Gap the night before, along with some men formerly belonging to John Imboden's brigade. Jackson sent them all, one hundred and twenty strong, to help Rosser.[86] Rosser attempted to rescue the prisoners near New Market on 6 March, but failed in the attempt.[87]

LAST STAND AT LYNCHBURG

Around 8 March Lomax sent dispatches recalling Jackson and McCausland to Millboro Depot. As soon as the brigades assembled, Lomax marched them to Lynchburg where a defense of the city was planned. On 14 March Lomax received orders from Early to bring his division to Richmond. The division arrived in Henrico County on 18 March, camped two days, then was ordered by Early to return to the Shenandoah Valley to recruit and organize resistance to federal troops occupying the region. Sheridan had left the Valley after destroying Early's force at Waynesboro, leaving only skeleton forces behind to garrison major towns such as Staunton and Winchester. Lee believed that Early could reorganize the troops that had scattered into the mountains to escape Sheridan. With most of Sheridan's soldiers no longer in the Valley, Lee hoped that Early might collect enough troops to reoccupy the region.[88] Lomax and his exhausted men and horses reached Churchville, five miles northeast of Staunton, on 27 March. On 30 March Early was relieved of his command and Lomax replaced him. After skirmishing with federal troops around Staunton for a week, Lomax concluded that reorganizing a Confederate army in the Shenandoah Valley was hopeless. On his own authority he started his old cavalry division back to Lynchburg. Although Lomax officially was in charge of a division of the Army of Northern Virginia, he had only William Jackson's brigade to command. Both Bradley Johnson's and John Imboden's brigades had been disbanded and reassigned. McCausland's brigade was retreating from Richmond with Robert E. Lee. Lomax and Jackson arrived back in Lynchburg on 6 April and began constructing defensive positions on the Richmond road. On the afternoon of 9 April 1865, McCausland and four hundred survivors of his brigade rode into Lynchburg with the news that Lee had surrendered the Army of Northern Virginia at Appomattox Courthouse that morning.[89]

Neither William Jackson nor John McCausland felt obligated to surrender. They had no knowledge of the surrender terms Lee had reached with Grant at Appomattox. Both feared that as Confederate officers they were likely to be charged with treason and imprisoned if not executed. McCausland especially was apprehensive because of his role in the destruction of Chambersburg, Pennsylvania the previous August. Both men decided to take what was left of their brigades and leave the area. McCausland led his men westward into Bedford County, but as they neared the small community of Liberty, they met some soldiers who had been paroled at Appomattox. When McCausland learned that Grant had agreed to simply allow the former rebels to go home after signing paroles, he disbanded his brigade and sent his men home.[90]

A RELUCTANT DISBANDMENT

Jackson left Lynchburg with the intention of slipping into North Carolina and joining the army of Joseph Johnston. Jedekiah Hotchkiss, topographical engineer for both Stonewall Jackson and Jubal Early, accompanied Jackson and the remnants of his brigade. The diary kept by Hotchkiss provided the only record of the final days of William Jackson's command. The brigade reached the border between Virginia and North Carolina on 12 April. Jackson had ventured only a short distance into North Carolina when he learned that large concentrations of federal troops were between him and Johnston's army at Durham. Hotchkiss was present in Jackson's dejected camp and noted that "few were left to follow General W. L. Jackson when he turned back toward the Valley."[91] Jackson and his men avoided federal patrols west of Lynchburg and reached Buchanan, Botetourt County, around 16 April. At Buchanan Jackson decided that the men could travel more safely in small groups, and he ordered the brigade to disband and reassemble at Staunton on 1 May.[92] Many of the men in Jackson's brigade left Buchanan and headed directly for their homes in West Virginia.

On 16 April 1865, Captain Joseph Badger of the Eighth Ohio Cavalry left Beverly with one hundred and fifty mounted men to search for bushwhackers and to post notices along the former Huntersville line announcing the terms of parole. Badger followed the Huntersville road through Marlin's Bottom to Knapp's Creek. He encountered a few men seven miles east of Huntersville who informed him that Jackson's brigade had disbanded and that the men were going home in small squads. Badger had moved a short distance toward Warm Springs when he met a family of refugees, mostly women and children. The women told Badger that a party of three hundred of Jackson's men, mounted and heavily armed, was on the road between Huntersville and Warm Springs. Badger moved forward cautiously and had traveled less than a mile when his advance scouts suddenly came under fire. Badger rode to the front of his column in time to see several men lunging up steep mountainsides to get away from the federal troops. One sniper was captured, and he admitted that he was a member of a company of around twenty-five men from Jackson's command headed for their homes. The party included Lieutenant Colonel Jacob Marshall of the Nineteenth Cavalry, Lieutenant Colonel Elihu Hutton of the Twentieth Cavalry, and Major William French Harding of the Twentieth Cavalry, all residents of Randolph County. Badger failed to catch any of Jackson's former officers. Badger completed the rest of his scout through Bath and Highland counties without incident. He noted in his report that the people he had met during his expedition were "completely conquered," and were "willing to submit on our terms."[93]

Jackson's men had been ordered to rendezvous at Staunton on 1 May. A large group of Nineteenth Cavalry veterans congregated near Staunton on 30 April only to discover that the town was occupied by federal troops. Colonel William Thompson sent Captain George W. Silcott into Staunton under a flag of truce to find out what terms the men would receive if they surrendered. Colonel Horatio B. Reed of the Twenty-second New York Cavalry, commander of the post at Staunton, probably was amazed at the audacity of Thompson's note. Thompson informed Reed that he was willing to discuss surrender terms only if Reed would agree to give him and his men a five hour head start to avoid capture in the event that the terms proved unsatisfactory. Although Thompson had signed his communication to Reed as "Colonel Nineteenth Virginia Cavalry," Reed sent his reply addressed to "Col. W. P. Thompson, Commanding Jackson's Brigade, Lomax's Division, &c." Reed advised Thompson that he would accept the surrender of Thompson's command on the same terms given to the Army of Northern Virginia: "officers and men to give their parole of honor not to take up arms against the United States until exchanged; all arms, horses, and public property to be turned over to the United States, officers to retain their side-arms, private horses, and personal baggage."[94] Thompson did not find Reed's terms acceptable. When he and his command failed to appear at Staunton the following day, Reed sent out a single scout to look for them. The scout reported to Reed that Thompson's party consisted of about one hundred men and that they had scattered into the mountains. Reed wrote to his superior, General William Russell, that he "did not think it proper to attempt to capture them, as it would occupy more time and labor than was justifiable."[95]

In some manner Jackson's widely dispersed men were advised that their rendezvous had been changed from Staunton on 1 May to Lexington on 3 May. According to Captain David Poe of the Twentieth Cavalry, about half of the brigade gathered at Lexington on the appointed day. Nearly half a century after the event, the rendezvous at Lexington still evoked nostalgia in his memory. Poe recalled:

> *Gen. Jackson tried to say something to those war worn veterans, but his emotions were too strong. He did ask us if he should surrender us, or if we would surrender ourselves, that he could get the same terms that Gen.*

*Lee got at Appomattox. The men said, "We surrender ourselves," but
some never surrendered. I had seen battles fought, buildings consumed
in flames, the face of the earth, as it were, strewn with dead and wounded,
both men and beasts, in fact, I had seen all the horrors of a wicked,
foolish war, and yet that day's scene was the saddest of them all.[96]*

William Jackson's movements between the time he disbanded his brigade on 16 April and the brigade's rendezvous at Lexington on 3 May were
not recorded by anyone. Jedekiah Hotchkiss— whose diary entries provided
the only clues to Jackson's whereabouts immediately after Lee's surrender—
lost track of him on 12 April when Jackson turned back north from the
North Carolina border. Hotchkiss apparently never saw Jackson again. He
reported a rumor that Jackson had disbanded his brigade at Buchanan on 16
April, and his entry for 2 May stated that "Rosser and Jackson, with a few
followers, left yesterday for the Southwest."[97] On 19 April, Union General
George Stoneman rushed a telegram to General George Thomas at Jonesboro,
Tennessee, warning Thomas to watch out for Jackson. "Echols, Vaughn, Jackson, etc.," Stoneman wrote, "with 1000 or 1500 volunteers, after having
stripped the country of horses, are now trying to make their way to Mississippi."[98] Rumors persisted that Jackson was somewhere in the Allegheny
Mountains organizing a guerrilla army to raid West Virginia. As late as 7
May 1865, Colonel Nathan Wilkinson at Clarksburg received a letter from a
home guard captain named H. H. Hartsock who reported that Jackson was
gathering a force to attack an unspecified target. Hartsock noted that he
thought Buckhannon and Beverly were unlikely targets because there was
nothing of value to steal in those towns. He believed that Jackson intended
to strike for Parkersburg, which Hartsock claimed Jackson would take a "fiendish delight" in destroying.[99]

The only records which placed Jackson at a particular place at a
definite time after Lee's surrender were Hotchkiss's brief diary entry on 12
April and David Poe's post-war memoir which placed him in Lexington,
Virginia, on 3 May 1865. Jackson disappeared after 3 May. He would not
reappear until ten weeks later when he rode into the federal camp at
Brownsville, Texas, and requested an application for parole.

7

REFUGEE

During the spring and summer of 1865 Mexico was a popular destination for officers and government officials of the defeated Confederate States of America. Many Confederate authorities were convinced that the victorious Union would exact retribution for the rebellion. The arrest and incarceration of Confederate president Jefferson Davis in mid-May 1865 alarmed many Confederate military and civil authorities in the South, but Davis's arrest did not surprise any of them. As head of state of the national government for the Confederacy, most southerners expected Davis to be tried and imprisoned if federal authorities could catch him. Many southerners blamed Davis for the Confederacy's collapse, and his arrest provided a convenient scapegoat for former Confederates concerned with their own roles in sustaining the rebellion.[1] However, when rumors began to circulate that Robert E. Lee had been arrested and charged with treason, Confederates still in the field took notice. Lee was revered throughout the South, and nearly all of his former officers and soldiers held him in such high esteem as a soldier and gentleman that they believed him to be immune from punishment for his role in the rebellion. Ulysses S. Grant had issued Lee a parole at Appomattox, promising that Union authorities would not molest him. Nonetheless, on 7 June 1865, a federal court in Norfolk indicted Lee and fourteen other Confederate officers for treason.[2] Contrary to rumors, Lee had not been arrested. However, the widespread belief that Union authorities had violated the terms of Lee's parole inspired many Confederates who had not surrendered to consider leaving the country. If Robert E. Lee was not safe from Union retribution, then Jubal Early, Kirby Smith, John McCausland and William L. Jackson certainly were not safe.

Early, McCausland and Jackson, among other Confederate officers, had managed to elude capture throughout April and May 1865. McCausland returned to his home in the Kanawha Valley, then quietly boarded a train for Canada.[3] Early and Jackson had made their separate ways through the deep South intending to cross the Mississippi River and join Kirby Smith's army in Texas. Smith, recognizing that continued resistance was futile, surrendered his army at Galveston, Texas, on 2 June. One of Smith's division commanders, General Joseph O. Shelby, declined to follow his superior officer's example. Shelby informed his troops that Smith had surrendered them. For his part, Shelby advised them, he was going to Mexico and anyone who wished to accompany him could ride along. About two hundred of Shelby's men chose to accompany their general into exile in Mexico. Riding across more than three hundred miles of Texas countryside, Shelby's "brigade" acquired nearly three hundred other former Confederates along his route. Kirby Smith and John Magruder joined Shelby's column near San Antonio. Near the end of June Shelby crossed the Rio Grande into Mexico.[4]

No rosters were kept of the men who traveled with Joseph Shelby to Mexico, but William L. Jackson and his half-brother, Thomas Stinchcomb, may have been among Shelby's troops. However, Jackson and Stinchcomb did not volunteer their services to the Mexican army as did Shelby. Jackson's and Stinchcomb's activities in Mexico were not documented, yet most of Jackson's biographers claimed that he went to Mexico for a short time.[5] However, Robert White, colonel of the Twenty-third Virginia Cavalry, in a post-war history of the Civil War in West Virginia did not mention that Jackson fled to Mexico.[6] White's history was published in 1899, only nine years after Jackson's death. The absence of documentation of William Jackson's exile in Mexico and omission of any reference to such an exile by a biographer who knew Jackson personally in the post-war period created questions about Jackson and Mexico which cannot be resolved through available records.

RETURN TO PARKERSBURG

One indisputable fact placed Jackson near the Mexican border in July 1865. On 26 July William Jackson and Thomas Stinchcomb appeared at the federal garrison in Brownsville, Texas, to sign paroles. They completed the formalities of surrender, including taking an oath of allegiance to the United States, without incident. Although Brownsville lay on the Mexican border opposite the Mexican town of Matamoros, nothing in the parole record of Jackson and Stinchcomb indicated that they had arrived at Brownsville from Mexico. Following the receipt of paroles and safe conduct papers, Jackson and Stinchcomb rode north into Texas. The half-brothers evidently traveled together as far as Mt. Pleasant, Texas. Stinchcomb remained in Mt. Pleasant where he spent the rest of his life as a successful merchant.[7]

William Jackson left his half-brother in Texas and continued to make his way east. Around the middle of September he appeared in Parkersburg, much to the delight of his former soldiers in Wood County, and much to the chagrin of Jackson's pre-war political and business associates. A Parkersburg newspaper published a terse announcement of Jackson's return:

Mudwall Jackson was lionized by the Southern Party at Washington's Bottom on Thursday (15 September 1865) by a ball and other attentions by which the Union citizens were scandalized and felt that it was only the license given to such orgies by the General Government that prevented them from giving him his due.[8]

The announcement of the reception accorded Jackson at Washington's Bottom set the tone for subsequent mentions of William L. Jackson in area newspapers.

James E. Wharton, editor of the *Parkersburg Daily Times*, had been an outspoken advocate for the Union cause in Wood County throughout the war. His pro-Unionism had not prevented his arrest by General David Hunter in 1864 and destruction of his printing press and office. Hunter had driven his undersupplied and bedraggled army to Parkersburg from Lynchburg following his humiliating withdrawal in June 1864. As Hunter's exhausted and starved soldiers straggled into Parkersburg, Wharton took note of their condition. He also noted that Hunter, his staff, and regimental officers had ridden steamboats from Charleston to Parkersburg, while the nearly eleven thousand infantrymen in Hunter's command were left to make their way overland to Parkersburg as best they could. Footsore and hungry, the federal infantry struggled across nearly one hundred miles of hostile territory between Charleston and Parkersburg. They were forced to live off a land stripped of supplies after three years of warfare, and they were harassed throughout the length of their journey by Confederate partisans. The troops began straggling into Parkersburg around the first of July. One survivor of the march noted later that "the clothing of the officers and men was in tatters and dirty, half were barefooted, and all worn down by the hardships of the expedition. To add to their misfortunes, the camp diarrhoea had set in . . . . We were truly forlorn and shipwrecked brothers."[9] Wharton found the condition of Hunter's common soldiers reprehensible. When he learned of a lavish dinner party given for Hunter and his commissioned officers at the luxurious Swann House hotel on Ann Street in Parkersburg, Wharton composed an editorial harshly critical of Hunter's management of his army. Wharton claimed that the troops were exhausted and that many had died of starvation on the retreat from Lynchburg. Following the editorial's publication, a group of Union soldiers under Hunter's orders arrested Wharton and destroyed his press. Wharton was taken to Cumberland, Maryland, where Hunter threatened to try him for treason. A heated letter from West Virginia governor Arthur Boreman secured Wharton's release and the dismissal of the charges against him. Hunter replied to Boreman and denied all of the allegations expressed by Wharton in his editorial. He advised Boreman to notify the West Virginia press that he would not tolerate the publication of articles in any newspaper critical of the condition of the army under his command.[10] Wharton, outraged over his treatment by Hunter, returned to Parkersburg and announced that he would sue Hunter when the war was concluded.[11]

Wharton forgot his proposed lawsuit against David Hunter during the fall of 1865. Instead he launched a vendetta against William L. Jackson. Numerous caustic remarks and editorials appeared in Wharton's paper throughout October and November 1865. Wharton had help condemning former rebels and William Jackson from the editor of the *Marietta* (Ohio) *Daily Times.* Every civil disturbance that occurred in the Parkersburg area in October and November 1865 was blamed on William Jackson and his former soldiers. According to the Marietta editor, "Bill Jackson's horse thieves" broke up a singing class at a church near Parkersburg with rowdy behavior. Wood County authorities were summoned, and the editor noted that "the interlopers fearing a flank movement, soon began to have lively recollections of what happened at Bulltown, and, imitating the example of their defunct master at that place were not long in making their heels do their duty."[12] In another incident a group described as "Mudwall Jackson's bushwhackers" disrupted a Bible study class at Zoar Chapel between Parkersburg and Marietta. This group of rabble rousers stood outside the church and created "a most unearthly noise, belching out terrible oaths, firing off revolvers, and making (the) night hideous with their howling."[13]

Jackson realized that his presence in Parkersburg created difficulties for his former soldiers. It was probably during November that he decided to settle in St. Marys. Before the war Jackson had been a popular and respected leader in the small river town. During his first term in the Virginia Assembly he had introduced the bill which created Pleasants County, and he had been the county's first prosecuting attorney. His wife was a native of St. Marys and her parents still lived there. However, Jackson quickly discovered that the people who had elected him to the Assembly to represent them in the early 1850s marched to a different drummer in 1865. Details of what happened to Jackson in St. Marys were not published in Parkersburg or Marietta newspapers beyond the fact that a violent demonstration against his presence in the town had occurred and Jackson had been forced to leave. He returned to Parkersburg.[14]

James Wharton noted Jackson's return to Parkersburg, and resumed his vilification of Jackson's character throughout November. In the 20 November issue of the *Parkersburg Daily Times,* Wharton made a passing reference to Jackson as a "guerrilla chief." Several of Jackson's former soldiers accosted Wharton near his office on 2 December and demanded a retraction of Wharton's flippant remark. When Wharton declined to retract his characterization of Jackson as a "guerrilla chief," one of the men challenged him to a duel. In the next issue of the *Daily Times* Wharton took a column and a half to answer the question, "Have We Rebellion Yet?" Wharton's comments in his front page editorial reflected Unionist attitudes in Parkersburg toward William Jackson and helped explain subsequent events:

> *A few days since Wm. L. Jackson came here. He was so called Col. in the Rebel army. He commanded a body of men who sacked a considerable portion of West Va. . . . We have been repeatedly told that he swore he would come into Parkersburg during the war. What for? Evidently to sack and pillage from Union men. . . . Thousands of persons had sleepless nights in Parkersburg under the threats of this same Jackson. . . . He was admonished that his presence among this people was offensive. Yet (he) came here. . . . On Saturday the editor of this paper was assailed by a dozen drunken men expressly to bully him into a promise to retract his expression that Jackson was a guerilla chief. We declined. . . . There were sundry assaults of this kind in language during that day . . . . Now, Messrs. Rebs or Jackson friends, when you get ready, if you are offended at what we say, pitch in. . . . We will take great provocation from others, but we tell the rebel sympathizers that they, on Saturday owed their lives to our courtesy and consideration for their condition. In ten minutes we could have raised a storm that would have cleared every rebel from Parkersburg."* [15]

THE OIL BUSINESS

William Jackson never stated publicly why he had returned to Parkersburg. He may have planned to resume his law practice. The West Virginia legislature passed a law in February 1865 denying the right to vote to any man who refused to testify that he had not borne arms against the government of the United States, the reorganized government of Virginia, or the state of West Virginia. The law did not proscribe attorneys from practicing their profession under the new system. Several of Jackson's Confederate associates reopened private law practices, among them Jonathan Bennett in Weston and William Lively in Glenville.[16] Jackson's brother-in-law and law partner, Jacob B. Blair, still maintained an office in Parkersburg, although Blair spent most of his time in Washington as a West Virginia congressman.[17] If Jackson planned to reopen his legal practice in Parkersburg, the animosity towards him by unionists in Parkersburg may have persuaded him to locate elsewhere.

The hostility directed at William Jackson in Parkersburg may have been motivated by Jackson's pre-war business activities rather than his politics. In 1859 a large deposit of petroleum reserves had been discovered at Burning Springs, Wirt County. Johnson Newlon Camden, a Weston merchant, invested heavily in development of the Burning Springs oil field. In 1860

Camden leased an oil well from William P. and John V. Rathbone of Parkersburg.[18] Camden's well struck a large oil deposit in January 1861. Hoping to raise cash to drill more wells, John Rathbone offered to sell one-half of his interest in the well to Camden for one hundred thousand dollars. Camden lacked sufficient cash to purchase Rathbone's offer for himself, but the well was producing oil in copious quantities. To raise the money to buy Rathbone's half-interest in the well, Camden organized a consortium of investors to contribute to the purchase price. Camden contributed enough money to the consortium to buy a full one-quarter share in the half share interest offered by Rathbone. He divided the remaining three-fourths of the half interest offered by Rathbone into one eighth shares. Camden priced these shares at twelve thousand, five hundred dollars for each one-eighth share. William L. Jackson, his cousin John J. Jackson, Jr. and William J. Bland, a Weston physician, pooled resources and purchased a one-eighth share.[19] Each of the three men contributed four thousand, one hundred and fifty dollars to the venture. Although he owned only one-third of a one-eighth share in the oil field, Jackson earned enough profit from his share that he leased an additional site and drilled his own well.[20]

When William Jackson left Parkersburg to join the Confederate army in May 1861, he may have entrusted his business interests to his brother-in-law Jacob Blair, a staunch unionist. Blair, despite his opposition to William Jackson's politics, probably intended to protect Jackson's financial investments. However, in July 1861 he was appointed to the United States House of Representatives replacing John S. Carlile, newly elected as one of loyalist Virginia's United States senators.[21] Blair left for Washington almost immediately, and in his absence Johnson Camden instigated a complicated plot to gain complete ownership of the Burning Springs oil field.

Shortly after Jacob Blair left for Washington, Camden complained to Rathbone that Confederate guerrillas interfered with production at Burning Springs to such an extent that business could not be conducted. He told Rathbone that only he and John J. Jackson, Jr. had stayed in Parkersburg after the outbreak of the war, and that Jackson had lost interest in producing oil. He asked Rathbone to cancel the agreement they had signed in January for Camden to buy one-half of Rathbone's interest in the Burning Springs field. Rathbone agreed, and Camden began trying to contact the other partners in his oil venture to secure their power of attorney to cancel the deal with Rathbone. John J. Jackson, Jr. and Andrew Weare readily agreed to Camden's proposal. Benjamin Byrne, Camden's closest business associate, was contacted in Lewisburg where he was serving with the Confederate army. Byrne signed a power of attorney. Weston attorney Matthew Edmiston and Lewis County businessman Matthew Harrison also signed powers of attorney for Camden.

The other four partners were not as amenable. William L. Jackson, William J. Bland and Snowden Andrews were all behind Confederate lines serving in the army. Gideon Camden, Johnson Camden's uncle, was a member of the Confederate Congress in Richmond. Normal mail delivery between the United States and the Confederate States had been disrupted since June 1861. Camden hired Horatio Eagle, a business agent whom Camden believed to be a strong unionist, to try to avoid the mail blockade and deliver letters to the four Confederates asking for their powers of attorney to cancel the lease with Rathbone. Eagle traveled to Cumberland, Maryland, in September 1861. In Cumberland he contacted a courier willing to carry Camden's letters to the Confederates. Eagle arranged to meet the courier on his return at Brady's Gate, Hampshire County, well within Confederate lines. When Eagle appeared at Brady's Gate to meet the courier, he was arrested by Confederate scouts and sent to Richmond as a spy.[22] When William Jackson was in Richmond in December 1861 securing his promotion to full colonel, he learned that Eagle was being held in the Henrico County jail. Jackson and Gideon Camden co-authored a letter to Jefferson Davis on 2 December 1861, explaining the circumstances of Eagle's being within Confederate lines. He was, they wrote, "induced to visit the neighborhood . . . where he was arrested, for the sole purpose of bringing to us a communication on important business in which we are deeply interested." Jackson and Camden did not ask for Eagle's release, but suggested instead that he be exchanged for a comparable prisoner held by federal authorities.[23] Eagle may not have been the staunch unionist Johnson Camden believed him to be. Another letter urging Eagle's release was written to Robert H. Smith, a Confederate congressman from Alabama, by E. W. McGinnis, a Mobile merchant. McGinnis asked Smith to intercede with Confederate Secretary of State Judah Benjamin on Eagle's behalf. In his letter to Smith, McGinnis noted that Eagle "has spent his money and used his influence at all times against the Black Republican party of New York (and) that he voted against them last fall and has always done so."[24] Eagle eventually was released from jail and allowed to return to Parkersburg. He did not bring Camden the powers of attorney he had been sent to collect.[25]

Despite failing to acquire the agreement of all of the partners to cancel the lease signed with Rathbone in January 1861, Camden and Rathbone proceeded to develop the oil field as though they were sole owners. Complaints against Confederate guerrillas interfering with production disappeared from Camden's letters. In July 1861 Camden and Rathbone formed a partnership in which they agreed to share profits from the sale of oil produced at Burning Springs. By April 1863 Camden and Rathbone shared profits amounting to over one hundred thousand dollars.[26] On 9 May 1863 Camden's and Rathbone's oil empire abruptly collapsed in spectacular fashion. Confederate General William E. Jones and his cavalry brigade attacked the Burning Springs oil field. The results did not please Johnson Camden and John V. Rathbone. Jones's graphically described the effect of his raid in his official report of the incident on 12 May 1863:

> *All the oil, the tanks, barrels, engines for pumping, engine-houses, and wagons—in a word, everything used for raising, holding, or sending it off was burned. The smoke is very dense and jet black. The boats, filled with oil in bulk, burst with a report almost equaling artillery, and spread the burning fluid over the river. Before night huge columns of ebon smoke marked the meanderings of the stream as far as the eye could reach. By dark the oil from the tanks on the burning creek had reached the river, and the whole stream became a sheet of fire. A burning river, carrying destruction to our merciless enemy, was a scene of magnificence that might well carry joy to every patriotic heart. Men of experience estimated the oil destroyed at 150,000 barrels. It will be many months before a large supply can be had from this source . . .[27]*

Camden and Rathbone were out of the oil business, but only for a short time. Camden organized the First National Bank of Parkersburg, engineered his own election as president of the bank, then loaned himself sufficient money to rebuild the oil works at Burning Springs. Some oil was produced by the summer of 1863, only three months after Jones destroyed production facilities, and by early spring of 1864 Camden and Rathbone again were earning profits from oil production at Burning Springs. In 1866 Camden and Rathbone sold their Burning Springs development to New York investors for over four hundred thousand dollars.[28]

One charge leveled against William L. Jackson by *Parkersburg Daily Times* editor James E. Wharton was the destruction of the Burning Springs oil field. Despite the facts that Jackson was not present when Jones's men destroyed the Burning Springs facilities and that part of the property destroyed belonged to him, Wharton claimed that Jackson "ranked Jones and could have prevented his burning Burning Springs."[29] Wharton was incorrect when he claimed that Jackson "ranked" Jones. William E. Jones was a brigadier general commanding his own brigade of cavalry in May 1863. William Jackson was a colonel commanding only the Nineteenth Virginia Cavalry regiment. If Jackson did play a role in selecting the oil field as a target for Jones's raiders, neither Jones nor Jackson's immediate superior, General John D. Imboden, mentioned the fact in their reports of the Jones-Imboden raid.

No records exist implicating Johnson Camden in a plot to drive William Jackson out of Parkersburg, but he had both the motivation and the means to make things uncomfortable for Jackson. Camden probably did not share

James Wharton's belief that Jackson could have prevented the destruction of the Burning Springs oil field, but he may have suspected that Jackson played a role in selecting the oil field as a target for Jones's raiders. Jackson probably realized that Camden and Rathbone were earning enormous profits from oil production, and he certainly knew that he was not receiving profits from his interest in the oil business. Camden may have believed that Jackson suggested destruction of the oil works as a measure of revenge against him and Rathbone. During the Civil War, Johnson Camden became a dominant capitalist in West Virginia, largely through his oil sales to the United States government. By the end of the war, he controlled the Parkersburg financial community. As president of the First National Bank in Parkersburg, Camden directed the allocation of money to finance new business ventures in the area. Without his endorsement, new businesses had small chance of success. As the leading business figure in Parkersburg, Camden had the capability of denying business to individual attorneys simply by referring clients to other lawyers. If William Jackson had reopened his law office in Parkersburg after the war, he may have been denied major accounts on the orders of Johnson Camden.

Camden was not simply opposed to Confederates or secessionists. According to his biographer, "Camden . . . was compelled to choose between his best interests on the one hand and loyalty to sentiments and traditions on the other. On the one side was stark realism with its strong impulses to economic gain, while on the other were the remnants of a decadent romanticism with strongly compelling social traditions."[30] Camden's brother-in-law was William P. Thompson, William Jackson's lieutenant colonel with the Nineteenth Virginia Cavalry and later its colonel when Jackson advanced to brigade commander. In 1866, Camden and Thompson formed the J. N. Camden Company and established a successful oil refinery in Parkersburg.[31] Thompson later became a multimillionaire as head of the National Lead Trust in New York and became a member of the board of John D. Rockefeller's Standard Oil Company.[32] Camden also was not opposed to William L. Jackson's family. George Jackson, William L. Jackson's brother, returned to Parkersburg after the war and became successful as an associate of Johnson Camden in the oil business.[33] If Johnson Camden played a major role in driving William Jackson out of Parkersburg, he must have done so for personal reasons. He may have resented Jackson for destruction of the Burning Springs oil field, or Jackson may have demanded compensation from Camden for the appropriation of his lease on the Rathbone property. Whatever the circumstances, if Johnson Camden had wanted William L. Jackson to remain in Parkersburg after the Civil War, no one else would have had the power or courage to force him to leave.

FALL FROM GRACE

Another factor, which hampered William Jackson's ability to restore his prestige in Parkersburg, was the decline in status of the Wood County Jackson clan during the Civil War. John J. Jackson, Sr. although strongly opposed to Virginia's secession, was equally hostile to the effort to create the state of West Virginia out of Virginia's territory. At the First Wheeling Convention in early May 1861, Jackson spoke in opposition to John S. Carlile's proposal that western Virginia counties secede from Virginia and form a separate state government. His stand against creating a new state outraged unionists in Parkersburg, and Jackson was defeated in a bid to represent Wood County at the Second Wheeling Convention in June.[34] Early in June Jackson had a dispute with federal authorities in Parkersburg. Jackson permitted the first Union troops to occupy Parkersburg to establish their camp on his farm. He asked the soldiers not to use a particular field on the farm, which he used to pasture geese, but tents were pitched in the forbidden area. Jackson rode into Parkersburg to complain to the Union commander, but his plea was dismissed in a brusque manner. Jackson publicly condemned the Union troops for abusing private property. Unionists in Parkersburg were offended by Jackson's condemnation of Union soldiers whom most citizens regarded as loyal protectors of the city and private property.[35]

Jackson campaigned strongly against the West Virginia constitutional referendum scheduled for 26 March 1863. The revised constitution, which detailed the process by which slaves in West Virginia would be emancipated, had to be ratified by West Virginia voters as a condition for Abraham Lincoln's signing of the West Virginia Statehood Bill passed by Congress on 10 December 1862. John J. Jackson, Sr., Sherrard Clemens, and John J. Davis among other opponents of the new state, focused on the constitutional referendum as a final opportunity to derail the separation of Virginia into two states. A convention was called to meet in Parkersburg on 12 March to develop a campaign to persuade western Virginia voters to reject the revised constitution. Arthur I. Boreman, a Parkersburg attorney, pre-war friend and associate of both John J. Jackson, Sr. and William L. Jackson, and a leader in the new state movement, spearheaded an effort to deny the convention an opportunity to meet. When Jackson, Clemens and Davis arrived at the Wood County courthouse for the meeting, they found the building locked and armed federal troops patrolling the court square. The meeting was cancelled, and John J. Jackson's political future in Wood County was destroyed.[36] After representing Wood County in the Virginia Assembly and serving as prosecuting attorney for two decades, Jackson never held public office again.

Two of Jackson's sons contributed to the family's fall from political power. James M. Jackson served Wood County as prosecuting attorney and colonel of the county militia at the outbreak of the war. When the reorganized

Virginia state government required public officeholders to subscribe to a loyalty oath in 1861, James Jackson refused to comply. He maintained that such an oath was valueless unless all citizens were required to take it. Because he refused to take the loyalty oath, the Wood County militia refused to allow Jackson to continue as their colonel. Arthur I. Boreman, who had replaced William L. Jackson as circuit judge in Wood County, removed Jackson from command of the Wood militia and replaced him with Rathbone Vanwinkle. Jackson lost even more respect when he was arrested in Clarksburg for displaying a rattlesnake flag and associating with known Confederate partisans. Jackson was released after only a few hours in detention, but the episode was reported in local newspapers. Wood Countians believed that Jackson, despite public statements to the contrary, was sympathetic with secession.[37]

John J. Jackson, Sr.'s youngest son also contributed to the lack of confidence in the Jackson clan among Wood Countians. Union authorities in Wheeling in 1864 arrested Jacob Beeson Jackson, who had succeeded William L. Jackson as prosecuting attorney for Pleasants County. According to news reports, Jackson was imprisoned in Atheneum Prison for making disloyal statements. Jackson said that "although he had taken the oath (of allegiance to the restored government of Virginia) he had done so as a matter of self interest and with such reservations as fully justified his conscience . . . . He said the President (Lincoln) was a damned old abolitionist and he (Jackson) was a rebel at heart and so was his father."[38]

James M. Jackson and Jacob B. Jackson regained the confidence of Wood County voters after the Civil War. James Jackson was elected to the West Virginia House of Delegates in 1870, served as a delegate to the Constitutional Convention of 1872, and served twenty years as a judge in Wood County.[39] Jacob Jackson was elected prosecuting attorney for Wood County in 1870, represented the county in the West Virginia House of Delegates, and was elected mayor of Parkersburg in 1879. In 1880 he was elected governor of West Virginia.[40] Unfortunately for William Jackson, the reputations of James M. Jackson, Jacob B. Jackson, and their father, John Jay Jackson, Sr., were at their lowest point when William returned to Parkersburg after the Civil War. Because of the questionable political position of the Jacksons during the war, the Jackson surname was regarded with suspicion by Wood County unionists and secessionists alike. William Jackson could not count on family influence and reputation to ease his transition back into Wood County society.

LOUISVILLE

On Saturday evening, 2 December 1865, William L. Jackson, his wife, and their three children boarded a steamboat and left Parkersburg for Louisville, Kentucky. A group of his former soldiers, loudly defaming *Daily Times* editor James Wharton, gathered at the wharf to see him off.[41] The Jacksons arrived in Louisville in mid-December. Coincidental with their arrival the Kentucky state legislature passed a bill removing all civil and political restrictions against former Confederates.[42] On 1 January 1866 Jackson opened a law office in Louisville. In January 1873 he was appointed circuit judge of Jefferson County, Kentucky. He served as a circuit judge for seventeen consecutive years. In mid-May 1883 Jackson came back to Parkersburg for the first time since 1865 to visit his dying brother George. Jackson was at his brother's side when he died on 27 May 1883.[43] Immediately after his brother's burial, Jackson left Parkersburg for the last time. He died in Louisville on 24 March 1890 and was buried in Cave Hill Cemetery.[44]

CONFLICTING OPINIONS

In 1919, John D. Sutton, a native of Braxton County, West Virginia, published a lengthy anecdotal history of Braxton County and adjoining areas. Sutton, a veteran of the Tenth West Virginia Infantry, wrote a lengthy chapter discussing events of the Civil War in central West Virginia. Sutton characterized William L. Jackson as an "extreme partisan" but "a poor military commander." According to Sutton, all of the "military genius of the Jackson Family" belonged to Stonewall. William Jackson's discipline, Sutton noted, "was not of that character that would give protection or inspire confidence and respect to a country helpless in the absence of civil government." Sutton dismissed with a single sentence the character of the men in Jackson's command; "He held a position between the regular army of the Confederacy and the ragged edges of the territory lying between the two opposing forces, and all the odds and ends that could be gathered together in a section of country without law and order, civil or military."[45]

John D. Sutton was not the first person to evaluate William L. Jackson as a "poor military commander," nor was he the first to indict Jackson's soldiers as "odds and ends." In 1863, Confederate quartermaster Edward McMahon charged that Jackson "made no preparation to meet the enemy" during William Averell's raid on Salem Depot.[46] In 1864, Robert E. Lee complained to Confederate adjutant general Samuel Cooper that the men of Jackson's command "have not impressed me favorably with regard to the discipline and efficiency."[47]

Balancing the critical assessments of Jackson and his soldiers by Sutton, McMahon and Lee was John McNeel's opinion that Jackson was "as brave a man as lived, and never refused to fight, when the attendant circumstances were anything like equal."[48] Lunsford Lomax, Jackson's last division commander, claimed that Jackson's men were his "best brigade."[49] Matthias Potts, a member of the Twentieth Virginia Cavalry, claimed that when the infantrymen of Ramseur's division saw Jackson's cavalry ride by, they took off their caps in respect for "Jackson's Brigade" which had "saved us at Winchester."[50]

THE MISSION

William Jackson hoped to recover northwestern Virginia from Union control when he formed the Nineteenth and Twentieth cavalry regiments in the spring of 1863. However, waging offensive campaigns to recover lost territory was not Jackson's assignment. The role of Jackson's regiments envisioned by Robert E. Lee was to scout the rugged borderland between the Shenandoah Valley and the Allegheny Mountains, and provide early warning of any federal movement in force toward Staunton and the left flank of Lee's Army of Northern Virginia. Lee considered Jackson's command as an extension of his own army, even though Jackson was not directly under Lee's command. One of the goals of the Jones-Imboden campaign in 1863, in which Jackson played a prominent role both in planning and execution, was to gather supplies, especially beef, for Lee's army. Jackson's attack on Beverly in July 1863 had been suggested by Lee to provide a diversion while he moved his army north to Gettysburg. No Confederate reports were filed giving details of Jackson's campaign against Bulltown, Braxton County, in October 1863, but Lee likely suggested that campaign as well, to cover his left flank and provide yet another diversion as Lee moved his army down the Shenandoah Valley in his first offensive since Gettysburg. Jackson's regiments did not become engaged in conducting offensive operations routinely until they were attached to Jubal Early's Shenandoah Valley command in the fall of 1864. Even then, the primary function of Jackson's brigade was to preoccupy federal troops who might be sent to Richmond to reinforce Grant's offensive against Lee. Indicative of the overall success of Jackson's mission to guard the western border and protect Lee's left flank is the fact that as late as March 1865, Jackson's headquarters were still at Warm Springs, Bath County, where Jackson had planted his regimental flag in March 1863.

IN RETROSPECT

Historians of the Civil War in West Virginia have failed to acknowledge the role played by William L. Jackson and his cavalry regiments in defending the Confederacy's western Virginia mountain border. Jackson himself was seldom included in any discussion of Civil War events in West Virginia. This curious omission of one of West Virginia's most active participants in West Virginia's Civil War history demands an explanation.

Throughout the war William L. Jackson declined to draw attention to himself. Having no military training before the war, Jackson may have been

unwilling to subject his operations to the scrutiny of other professional soldiers. As Stonewall Jackson's cousin, he probably had no wish to invite com-
parisons between himself and his legendary relative. Military archives have
failed to uncover a photograph of William L. Jackson in his Confederate
uniform. After the war Jackson wrote no memoirs. Historical journals, which
abounded in the post-war period, contained no articles or letters written by
Jackson. If Jackson maintained a file of personal papers, they have not been
discovered. The only known letters of Jackson during the war, to his wife, are
included at the end of this work.

If Jackson had ambitions of receiving post-war recognition for his military service, he may have done himself a disservice by relocating to Louisville
after the war. In Louisville, Jackson was only one of dozens of former Confederate officers living and working in the city. Despite his high profile surname, everyone knew that William L. Jackson was not Stonewall. Reporters
did not badger him for interviews, and Jackson did not seek out reporters to
tell his story. Jackson had done nothing sufficiently noteworthy during the
war to earn instant name recognition. Unlike John McCausland, he could
not list a Chambersburg in his resume. The only successful raid in which
Jackson participated was identified with John Imboden and William Jones.
Imboden's opinion often was sought as an expert on mountain campaigns.
No one invited William Jackson to express his opinion of Civil War campaigns in western Virginia's mountains. Jackson was not martyred in battle
like Albert Jenkins and William Jones. He declined to engage in controversial post-war debates as did Bradley Johnson and Jubal Early. From the point
of view of period historians and reporters, William Jackson was not interest-
ing to readers.

A curious exchange of notes in several issues of the journal *Confederate
Veteran* in 1909 and 1910 emphasized Jackson's problem earning recognition as a military commander. In an article describing the Battle of New
Market, Virginia on 15 May 1864, author J. N. Potts inserted a remark
about William Jackson. "No Confederate soldier," wrote Potts, should refer
to William L. Jackson as "Mudwall" Jackson, for there was not a more pol-
ished gentleman nor a more gallant and competent officer in the Confederate army than this same Gen. William L. Jackson."[51] Three months later Dr.
M. S. Browne of Winchester, Kentucky commented on Potts's remark. Browne
claimed that "Mudwall" Jackson actually was General Alfred E. Jackson from
Tennessee. Browne suggested that Potts's article contained a typographical
error. Mudwall Jackson, Browne wrote, was "not Gen. William H. Jackson
of Tennessee (I infer that William H. was meant instead of William L.)"[52]
The following month Milton W. Humphries added a postscript to a letter he
wrote to the *Veteran* concerning the battle at Cloyd's Farm. Humphries noted:

I was a little surprised at the note about "Mudwall" Jackson, which seems to imply that there was no Gen. W. L. Jackson; but he was, in fact, the man who in Virginia was called "Mudwall" to distinguish him from his famous cousin, "Stonewall." They both were born in the same town, Clarksburg, W. Va. He commanded a brigade of cavalry during the latter half of the war, and was very active in the campaign of 1863 in (West) Virginia.[53]

Jackson also failed to achieve post-war recognition due to the lack of regimental memoirs by his soldiers. Only four of Jackson's cavalrymen published memoirs: David Poe, John Henry Cammack, Matthias Potts and Daniel DeWees. Poe, Cammack and Potts were members of the Twentieth Virginia Cavalry. DeWees was the only member of the Nineteenth Cavalry known to have published a memoir. These recollections focused on the men's personal experiences and seldom addressed a broader view of their regiments' operations. Only Poe's memoir contained insight into William Jackson's character and performance as an officer. Cammack and DeWees spent little time on Jackson's roster and provided few memories of activities of the Nineteenth and Twentieth cavalries. Most of the soldiers in Jackson's command were uneducated farmers from central West Virginia, few of whom were literate. While they all had stories to tell, most of them lacked the means and opportunity to relate their experiences.

Another reason for Jackson's disappearance from the historical narrative of the Civil War in West Virginia may lie in the fact that most public memories of his operations were unpleasant. People in Upshur County had no desire to remember the raid on Centerville in which Jackson's men captured eighty-seven members of the Upshur County militia. Forty-three of the civilian soldiers died in southern prisons. Although Jackson was not present at Centerville, Upshur County citizens associated the disastrous raid and its devastating consequences with Jackson's men. Wood Countians blamed Jackson for the destruction of the Burning Springs oil field and lived in constant fear the he would lead a raid on his former hometown. Frequent raids by Jackson's men against civilians, some of whom were southern sympathizers, provoked a public outcry against these independent operations. As the commanding officer of the men involved in such raids, responsibility for stolen horses and burned barns was laid at the feet of William Jackson. Before the war Jackson was described as "the most widely known, as well as the most popular man in all that part of Virginia."[54] By the end of the war, Jackson was characterized as a man who would take a "fiendish delight" in sacking Parkersburg.[55] Few West Virginians would have been inclined to respect the memory of a man whom many citizens believed was capable of executing twenty-eight captured Union soldiers in cold blood.[56]

Finally, William L. Jackson had no place in West Virginia history after the war. Forced out of Parkersburg by business and political rivals, Jackson had no power base from which to strike back in his own behalf. Had he chosen to remain in West Virginia and join the effort to restore civil and political rights to former Confederates, he may have risen to the same political heights enjoyed by Allen Caperton, Jonathan Bennett and his cousins James and Jacob Jackson. However, these men retained the respect of their communities in the post-war period, a luxury not afforded to William Jackson. His only support in Wood County came from his former soldiers, whose activities were reduced to lurking outside churches and disrupting Bible study and singing classes by howling and firing revolvers.

William L. Jackson's massive red marble monument in Louisville's Cave Hill Cemetery carried the inscription:

As Judge, Legislator, Auditor, and Lieut.-Governor in Va., as a General in the Confederate Army and as a Judge for seventeen years of the Ninth District in Kentucky, he was faithful to every trust and merited and had the confidence of his countrymen.

Although Jackson's post-war Kentucky colleagues were lavish in their recognition of his achievements, West Virginia historians chose to ignore Jackson and dismiss his contributions to western Virginia's political and military history.

During Jackson's assault on Union lines at Beverly, Randolph County, in July 1863, Jacob Wamsley, Captain of Company D of the Nineteenth Virginia Cavalry, urged his men forward with the cry, "Come on! Don't let the damned Yankees whip us on our own soil!"[57] Wamsley's rallying cry epitomized William Lowther Jackson's attitude throughout the Civil War. He defended his own soil, the mountain counties of western Virginia, with fortitude and energy for four harrowing years. Jackson and his rag-tag regiments of farm boys, fathers, sons, brothers and cousins, withstood the overwhelming power of the professional army of the United States, and never surrendered. When Jackson returned to Parkersburg in September 1865 his former political colleagues and business partners took only three months to accomplish what the Union Army had failed to do in four years: they whipped William L. Jackson on his own soil. Once the politicians and capitalists whipped the General, historians buried both him and the dedicated citizen-soldiers he had led in defense of their native state. William Lowther Jackson and the soldiers of the Nineteenth and Twentieth Virginia Cavalry regiments are worthy of resurrection.

WILLIAM L. JACKSON
LETTERS

West Virginia Regional History Collection
West Virginia University
Morgantown, WV

Roy Bird Cook Collection
Accession # 1561
Series II
Box 2, Volume 1

The forty-four items of correspondence published here constitute the only known cache of private papers belonging to William L. Jackson. The papers are published verbatim as an appendix because they provide uncommon insight into Jackson's outlook on secession, the Civil War, and his colleagues during the first year of the war when he served as colonel of the Thirty-first Virginia Infantry Regiment. Jackson's gradual disenchantment with the Confederate hierarchy and bureaucracy can be traced almost weekly from June of 1861 to April 1862.

The letters touch on a variety of topics well-known to West Virginia Civil War historians – the disastrous Rich Mountain campaign, the bickering among John Letcher, Henry Wise and John Floyd, Robert E. Lee's questionable leadership in the Cheat Mountain campaign, the political in-fighting among Virginia's military personnel. There are no revelations or smoking guns in Jackson's letters that change the traditionally held views on these issues, but they do serve as further validation of the Civil War climate in western Virginia.

One theme that stands out in Jackson's letters is his devotion, confidence and trust in his wife, Sarah Creel Jackson. Virtually nothing is known about Mrs. Jackson, but she emerges in these letters as her husband's intellectual equal, a fact fully acknowledged by him. Sarah Jackson's assessments of military movements and political machinations are as perceptive as those of William L. Jackson.

Reading the Jackson letters in chronological order clearly charts the progress of the fire-eating secessionist who wrote in June 1861 that "we will drive the enemy out of our land," to the jaundiced military realist of April 1862 who noted that "it is impossible not to feel anxious about the result." Jackson's words in these letters are worth a thousand pictures.

LIST OF LETTERS

Note: All letters are from William Lowther Jackson to his wife, Sarah Creel Jackson, unless otherwise noted. This list includes the date of the letter, the place at which it was written, and a brief note of content.

1. Early June 1861. Laurel Hill, Barbour Co. Given command by Garnett.

2. 21 June 1861 (Friday). Parkersburg, VA. Pass issued to Sarah Jackson by Robt. L. McCook, Col. 9th Regt. VA Vols (USA).

3. 27 June 1861 (Thursday). Laurel Hill. George in Richmond.

4. 20 July 1861 (Saturday). Monterey, VA. Rich Mountain and retreat from Laurel Hill. Garnett's death.

5. 30 July 1861 (Tuesday). Laurel Fork, 11 Miles West of Monterey. Laurel Hill. George at Monterey.

6. 14 August 1861 (Wednesday). Greenbrier. Western Virginia strategy.

7. 22 August 1861 (Thursday). Camp Bartow. Bad weather, Wise and Floyd. McCullough.

8. 27 August 1861 (Tuesday). Camp Bartow, Travellers Repose. Lee, T. J. Jackson, Wise, Floyd, northwestern Unionists.

9. 29 August 1861 (Thursday). Camp Bartow, Travellers Repose. Bad weather, Floyd and Wise.

10. 1 September 1861 (Sunday). Camp Bartow, Travellers Repose. Pierpont government, sickness.

11. 2 September 1861 (Monday). Camp Greenbrier. Pass issued to Sarah Jackson by Bob Moorman, Comdr., Greenbrier Cavalry.

12. 3 September 1861 (Tuesday). Camp Bartow, Travelers Repose. Discourages Sarah from visiting.

13. 19 September 1861 (Thursday). Travellers Repose. Lee, Anderson, Donalson, Tygarts Valley, Huttonsville.

14. 23 September 1861 (Monday). Travellers Repose. Floyd and Wise, James Bennett. Rape of a southern woman in Upshur Co.

15. 26 September 1861 Thursday). Travellers Repose. Floyd and Wise, Lewisburg.

16. 1 October 1861 (Tuesday). Travellers Repose. Cheat Mountain (fragment).

17. October 1861. Battle of the Greenbrier (fragment)

18. 7 October 1861 (Monday). Travellers Repose. To General Henry R. Jackson. resignation.

19. 8 October 1861 (Tuesday). Travellers Repose. Resignation.

20. 11 October 1861 (Friday). Sarah Jackson to WLJ. Lee and Kanawha campaign.

21. 12 October 1861 (Saturday). Travellers Repose. Reynolds.

22. 16 October, 1861 (Friday). Tuckwillers. Sarah Jackson to WLJ. Resignation, Letcher, Floyd, Lee.

23. 18 October 1861 (Friday). Travellers Repose. Loring, Letcher, Confederate States service.

24. 22 October 1861 (Tuesday). Travellers Repose. Letcher, Northwestern Virginia.

25. 25 October 1861 (Friday). Tuckwiller's. Sarah Jackson to WLJ. Letcher, Jenkins, Loring, Fayetteville.

26. 27 October 1861 (Monday). Traveller's Repose. Resignation, money.

27. 2 November 1861 (Saturday). Traveller's Repose. Resignation.

28. 16 December 1861 (Monday). Richmond. Special Order #267 signed by Jno. Withers, AAG.

29. 5 January 1862 (Sunday). Richmond. WLJ to Sarah Jackson. Assembly convening, prospects of command, comment on actions in Tennessee and North Carolina.

30. 10 January 1862 (Friday). Camp Allegheny, Travellers Repose. WLJ to Sarah. Letter is dated erroneously as "1861". Weather, illnesses in regiment, George in action at Greenland Gap.

31. 16 January 1862 (Thursday). Huntersville. WLJ to Sarah. First letter from new command at Huntersville. Comments on demoralization.

32. 21 January 1862 (Tuesday). No. Monterey, Camp Allegheny. Gen. E. Johnson to Col. WLJ. Reinforcements, encouragement, Stonewall at Romney.

33. 25 January 1862 (Saturday). Huntersville. WLJ to Wm. Cooper, Robt Bradshaw, and Stephen Morgan. Thanking the 31st Regt. for a sword.

34. 26 January 1862 (Sunday). Camp Aleghany. Gen. Johnson to WLJ. Instructions.

35. 3 February 1862 (Monday). Huntersville. WLJ to Sarah. Conditions at Huntersville. Mentions "Sliding Sallie."

36. 13 February 1862 (Thursday). Huntersville. WLJ to Sarah. Weather, events at Parkersburg.

37. 20 February 1862 (Thursday). Huntersville. WLJ to Sarah. Fort Donaldson, Parkersburg. Locates Sarah in Richmond.

38. 24 February 1862 (Monday). Camp Allegheny. WLJ to Sarah. Death of stepfather Thomas Stinchcomb. In command while Johnson is in Richmond.

39. 14 March 1862 (Friday). Camp Allegheny. WLJ to Sarah. Again indicates that Sarah is in Richmond. Guerrilla warfare. Mentions "exploits of the Virginia" and victories by Price and VanDorn.

40. 18 March 1862 (Tuesday). Camp Allegheny. WLJ to Sarah. Gloom and doom. Mentions Stonewall's retreat.

41. 20 March 1862 ((Thursday). Camp Allegheny. WLJ to Sarah. Pocahontas militia.

42. 30 March 1862 (Wednesday). WLJ to Sarah. Camp Alleghany. WLJ to Sarah. Moving camp.

43. 9 April 1862 (Wednesday). Camp Shenandoah. WLJ to Sarah. George at McDowell. Alf Jackson with William.

44. 14 April 1862 (Monday). Camp Shenandoah. WLJ to Sarah. Skirmish near Monterey. Asks for postage stamps. Mentions battle at Yorktown.

1. William L. Jackson to Sarah Jackson

June 1861?[1]
Headquarters, Laurel Hill
My dear Wife:

I have but time to write you a line. I am in good health and stand camp life very well. I joined the army at Huttonsville,[2] and was placed in command of the Infantry. Since the arrival of Genl. Garnett,[3] a regiment was formed[4] and under my command marched to this place where we are waiting for the reinforcements now on the way. I feel a presentment that I will escape unharmed, and be with my dear wife and children again. I succeed well. Be certain that I will conduct myself as a brave man should. Do not believe any rumors. I see men alive, who are in the papers represented as dead. Our reinforcements are coming, and we will drive the enemy out of our land.

2. Safe conduct pass from Col. Robert L. McCook to Sarah Jackson

June 21st 1861

The bearer of this, Mrs. W. L. Jackson, with her three children, will be passed from this place to Weston in Lewis County Virginia by way of Staunton

Turnpike. She takes with her two buggies and must not be interfered with by any person friendly to the Government of the United States.

Robert L. McCook[5]
Col. 9th Regiment O V
Commanding at Parkersburg

3. William L. Jackson to Sarah Jackson

Camp at Laurel Hill
June 27, 1861

I cannot say anything about our force, as this letter may fall into the hands of the enemy. Be assured that when we do fight, we will be victorious. I have written a letter to you by a man from Braxton, which you will get if you are in that country.

P.S. I wrote in my former letter, that I was in command of a Regt. George[6] is safe in Richmond when last heard from. He was to get a good appointment.

4. William L. Jackson to Sarah Jackson

Camp at Monterey, Va.
July 20th 1861

I send you a messenger, my friend and the namesake of my father, Wm. L. J. Corley,[7] to inform you that I was in the five days fight at Laurel Hill, and in the retreat from that place, on the route of which there was a fight in which Genl. Garnett was killed, and that amidst hardships unparalleled in history, I brought my regiment through in safety to this place, and am un-wounded and in good health. I have been apprehensive that you might hear some bad rumors about me, and therefore send this trusty man.

The disastrous defeat at Rich Mountain, for we were successfully hold-ing our position, enable the enemy to surround us and cut us off, or starve us out, and hence we were compelled to retreat. The prospects are now gloomy but I hope they will soon brighten. The force attacking us was overwhelming and our General was outgeneraled. There is a dispatch here today that Beauregard has whipped Genl Scott at Alexandria.[8] I hope this is true. When-ever I can get leave of absence I will come to see you. It may not be safe for you to stay in Braxton. Corley will guide you to a safe place in Webster where you had better stay. Write me a long letter by Mr. Corley. George is here in command of the cavalry, in fine health. Mr. C. who is intelligent will give you all details.

5. William L. Jackson to Sarah Jackson

Laurel Fork, 11 miles west of Monterey
July 30, 1861

Mr. McCuchen has just informed me that he traveled with you from Lewisburg to Callaghan. I deeply regret that you did not come to Monterey. You did right in leaving Parkersburg. I never felt safe until I learned from Mr. Bastable[9] that you had left.

It is true in the retreat from Laurel Hill I tried how long a man could do without food. I found that two days and two nights was about as much as I could stand, after having been previously very indifferently fed and slept for five days and nights. No man in the army has been harder worked than I have been. I am now a long distance from any house, in the mountains surrounded by dense forests. The victory at Manassa shows that the south cannot be subjugated. Our independence will be recognized. I believe since the defeat at Masassa that the troops of the Northern Army will be withdrawn from the Northwest. If so, we will march in, take possession, with a force that cannot be drive out. At any rate force enough will be sent to us to drive them out.

For the next two weeks write to me at Monterey, the letters will be forwarded. George is at Monterey.

6. William L. Jackson to Sarah Jackson

Camp on the Greenbrier
August 14th, 1861

I now believe that the war in N. W. Va. Will be carried on right. The defeats here have opened the eyes of our Government. The enemy will be attacked from several different points, and by strong forces. Genl. Lee is now at the head of affairs. We arrived at this point without difficulty. Our position is a strong one, and we will be strongly reinforced today. I am still of the opinion that in the first great fight, we here will not take much part. Yet it is important that our force should be here. Although I had no military education, I have the confidence of the commanding officers, and am deemed so efficient that my demand to be permitted to see you has been kindly refused, and in the most complimentary terms.

7. William L. Jackson to Sarah Jackson

Camp Bartow, Hdqrs. 31st Regt Va Vols
Travellers Repose P. O., Va.
August 22d, 1861

On yesterday upon my return from a five day scout, Mr. Taylor sent for me to deliver from his own hand, your kind letter. I found Mr. Taylor badly broke out with the measles. I was quite unwell on my return having been rained upon for five days, but I am much better today and Dr. Bland says that I will be entirely well by tomorrow. If I don't get better I intend to come to you. I fear I am more homesick than anything else. If as I begin to suspect, we are merely here to guard this pass, and not to make any advance, if I cannot get a furlough, I will resign. To do nothing but ambush in the woods in constant cold rains is more than I can stand. There is a limit to human endurance and tough as I have been I begin to realize the fact. Besides I begin to think we are not to have any fight here. The name of this camp is "Camp Bartow." Address your letters as I have headed this. Let me have your opinion about my resignation, if my conjectures as to what we are to stay here for is correct. I infer from what all the Wood Co men who were with Genl Wise, but who have come to my Reg. say, that he is too peevish and curses his men too much. Floyd knows better how to manage men, and yet be obeyed. That is part of my forte. We have just got the news of Genl. McCulloughs victory in Missouri.[10] The independence of the Confederate States must soon be recognized. The North cannot stand a long war as well as the South, and it must be apparent that we can never be subjugated. When the enemy retire from the Northwest I look for them to do much damage, and even some of the cowardly Union men will not escape. Those who invited them in to fight for them, too cowardly to fight themselves, will get some kicks and cuffs.

8. William L. Jackson to Sarah Jackson

August 27th 1861
Camp Bartow, Travellers Repose P. O., Va.

I have no news of interest. The impression seems to exist here that Genl Lee has a brilliant plan for the campaign in the Northwest. Floyd and Wise are to sweep the Kanawha Valley, Loring is to advance on Huttonsville, we are to advance on this pike, and Genl. Tom Jackson, or some other General with a large force, is to advance by way of the Northwestern Turnpike, destroying the railroads as they go. Of course these movements are to be simultaneously made. He is but delaying untill he can get force enough to carry out this plan. With force enough the enemy will scarcely make a stand if attacked according to the above plan. I have great confidence in General Lee. He sees the dificulty of his position, and is preparing to meet the emergency. When he does move, success is ours. The enemy are not as strong in the Northwest as they were. McClelland took some Regiments with him, and many of the three months men have been mustered out. The North now has dificulty in raising Volunteers. The Volunteers from the Western States will be needed by Fremont in Missouri. Men who made their escape and come here, report that Union men in our country are becoming terribly alarmed. The Pittsburgh papers are beginning to call them cowards. Poor devils, the time is soon coming when all parties will treat them with contempt. The argument of Genl. J.,[11] Boreman[12] and Beerd[13] was that all who were union men would not have to fight. They appealed to the cowardice of our population, and cowardice was the cause of most of the unsoundness in our country. Now they are called upon to volunteer, and are threatened with a draft. I want them to be driven into a fight. If however there is a draft resorted to, there will be some good hiding in the hills and caves. The movements of Genl Lee are very secret. He keeps everything to himself. This is right. I cannot therefore express any opinion as to the time our forward movement will be made.

9. William L. Jackson to Sarah Jackson

August 29th 1861
Camp Bartow, Travellers Repose P O, Va

There is no direct mail from Huntersvill[14] to this place although one is proposed. I get well very slowly. There is so much bad weather. Since I started from Laurel Hill I have seen but five days of good weather. We have constant cold heavy rains. There never was such a climate as this. Our men sicken and many die. Indeed when the war is over it will be found that more have died in camp than on the battle field. I hope we will get beyond these mountains, and in a better climate before long.

Floyd and Wise must now be some distance beyond you on their way to Kanawha. Stay by all means where you are.

I have no news to write. Genl Lee has his plans, he is not yet ready, and besides keeps his plans to himself. Of one thing you may be assured that when the blow is struck, it will be effective and complete.

I have now given my warrior wife all the news.

10. William L. Jackson to Sarah Jackson

Septr 1st 1861
Camp Bartow, Travellers Repose P O, Va

This letter I will send by private hand to be mailed to you at Staunton. Well, we are not making any forward movement. Here we are guarding this pass. What is remarkable we have had three days of good weather. How long it will last, it is impossible to tell. The papers and everybody not here expect great battles here immediately. I see no indications of the kind. Genl Lee will move when he is ready, and not until. I hope when he does move, that he will be compelled to take "no step backwards." How is George Barley?

Mr. Blankensop from Brooke County made his escape and is here. He reports a great reaction in the northwest in our favor. The Pierpoint Government[15] is becoming odious. Union shriekers are panick struck, and many preparing to leave. Pierpoint has his family in Washington, Pa., and stays there every night, going and returning by Hempfield railroad. He had no news from Parkersburg. Who is my successor as Judge? What a time I will have in trying him for treason. But he will have to be caught first.

Many of my men are sick. They have every disease – measles, mumps, jaundice, dysentry, and typhoid fever. Out of about five hundred men present, I have this morning only 231 men fit for duty. There has been so much hardship and exposure.

11. Military Pass signed by Bob Moorman[16] for Sarah Jackson

Sept 2d 1861
Camp Green Brier Cavalry

The bearer of this, Mr. Fells, has under his charge Mrs. Jackson, wife of Col Jackson, C. A., who he is conveying to the encampments of her husband upon Alleghany Mountain.

Of course every southern soldier will treat Mrs. J and her companion with courtesy and will not detain or delay them upon their mission of kindness to our sick soldiery.

Bob Moorman
Comdt. Greenbrier Cavalry[17]

12. William L. Jackson to Sarah Jackson

Sept 3d 1861
Camp Bartow, Hd. Qrs. 31st Regt. Va Vols.
Travelers Repose

It will be impossible for me to get a furlough now as we are in the face of the enemy, and my health is improving, and an advance movement daily expected. I have never mentioned the subject of resignation to anyone but my Darling as it is a delicate subject. I am now convinced that my regiment would go to pieces were I to resign, besides there would be injurious reflections attaching to me through life. I am in for the war until I can hold court in my circuit, when there will be a necessity for my resignation. If before that period arrives winter should set in, and army movements here rendered impossible, I can then get a furlough.

Much as I would like to see you, yet you must not come. Within twenty miles of this place there is no place where you can stay. Those families who have been able to entertain have left for the interior, and those compelled to stay have the sick of the army crowded upon them with all manner of diseases. You cannot sleep in camp on dirty and sometimes wet straw. Such a trip might lose you your life. Stay where you are.

13. William L. Jackson to Sarah Jackson

Sept 19th 1861
Travellers Repose

Wm. Patton has just informed me that he starts in a few minutes for Lewisburg and will carry a letter to you. I have written twice since you were here. I have no news of interest. Army affairs are the same. We have a report here this morning that Genl Lee is advancing. I was much disappointed that my regiment was not permitted to go on to Genl Lee. It seems that on the morning Rust[18] was to have attacked the enemy on Cheat, Genl Lee had a force under Genl Anderson[19] at Huttonsville and one under Genl Donaldson[20] between that point and where Rust was, the former had driven back the federals, and destroyed the telegraph and taken about nine prisoners. If Rust had made the attack or sent Donaldson word that he would prevent the Yankees from harrassing his rear, the enemy would have been driven out of Tygarts Valley, and we would now be in the Northwest. But the expedition was terribly managed, and we are now in a worse position than we were before it started. We have the rumor of Floyds fights, and of his falling back.[21] I hope he will not be compelled to fall back far.

Address to Travellers Repose, leave out "Camp Bartow" as there is another Camp of that name.

Today the weather is fair.

14. William L. Jackson to Sarah Jackson

23d Sept 1861
Travellers Repose, Pocahontas Co., Va.

As yet I have received no word from you since you left me. Try this direction in your next – "Col. Wm. L. Jackson, 31st Regt. Va. Vols, Genl H. R. Jackson's[22] Brigade, Travellers Repose P. O. Pocahontas Co. Va."

I have no news of interest. We are still here. The weather has been very cold for the last two days. I am about well. Report says that Floyd and Wise will be strongly reinforced. I wish my regiment would be ordered to them. But I have no hope of such an order. It is supposed that Genl. Lee will go to Floyd with large reinforcements, take the Kanawha Valley, and go in behind the enemy here, at Weston, etc. Time will develop the truth of these rumors. James Bennett[23] made his escape from Lewis and is now here on his way to Richmond. He reports a frightful state of affairs in Lewis, Upshur and Braxton. Detachments of the enemy who go out to kill or arrest secessionists have violated a number of women, among them the wife of Col. Peterson of Lewis,[24] and Mrs. Ben Bassil[25] of Upshur. Mrs. B. was violated twice. Ben Bassill is here but does not know of his misfortune. I believe it would set him crazy, and we therefore keep the information from him. Many of my men are quite sick and two have died since you left. That expedition was a terrible affair and a worse failure.

15. William L. Jackson to Sarah Jackson

Sept 26th 1861
Travellers Repose Pocahontas Co Va

I have been anxious about you for the last several days, owing to the advance of the enemy upon Floyd and Wise, and their falling back so near Lewisburg.

I do not think we can winter here. Our Generals do not indicate their intentions. We are now entrenching and fortifying this post, as if an attack was expected, or a force to be left here all winter. I don't think we will be attacked at this place. Our sick have all been sent back to Crabbottom. As soon as the Paymaster arrives I intend to send Patton to you with some money.

No news, no army movements. Our men are busy cutting down trees and digging entrenchments. Floyd made a gallant fight at the Ferry.[26] How I wish to be attached to his division of the army.

16. William L. Jackson to Sarah Jackson

Oct 1st 1861
Travellers Repose Va

No letter from you yet. We have no news here. The great fighting is expected to occur in the Kanawha Valley. We are still entrenching, etc. I expect however if we cannot get forward, that we will fall back to Buffalo Gap or Staunton for the winter, but we will stay here as long as the weather will . . . (remainder of letter missing from file).

17. William L. Jackson to Sarah Jackson?

(Letter fragment, no date, but written between 3 October and 7 October, 1861. The Battle of the Greenbrier discussed in the letter fragment occurred on 3 October 1861.)

. . . fight today. They retreated to Cheat Mountain. If they deem it important to drive us from this position they may try us tomorrow. If so we will whip them again. We are now better prepared and our men in better spirits. Each man believes himself the nerve of the fight, or feels confidence in our ability to defeat any attack. Our position is now a very strong one. We could not successfully follow the Yankees in their retreat as they greatly outnumbered us. Our force was about twenty eight hundred fighting men, theirs not less than seven thousand.

18. William L. Jackson to Gen. Henry R. Jackson

Oct. 7, 1861
Camp Bartow on Greenbrier River
Hdqrs 31st Regt Va Vols.

General –
Having been on the 15th day of June 1861 by Brig Genl R. S. Garnett assigned to the command of a Regiment of Va Vols (a Regiment which I was requested to form by Genl Garnett and which is composed of companies from my own section of the state) since numbered the 31st Regt. Va Vols, and having been with that Regiment ever since participating in the fight and retreat of Laurel Hill, and the battle of Greenbrier River; I am now officially informed that Captain Samuel H. Reynolds,[27] Virginia Volunteers, is promoted to be Colonel and assigned to the command.

Under the circumstances my self respect compels me respectfully but peremptorily to resign the position of Lieut Col of Va Vols. I will endeavor in some position consistent with my self respect to serve Virginia and the Confederate States.

19. William L. Jackson to Sarah Jackson

Oct. 8th 1861
Travellers Repose, Pocahontas Co, Va

On yesterday I received official notice that Capt. Samuel H. Reynolds, Virginia Volunteers, had been promoted to be Colonel and assigned to the command of this Regiment. Who Col. R. is I do not know. He has not yet arrived. I have resigned my position, but will have to wait until my resignation is accepted. The course I have taken is warmly approved by Col. Johnson and all the officers and men. Col. Johnson endorsed on my letter of resignation substantially as follows: "I respectfully recommend the acceptance of the within resignation. Such treatment of a brave and gallant officer will drive honorable men from the service, and if persisted in will destroy the tone of the Army." Officers and men of my Regiment are furious.

Letcher is at the bottom of this movement. So warm are the protests made against the change that the War Department may recind the order assigning Reynolds to the Command and reinstate me, by promotion. The Regiment today started Robert Johnson to Richmond to remonstrate. I fear the change will demoralize my Regt. I will not remain in this Regiment in a subordinate position, having been in the command so long, in sunshine and storm. The indications of the affection on the part of my officers and men, gratify me. They do not admit that I cannot, consistent with self respect, persue any other course than to resign. If no change takes place, I will soon be with my loved ones, and if forces joining to the Northwest cannot advance, and are compelled to go into winter quarters, I shall take mine with you.

20. Sarah Jackson to William L. Jackson

October 11th 1861

Genl Lee moves today toward Charleston. I hope he will not stop until he reaches the Ohio River. Several Companies have passed here this evening, going to reinforce him. Three Regt. are expected go on this week, and it is thought he will have at least twenty thousand men. I am in hopes that you will not have to "retreat" again, that you will have the pleasure of moving forward.

I shall not leave here until I know something certain about the movements of the Army. If you fall back I shall go to Staunton.

21. William L. Jackson to Sarah Jackson

Oct. 12th 1861
Travellers Repose

Patton and Clark are about to leave and I have but time to drop you a line. Col. Reynolds has arrived. He is a son of Johnson Reynolds of Lewisburg. I cannot tell when I will be let off, but hope in a few days. I am most anxious to see you and our dear children. My health is good, write when you receive this.

22. Sarah Jackson to William L. Jackson

Oct. 16th, 1861
Tuckwillers

Mr. Clark and Patton called yesterday and gave me your letter. I had received one the day before informing me of your resignation. I approve of your course, but think you will be promoted. I cannot believe the War Department will see a brave men treated so mean. Of course Letcher is at the bottom of this movement. What a miserable old brute he must be.

I fear Floyd's movements down the Valley will amount to nothing. There is a report here today that the Yankees are coming on the Wilderness Road. If that is true, Floyd will be obliged to turn back. A man just passed here on his way to Lewisburg for ammunition and says that he feels sure that Lee will fight soon.

23. William L. Jackson to Sarah Jackson

Octr 18th 1861
Travellers Repose

I have received within the last three days yours of the 5th, 7th & 11th inst. The latter arrived before the others, showing the great irregularity of the mails.

I have not heard from my resignation. Genl. Loring has made an order by which all furloughs must come through him. I can hear from my resignation as soon if not quicker than I can from him. Our operations here for the winter are about over. In the spring before the campaign can well open, this Regt. will be mustered out of service. They will re-enlist again under me, and upon that representation being made, old Letcher will be bound to commission me a full Colonel. So I can spend the winter with you while nothing can be done, and when needed can enter the service. I cannot accept a commission from the Confederate States as it would vacate my office of Judge. The War Department has much to do, and it may be some time before my resignation is acted upon. The enemy has not made another attack upon us, nor do I think they will. Our position is now very strong, and I do not think they relish their last visit.

24. William L. Jackson to Sarah Jackson

Octr 22nd 1861
Travellers Repose Va

The effort of Letcher to degrade me will fail, whatever may be the course of the War Department. By the arrangement between the Confederate States and Virginia, the Governor has the appointment of the Staff officers of all the Regiments of Virginia Volunteers. Under this arrangement Letcher superceded me in this command. I do not hope therefore to be reinstated, and shall insist upon my resignation. In the spring, when the time of my men will expire, and there is a call for volunteers, all will be right, for the men composing my Regt will not reenlist under anyone but me. Of the Col. who supercedes me I will express my opinion when I see you. He however is not to blame.

There is no hope for the redemption of N. W. Va. during this season. The whole campaign has been a series of blunders. Millions of money and thousands of the best blood of the south must expiate these blunders. "With how little wisdom the world is governed."

No news here. We are still fortifying our position.

25. Sarah Jackson to William L. Jackson

Oct. 25th, 1861
Tuckwiller's

I have seen many of your friends and they are all very indignant at Old Letcher and approved your course. Capt. Sweeny[28] told me that everyone he saw from the North West in Richmond said you should be promoted and that Charlie Russel[29] said that he would go to see Letcher, that you could not be spared from the service now. I think that Floyd will soon come back and go into winter quarters near here. When last heard from he was near Fayett C. H. and it was thought he would have a fight. Col. Jenkins[30] left here last week with almost a regiment of cavalry to join Gen'l. Loring's brigade. His men were all dissatisfied to think they had so much marching and seen such hard times, and then had not been in a fight. Most of them were anxious to go to Kentucky.

26. William L. Jackson to Sarah Jackson

October 27th 1861
Travellers Repose, Pocahontas Co. Va.

I have an opportunity to send you a letter by Mr. Michael. We have occasional picket fights with the Yankees and they make now and then marauding expeditions. A few days since some two hundred of them visited our friends the Hartmans, and the town of Greenbank. They committed no other outrage than the stealing of horses and cattle. Mr. Hartman[31] lost two of his best horses.

No word of my resignation as yet. I am so impatient. Every day I expect to start for home. Twenty days have elapsed since I forwarded my resignation. Justice must be done, or my resignation must be accepted. This Regiment does not lose my name. All call it, even now, "Jackson's Regiment." The piece of cannon still bears my name, and the officers and men display an affection for me, so much so that it grieves my heart to leave them. They all however applaud my course, and declare that they will not reenlist unless it is under my command, then I know my wife will be gratified to learn the impression I have made on all around me. My resignation has to pass through the "Circumlocution Office," but cannot now be longer delayed.

P.S. I send you $250. Pay your board with Confederate money, keeping your Virginia notes, so as to have both kinds to prevent any accident.

27. William L. Jackson to Sarah Jackson

November 2d 1861
Travellers Repose Pocahontas Co Va

I had hoped that I had written my last letter to you from this place, but no word yet of my resignation. I now know that my resignation will be accepted, but I am to have a Regt next spring.

We have no news except an occasional picket fight. In one which occurred the other day we killed three, have two wounded prisoners, and took eleven muskets. We must have wounded several others.

The weather is very terrible.

28. War Department Order

Decr 16th 1861
Richmond, Va.
Special Order No. 267

Col. Wm. L. Jackson is assigned to duty with the 31st Regiment Va vols and will report to Brigr Genl W. W. Loring Commanding Army of the North-West.

By Order of the Secretary of War

Jno. Withers, AAG

29. William L. Jackson to Sarah Jackson

Jany 5th 62
Richmond Va

I arrived here this morning. Congress does not meet until Monday next, but the General Assembly convenes Wednesday next. The members are coming in rapidly. I will be strongly urged for the position of Brig Genl, and intend to touch every spring. Rumors today are not favorable from Tennessee. It is said that Bragg is falling back.[32] An attack upon Wilmington is apprehended, and troops are passing through here for that place.[33] Write to me care of Bennett.[34]

30. William L. Jackson to Sarah Jackson

Jany 10th 1861 (sic)
Camp Allegheny, Travellers Repose Va

The weather is now moderate and we have plenty of mud. How long this will last is uncertain. In two hours from now we may have a hurricane or hail storm. Our men are very busy making cabins. The Yankees keep to their mountain fastness. Did you get my watch? I recollect placing it under the head of the bed so that I could see the time without getting up. The letter with the books is the only one I have received.

We have another case of Erysipelus this morning. It is the fatal kind. Dr. Bland[35] fears it may become an epidemic. Our men are hard worked and I fear many of them at the end of the time will not revolunteer. I may not have a regiment after the middle of May.

George has had a little fight with the Yankees and Union men, routing them, killing several, wounding nine, and running the balance. This occurred at Greenland beyond Petersburg in Hardy County.

31. William L. Jackson to Sarah Jackson

Jany 16th 1862
Huntersville Va

I arrived here on the morning of the 14th Inst. And assumed command of this post. I find everything in confusion. I have now about one hundred and twenty men, and am to have by tomorrow or the next day one hundred more. The position is wholly indefensible with such a force, and yet I am expected to hold it. I am in the delightful position of being sacrificed, if the enemy attack me with anything like the force they had when they made their attack. Well, "here's a heart for every fate." I am very busy organizing this demoralized command. It may be that Genl Johnson will relieve me as soon as I succeed in doing so, at any rate as soon as I can honorably do so I will insist on being relieved.

32. Edward Johnson to William L. Jackson

Jany 21, 1862
Monterey, Camp Allegheny

Col.

Your communication relative to affairs at Huntersville has been rec. I approved the course you have taken and am very glad that you adressed the citizens. I trust your effort have been successful in rousing the cooperation and active assistance of the citizens of that vicinity, in the event of another attack from the Yankees which I do not much apprehend. Their late attack I feel confident might have been successfully repelled by the determined resistance of 200 resolute men at a point about two miles from Huntersville.

The two companies of 58th Va Vols will have reached you I hope before this. Please report their strength, and also the character of the officers in command. It is difficult to find a suitable officer for that position. I have thought that the two cos. 58th with the troops now at Huntersville, Cum. Co.[36] & Pocahontas Rescuers and Cavalry, would be a sufficient force to hold the position. I could also send two pieces of artillery. I think the very inclement season will put an end to operations. A regiment at least should have been left at Huntersville to garrison that place. Please report as to the facilities for supplying troops, a regiment say, at that point.

It has not been my intention to keep you there permanently except with a command suitable to your rank, and unless I could find no one suitable to the position. It is much desired by the Citisens that you should remain and in the event of sending a Regiment I might possibly find it necessary to do so.

I have written to have an express established between __?__ and Huntersville. I am sorry to learn that a large amount of stores have been taken by the Citisens. If these can be recovered I hope you will do so if possible. It is asserted that there are many unsound men in the county. I trust this is not so.

Try and get Citisen Scouts to give the earliest possible information of the movements of the enemy. In extremity in twelve hours I can detach a force from here of several hundred men via Greenbank. It is always important for scouts to ascertain the strength of the enemy as much as possible. Have the troops well supplied with ammunition. Should any important intelligence reach you send it via Greenbank by special messenger.

P. S. Our troops are in Romney. The enemy left in haste. It is thought that Jackson is giving in. If so the enemy near us will be a little uneasy. Our troops have suffered much from cold. The enemy here crossed on an ___?___ to cross the river by reason of their baggage. This I get from Col Stevenson direct. ___?___ in fact the valley is our fear from Yankees.

33. William L. Jackson to Wm. P. Cooper[37], Robert P. Bradshaw[38], and Stephen A. Morgan[39]

Jany 25 1862
Huntersville, VA

Gentlemen:

I have received the handsome sword you have sent me by Captain Hill, as a present from the 31st Regiment Virginia Volunteers, my friends and comrades in arms, and the kind letter accompanying it.

I cannot express to you, Gentlemen, how deeply I appreciate the kindness manifested toward me in your letter, or how sacredly I prize this sword, the generous gift of the living and the dead.

A testimonial from gallant men who have won imperishable renown on a glorious field I accept with pride and with gratitude. Believe me this gift shall be treasured always in proud remembrance of the brave spirits who gave it, and whom it has been my greatest honor to command.

34. Edward Johnson to William L. Jackson

Jan 26th 1862
Camp Alleghany

Col.

I shall see that you are provided with ammunition and other articles required. Please report your entire strength. The enemy are said to be very weak in our front. The 9th and an Ohio Regt. are said to have gone to Ky. Try and ascertain reliable accounts of the enemy, movements, strength, etc. Let the insubordinate members of your command know that they will be sent here and severely dealt with for violation of orders. Destroy all the whiskey you can lay your hands on. I hardly think that military operations can be conducted in this region at this season, but we must be prepared. I could easily reinforce you from here if given of the enemy's approach.

35. William L. Jackson to Sarah Jackson

Feby 3d 1862
Huntersville

While I am writing the snow is now six inches deep, and falling heavily. On yesterday I received yours of the 26th Jany which you say you handed to Mr. Hart. Write how long it takes my letters to reach you sent by express. No movement of the enemy in this section. I am now in a more comfortable position so far as force is concerned, than I have been for some time, but Huntersville is an awful mean place. At Allegheny we were all becoming comfortably fixed, and were living well. Here there is nothing. There are no families, my soldiers occupy the houses not burned, and the whole country has been stripped by the forces formerly here. I think Genl Johnson will relieve me in a short time. Genl. Johnson informed me when here that he would have relieved me before but the sound people in this country all desired me to be in command, and indeed that his sending me here was at their request. This is a compliment but I feel that I ought to be with my Regiment. My Regiment now receive many presents, some from the extreme South. The letters all speak of "the gallant 31st."

I never enjoyed better health. The exercise I take agrees with me. "Sliding Sallie" improves, except that she has the scratches. She carries me nicely. I keep her in a good stable, and have her well attended to.

36. William L. Jackson to Sarah Jackson

Feby 13th 1862
Huntersville Va

Yours of the 7th Inst was received yesterday by mail. Yesterday there was a report from some of our scouts of a large advance of the enemy upon us, and I had my whole force out for a fight during the entire day. It was a false alarm. No enemy near. Today the sun is shining brightly. We have had no very cold weather, but it has been bery changeable and disagreeable. I received a letter from Kenna B. Stephenson,[40] dated the 5th Inst. from Woodstock. He says he has been in the 10th Va Regt at Managa and returns to it in a few days. In the spring he intends to join me "until the infernal Yankees are whipped."

They had his brother Jim in Jail at Parkersburg but he made his escape. Kenna received a letter from the Revd Mr. Lepps[41] written from New Creek. Mr. L. had to leave his congregation on account of his secession proclivities. Mr. L. writes that Wood Co is for the South by two hundred majority. I never did like Lepps, but as he is a Secessionist I will have to do so. Nothing of interest transpiring here. As I predicted Roanoke Island has fallen. I am glad the Yankees did not get Genl Wise, and that the wound of O.J.W.[42] is not mortal. Very gloomy news however.

37. William L. Jackson to Sarah Jackson

Feby 20th 1862
Huntersville, Va

I do not suppose that a furlough would be granted me as field officers are scarce on this line of operations. Genl Johnson is now in Richmond on business. He will not be absent long. Before this reaches you the new permanent Government will be put in operation. You will have seen the inauguration. May the Government be perpetual.

This express did not arrive last night owing to high water, and I missed the paper of the 18th. We will get today the paper of the 18th & 19th. I hope we have achieved a great victory at Fort Donaldson. We need a great victory now. Its effect upon Europe would be immense. I saw two young men from Harrison Co. on yesterday. One was anephew of Gov Johnson and the other was a Bartlett[43] whose mother was a Chapin. They knew very little about Clarksburg or Parkersburg, but think they heard that our house was being used as a hospital. This is plesant information. I leave here on Saturday. Two deaths occurred last night, and sickenss is on the increase. Old Charles Lewis is dead. He was the father of Chas. S. Lewis.

Today the weather is blowing cold. I prefer the cold to the miserable damp weather we have had. The people of the country and the officers and soldiers of this command express great regreat at my intended departure. All seem to have the utmost confidence in me. I have found that the true way to inspire confidence is to do your duty, and act impartially. A firm man can be kind and sociable, and yet be strictly obeyed.

38. William L. Jackson to Sarah Jackson

Feby 24th 1862
HdQrs 2d Brigade N W Army, Camp Allegheny

On my arrival here yesterday I found your kind letter of the 20th inst. I am truly glad Father Parks[44] came through.

Poor Mr. Stinchcomb,[45] I have been expecting to hear of his death. I am pleased to hear that I have still many friends in the North West. Wherever I have a friend there he is true to the South. I am now well.

I am commanding this post in the absence of Genl. Johnson. The whole force on this and the Huntersville line is under my control. Genl Jn is expected here by the 6th day of March. My labors are very arduous. I am however used to hard work. My men gave me a warm reception last night and I made them a speech. They are delighted at my return.

No news of interest here. The wind is blowing almost a hurricane, and it is very cold. There is very little sickness here. I am so glad I am not at Huntersville.

39. William L. Jackson to Sarah Jackson

March 14th 1862
Camp Allegheny

The Yankees are quiet, and my men have recovered mostly from our march to Franklin. The weather is changeable from warm to cold, wet to dry, etc. There is however very little sickness here. I enjoy very fine health. Capt Will Thompson[46] has been here and left for Richmond. I do not write by him, as he will spend some days in Staunton.

I fear that many of my men will not reenlist. They all have the Guerrilla fever. There is a wild, roving and daring life connected with that system, and certain freedom from discipline and restraint, dazzling to the most of them.

Capt. Ballard will call on you before he returns. Mail communication is irregular from Richmond, and your last is dated on the 4th. Paper is scarce, but the train has arrived and I expect a supply. We are all delighted at the exploits of the "Virginia" and the reported victory of Price and VanDorn. Our loss is great, but even in victories our joy is always ringed with sorrow.

40. William L. Jackson to Sarah Jackson

March 18th 1862
Camp Allegheny

Indeed our affairs look so gloomy that I have no assurance that I will have the opportunity to write to, or hear from you, long. I fear our Government have not taken the proper precautions to meet the great emergency now soon at hand. The enemy are pressing us on all sides, and wherever they strike success attends their efforts. Whenever our armies are defeated, the people of the South will submit. The people are not blest with the gift of endurance, and if our armies now in the field are defeated, they will compel a treaty of peace, degrading as that may be. We have many submissionists in our midst, in disguise, and if continued defeats attend our armies, they will throw off their masks. True there are many who will die before they submit, but they can do little without the support of the masses. It is well for us to look the dangers now surrounding us steadily in the face. Important positions have been taken by the enemy. So deep laid are their plans, it seems as if they can and do take any city they choose. Richmond may not be alto-gether safe. Tom Jackson is now falling back, and unless we are soon ordered back, or a great victory attends our armies in Virginia, this force here will be cut off, and surrounded by overwhelming forces.

The sooner you purchase the gold the better, for if bad news continues to come, you cannot buy it at any price with your money.

41. William L. Jackson to Sarah Jackson

March 20th 1862
Camp Allegheny

The militia of this County have been ordered out by the proclamation of the Governor, and between one and two hundred have gone over to the enemy. This is Pocahontas County, and such is the spirit of our people here. Other of the "Milish" are dodging. No news here of interest. The weather very damp. I enjoy good health.

42. William L. Jackson to Sarah Jackson

March 30th 1862
Camp Allegheny

The snow here has disappeared and we have now rain in its place. The climate here is very changeable.

We are to move back towards Staunton in a few days. This is a secret. Our destination is not permanently fixed. I think we will stop at Shenandoah Mountain about twenty-five miles this side of Staunton. Our extra baggage has started back. Alph Jackson was not in the fight near Winchester, I am informed. He had resigned, and was in Staunton a few days before on his way to Dagger Springs.

43. William L. Jackson to Sarah Jackson

April 9th 1862
Camp Shenandoah, Augusta Co. Va

George is at McDowell ten miles from this place. He is well. Alf Jackson is here, and on yesterday was elected a Lieutenant in his old company. I have written you to go to Wytheville. I would like to see you before you go but that is impossible. I cannot leave nor is it advisable for you to come. The weather has been very bad for three days. We are all very much exposed and I am so cold I can scarcely write.

44. William L. Jackson to Sarah Jackson

April 14th 1862
Camp Shenandoah Va

Our eight hundred men marched to the hill this side of Monterey, found the enemy in too strong force, and fell back here. There was some skirmishing, but none of our men hurt. It is supposed we killed and wounded some of the Yankees. George is now falling back from McDowell to this point. Moss with his Regt is at Monterey. The Yankees say that they intend to march to Staunton in a few days. They are now about a thousand strong, and are being reinforced. If they make the attempt, there will be a pretty fight. The weather is disagreeable.

Please send me forty postage stamps. I fear that Beauregards last fight was a drawn battle.[47] A great fight is certainly impending near Yorktown.[48] It is impossible not to feel anxious about the result.

I cannot get a leave of absence, but have confidence that you can take care of yourself and the children.

CHAPTER NOTES

CHAPTER 1

1. Charles Knowles Bolton, *Scotch Irish Pioneers in Ulster and America* (Boston: 1910; Baltimore: Genealogical Publishing Co., 1972), 37.
2. Ibid., 37-38.
3. William King, quoted in Bolton, *Scotch-Irish Pioneers*, 45.
4. Hugh Boulter, quoted in Bolton, *Scotch-Irish Pioneers*, 48.
5. James G. Leyburn, *The Scotch-Irish, A Social History* (Chapel Hill: University of North Carolina Press, 1962), 172-175.
6. Roy Bird Cook, *The Family and Early Life of Stonewall Jackson* (Richmond: Old Dominion Press, 1924), 17-18.
7. James I. Robertson, Jr., *Stonewall Jackson: The Man, The Soldier, The Legend* (New York: MacMillan, 1967), 1-2, 790n.
8. Ibid., 2, 790n. Robertson was the first Jackson historian to reveal the information that both John Jackson and Elizabeth Cummins were transported convicts. Robertson received documentation of this startling revision of the Jackson family saga from a Jackson descendant, John M. Jackson of Little Rock, Arkansas. Jackson's own research into his family antecedents uncovered London court transcripts of the trials of the patriarch and the matriarch of the central West Virginia Jackson family.
9. No record of the Jackson-Cummins marriage has been found. 1755 was established in early family tradition as the date of the marriage.
10. Leyburn, *The Scotch-Irish*, 200-214.
11. Cook, *Family and Early Life*, 18.
12. Hu Maxwell, "Lands and Landowners," in Hu Maxwell and H. L. Swisher, *History of Hampshire County, West Virginia* (Morgantown: A. Brown Boughner, 1897), 392-399.
13. Otis Rice, *The Allegheny Frontier* (Lexington, KY: University of Kentucky Press, 1970), 59-69.
14. Edgar Sims, *Sims Index to Land Grants in West Virginia* (Charleston: State of West Virginia, 1952), 302. When John Jackson first claimed land at the mouth of Turkey Run, the area was under the jurisdiction of Augusta County. In 1776 the Turkey Run area became part of Monongalia County. In 1784 Harrison County was created from Monongalia, and Turkey Run was included in the new county. Jackson received a clear title to his land from the Virginia Land Office in 1787, seventeen years after he first claimed the land by a settlement right. The grant specified that the land lay in Harrison County. (See Grant Book 2, p. 472, West Virginia State Auditor's Office, Charleston, WV.) This area became part of Lewis County in 1816, and finally Upshur County in 1851.

15. Alexander Scott Withers, *Chronicles of Border Warfare*, Reuben G. Thwaites, ed. (Cincinnati: Robert Clarke Co., 1895), 121, 341-2.

16. Ross B. Johnston, comp. *West Virginians in the American Revolution* (Baltimore: Genealogical Publishing Co., 1977), 146, Robertson, Stonewall Jackson, 3, and Cook, Family and Early Life, 20. Robertson claimed that John, George, and Edward Jackson enlisted as privates in the Continental Army and that at the end of the war John held a commission as captain. No documentation was found to support Robertson's statement. George Jackson filed an affidavit of his war service with the Harrison County Court as part of the process for claiming a service pension. No evidence was found to establish whether or not he received a pension for his war service.

17. *Sims Index*, 302-3, 379-80, 675-76.

18. John Alexander Williams, *West Virginia: A History* (New York: W. W. Norton, 1976), 38-41; Cook, *Family and Early Life*, 18-22; Robertson, Stonewall Jackson, 3. Williams discussed the Jackson family's role as western Virginia aristocrats, equivalent in power and influence if not in wealth and manners, to eastern Virginia Tidewater planters. County court minute books have been preserved for both Randolph and Harrison counties. These records contain multiple references to the Jacksons including their various appointments to county offices.

19. Cook, *Family and Early Life*, 19-20.

20. Withers, *Chronicles*, 341-2.

21. Robertson, *Stonewall Jackson*, 791; *West Virginia Heritage Encyclopedia, Vol. 12* (Richwood, WV: Jim Comstock, 1976), 2472.

22. Johnston, *Revolution*, 146. George Jackson stated that he married Elizabeth Brake, daughter of Jacob Brake, at Moorefield on 13 November 1776 in his declaration of Revolutionary War service submitted to the Harrison County Court. There is no official record of the marriage in Hampshire County.

23. Stephen W. Brown, *Voice of the New West* (Macon, GA: Mercer University Press, 1985); Dorothy Davis, John George Jackson (Parsons, WV: McClain Printing Co., 1976). These two biographies of John George Jackson thoroughly documented Jackson's political and economic careers.

24. *West Virginia Heritage Encyclopedia*, Vol. 12, 2472.

25. Beverley W. Bond, Jr., *The Foundations of Ohio* (Columbus: Ohio State Archaeological and Historical Society, 1941), 376-377.

26. Dorothy Davis, *John George Jackson* (Parsons, WV: McClain Printing, 1976), 53.

27. Ibid. William Lowther Jackson's birth is listed on a foldout genealogical chart inserted in this volume. Davis states that her source of dates was photocopied from the pages of the George Jackson Family Bible belonging to descendants of Mary Allen Cassady, George Jackson's great-granddaughter.

28. *West Virginia Heritage Encyclopedia*, Vol. 12, 2472.

29. Brown, *Voice of the New West*, 95-100.

30. Cook, *Family and Early Life*, 19.

31. *Clarksburg Intelligencer*, 19 March 1825 carried a notice of militia musters in Randolph, Lewis, Tyler, Harrison, and Wood counties. William L. Jackson, aide-de-camp, signed the notice. White, "West Virginia," 132, stated that Gen. William L. Jackson's father was "Col. William L. Jackson." No records document William L. Jackson serving in any capacity other than aide-de-camp. The same biography identified William L. Jackson's father as Edward Jackson, not George.

32. Cook, *Family and Early Life*, 29.

33. "Will of Edward B. Jackson," 11 September 1826, Harrison County, Virginia, Will Book 4, p. 131, Office of the County Clerk, Harrison County courthouse, Clarksburg, WV.

34. "Will of George Jackson," 25 May 1831, Muskingum County, Ohio, recorded Harrison County, Virginia, November 1835, Will Book 5, pp. 198-203, Office of the County Clerk, Harrison County courthouse, Clarksburg, WV.

35. Harrison County, Virginia, *Register of Marriages for the Year 1820*, n.p.; Harrison County, Virginia, Will Book 6, p. 141. Only the year of William L. Jackson and Harriet Wilson's marriage was recorded. Benjamin Wilson was named as Harriet's father on the marriage bond. Harriet was identified as a daughter of Patsey (Davisson) Wilson in her will dated 22 June 1855. William L. Jackson, Jr., was selected by his grandmother as executor of her will.

36. Henry Haymond, *History of Harrison County, West Virginia* (Morgantown, WV: Acme Publishing Co., 1910), 388-9.

37. Minnie Kendall Lowther, *History of Ritchie County, West Virginia* (Wheeling, WV: News Lithograph Co., 1911), 108-112.

38. Withers, *Chronicles*, 234-5.

39. Haymond, *History of Harrison County*, 388.

40. Brown, *Voice of the New West*, 188-204.

41. Harrison County, Virginia, Minister Returns, 1802, n. p., Office of the County Clerk, Harrison County courthouse, Clarksburg, WV.

42. Davis, *History of Harrison County*, 113-115; Brown, Voice of the New West, 38-39.

43. Robert White, "West Virginia," *Confederate Military History, Vol. 3* (Wilmington, NC: Broadfoot, 1987), 131.

44. Haymond, *History of Harrison County*, 386-9.

45. Stephen W. Brown, *Voice of the New West* , 185-205.

46. C. R. Williams, *Southern Sympathizers: Wood County Confederates* (Parkersburg, WV: Inland River Books, n.d.), 15. Williams wrote that William L. Jackson, Jr. was left an orphan at the age of ten. Jackson's mother died in Parkersburg in the 1890s. She outlived two husbands and all three of her sons. No record of William Lowther Jackson, Sr.'s death or the circumstances concerning his death exist in Harrison or Lewis County.

CHAPTER 2

1. Brown, *Voice of the New West*, 200. The most vocal opponent of the Monongalia Navigation Company was Benjamin Wilson, Jr., William Jackson's father-in-law. Whether or not Wilson's opposition to the navigational scheme influenced William's decision to withdraw from the company's board of directors is not known.

2. William Jackson died intestate and no estate sale was held for his property in Harrison or Lewis counties. Presumably he died without debts and his widow inherited the entire estate.

3. Harrison County, Virginia, *Register of Marriages for the Year 1838*, n.p., Office of the County Clerk, Harrison County Courthouse, Clarksburg, West Virginia. Thomas Stinchcomb and Harriet B. Jackson were married 16 August 1838.

4. *1860 United States Census (Free Schedules)*, Wood County, Virginia; p. 121, Family 929; National Archives Microfilm M-653, Roll 1384.

5. Wes Cochran, ed. *1850 Census of Ritchie County, (West) Virginia* (Parkersburg, WV: Wes Cochran, n.d.), 14.

6. *Acts of the Assembly, Chapter 52, 1843* (Richmond: William L. Ritchie, 1843), 35-37; Lowther, Ritchie County, 443.

7. *In Memoriam, General John Jay Jackson* (Washington: W. H. and O. H. Morrison, no date), n.p. This pamphlet probably was published soon after J. J. Jackson's death, 1 January 1877. A photocopy of the volume is in the Wood County Public Library, Parkersburg, WV.

8. Brown, *Voice of the New West*, 9, 11-13, 100, 240.

9. Wood County, Virginia, *Register of Marriage for the Year 1823*, p. 1. Office of the County Clerk, Wood County Courthouse, Parkersburg, WV. Jackson and Emma Beeson were married 29 June 1823.

10. *West Virginia Heritage Encyclopedia, vol. 12*, 2475-76. Documentation of John Jay Jackson's public life can be found in numerous sources. Newspapers in western Virginia and Richmond contained many references to his legislative activities, and Wood County records prior to 1850 listed him as a participant in many business ventures. However, probably due to the questionable circumstances of his birth, Jackson genealogists generally have ignored him and his prestigious sons. Several published genealogies of the West Virginia Jackson family did not list John Jay Jackson as a son of John George Jackson, and none of John Jay's children were recognized as Jackson descendants.

11. Harvey Mitchell Rice, *Jonathan M. Bennett* (Durham: University of North Carolina Press, 1943), 253.

12. *West Virginia Heritage Encyclopedia, Vol. 3*, 460.

13. Ibid., Vol. 12, 2474, 2478.

14. *Parkersburg Gazette and Courier*, 18 November 1847.

15. Lowther, *Ritchie County*, 429.

16. *Parkersburg Gazette and Courier*, 16 February 1848.

17. Ibid., 2 December 1848.

18. Ibid., 25 January 1849.

19. Ibid., 10 February 1849.

20. *Wheeling Intelligencer*, 21 April 1849.

21. *Parkersburg Gazette and Courier*, 23 February 1850.

22. Ibid., 20 April 1850; 27 April 1850.

23. Robert L. Pemberton, *History of Pleasants County, West Virginia* (St. Mary's, WV: Oracle Press, 1929), 53-57.

24. Charles H. Ambler and Festus P. Summers, *West Virginia: The Mountain State* (Englewood Cliffs, NJ: Prentice-Hall, 1940), 168-172; Virginius Dabney, *Virginia: The New Dominion* (New York: Doubleday, 1971), 221-223.

25. *Acts of the Assembly, Chapter 27, 1850-51* (Richmond: William L. Ritchie, 1851), 25-26.

26. *Wood County, Virginia, Will Book 4*, p. 361. Office of the County Clerk, Wood County Courthouse, Parkersburg, WV. William L. Jackson and Sarah Creel were married in Tyler County, but a record of the marriage could not be found among the incomplete early records of Tyler County. Sarah Creel Jackson's identity was established through the will of her grandfather, George Neale. Sarah was a beneficiary in Neale's will, and she was identified as "Sarah E. Creel, wife of Wm. L. Jackson."

27. *Ritchie County, Virginia, Register of Marriages for the Year 1850*, Book 1, p. 6, l. 6. Office of the County Clerk, Ritchie County Courthouse, Harrisville, WV.

28. *Parkersburg Gazette and Courier*, 27 January 1849.

29. *1860 United States Census (Free Schedules), Wood County, Virginia*, p. 131, Family 1010, National Archives Microfilm M-653, Roll 1384.

30. *Parkersburg Gazette and Courier*, 4 July 1857.

31. Ibid., 21 December 1850.

32. Ibid., 14 February 1851.

33. Ibid., 1 March 1851.

34. Ibid., 22 March 1851. Details of the political maneuverings to secure passage of the railroad bill and Jackson's critical role in the process were described in a lengthy letter published by Sterrett as part of his apology. The letter was signed "Putnam," but the identity of "Putnam" was never revealed.

35. Robertson, *Stonewall Jackson*, 80-1.

36. Thomas J. Jackson to Laura Arnold, 2 April 1851, quoted in Thomas Jackson Arnold, *Early Life and Letters of General Thomas J. Jackson* (Richmond: The Dietz Press, 1957), 171-172.

37. *Pleasants County, Virginia, Minute Book 1, 15 May 1851 Session*, Office of the Circuit Clerk, Pleasants County Courthouse, St. Mary's, WV; Pemberton, Pleasants County, 56.

38. *Concise Dictionary of American Biography* (New York: Charles Scribner's Sons, 1964), 470.

39. William Edwin Hemphill, Marvin Wilson Schlegel, and Sadie Ethel Engelberg, *Cavalier Commonwealth* (New York: McGraw-Hill, 1963), 278-9.

40. Rice, *Jonathan M. Bennett*, 57-58. Complete text of Jackson's speech was recorded in the Journal of the House of Delegates, 1852, p. 72.

41. *Parkersburg Gazette and Courier*, 16 February 1848.

42. Ambler and Summers, *West Virginia*, 172-176.

43. *Parkersburg Gazette and Courier*, 18 December 1852.

44. Rice, *Jonathan M. Bennett*, 58.

45. Robert K. Krick, *Lee's Colonels* (Dayton: Morningside, 1991), 206.

46. John Hays to David Hays, 9 April 1852, quoted in Nancy Ann Jackson and Linda Brake Meyers, *Col. Edward Jackson 1759-1828* (Franklin, NC: Genealogy Publishing Service, 1995), 167.

47. *1860 United States Census, Wood County, Virginia.*

48. *Parkersburg Gazette and Courier*, 26 April 1856.

49. Pemberton, *Pleasants County*, 61.

50. "Deed of Sale from William L. Jackson, Commissioner, to Alexander H. Creel," 14 May 1856; "Deed of Sale from Alexander H. Creel to William L. Jackson," 14 May 1856, *Pleasants County, Virginia, Deed Book 1*, p. 454. Office of the County Clerk, Pleasants County Courthouse, St. Mary's, WV.

51. *Parkersburg Gazette and Courier*, 4 July 1856.

52. Rice, *Jonathan M. Bennett*, 81-83.

53. *Weston Herald*, 2 November 1857; Rice, *Jonathan M. Bennett*, 113.

54. Otis K. Rice, *West Virginia* (Lexington, KY: University Press of Kentucky, 1985), 109-110.

55. Dabney, *Virginia*, 290.

56. Thomas J. Jackson to Jonathan M. Bennett, 17 April 1860, quoted in Rice, *Jonathan M. Bennett*, 260.

57. Rice, *Jonathan M. Bennett*, 113.

58. *1860 United States Census (Free Schedules), Wood County, Virginia*, p. 121, family 929; Matheny, Wood County, 31.

59. Thomas J. Jackson to Laura Arnold, 1 December 1860, quoted in Arnold, *Early Life and Letters*, 290. Thomas Jackson was impressed with William Jackson's wife, Sarah Creel

Jackson. He mentioned her in detail in both letters he wrote to his sister about his visits with William and Sarah in Richmond. In one letter he asked his sister to explain the relationship between him and Sarah Creel Jackson. Thomas Jackson and Sarah Creel Jackson were second cousins through the Parkersburg Neale family.

CHAPTER 3

1. Elizabeth P. Cometti and Festus P. Summers, eds., *The Thirty-Fifth State: A Documentary History* (Parsons, WV: McClain Printing Co., 1966), 286-7.

2 . Herman E. Matheny, *Wood County, West Virginia, In Civil War Times* (Parkersburg: Trans-Allegheny Books, 1987), 6-15. Matheny's massive study of Parkersburg during the Civil War focused on the Union-Confederate split within the county, a fact often ignored since Parkersburg was occupied by Union forces throughout the war.

3. *West Virginia Heritage Encyclopedia, Vol. 12* (Richwood, WV: Jim Comstock, 1976), 2476.

4. Ibid., 2474.

5. Ibid., *Supplementary Vol. 8*, 60.

6. John G. Morgan, *West Virginia Governors* (Charleston: Charleston Newspapers, 1981), 39.

7. *Wheeling Intelligencer*, 4 January 1861.

8. Matheney, *Wood County*, 8.

9. *Parkersburg Gazette and Courier*, 21 December 1850.

10. Dabney, *Virginia*, 290-2.

11. Emory M. Thomas, *The Confederate Nation* (New York: Harper & Row, 1979), 85

12. Ambler and Summers, *West Virginia*, 188.

13. *Wheeling Intelligencer*, 7 February 1861.

14. Anna Pierpont Siviter, *Recollections of War and Peace 1861-65*, Charles A. Ambler, ed. (New York, G. P. Putnam's Sons, 1938), 45.

15. Ambler and Summers, *West Virginia*, 192.

16. *Marietta Intelligencer*, 24 April 1861.

17. Hemphill, Schlegel and Engelberg, *Cavalier Commonwealth*, 290.

18. Richard Orr Curry, *A House Divided* (Pittsburgh: University of Pittsburgh Press, 1964), 1.

19. Virgil A. Lewis, *Second Biennial Report: West Virginia Department of Archives and History* (Charleston: State of West Virginia, 1908), 158-161.

20. Curry, *A House Divided*, 34.

21. Matheny, *Wood County*, 28.

22. Ibid., 27-31. Matheny included an 1865 street map of Parkersburg as end pages. The map clearly marks city streets from the telegraph office to the courthouse.

23. Ibid., 29, 472. Matheny stated that the militia muskets were rusted flintlocks and would not fire.

24. *Wheeling Intelligencer*, 20 April 1861, Matheny, *Wood County*, 30, and J. R. Scullin, "Reminiscences of Early Parkersburg," in *Parkersburg News*, 1 September 1925. Scullin described the Parkersburg riot from his vantage point as a participant. He did not witness the fight between the Jacksons.

25. Matheny, *Wood County*, 35-37.

26. *Marietta Intelligencer*, 8 May 1861.

27. Ibid.

28. Curry, *A House Divided*, 158. Marshall M. Dent, editor of the *Western Virginia Star*, made the remark.

29. Ibid., 38-39.

30. *The War of the Rebellion: A Compilation of the Official Records of the Union and Confederate Armies, Series I, Vol. 2* (Washington: U.S. Government Printing Office, 1880), 47-48.

31. *Marietta Home News*, 27 April 1861. *Leslie's Illustrated Weekly*, 21 August 1861 featured an engraving of "Federal Troops Landing at Parkersburg."

32. *Parkersburg News*, 22 March 1939. Lily Jackson's role in guiding the Union troops to Prospect Hill was recalled in a memoir by Kate Harris, and *News* reporter. Harris stated that Ms. Jackson's service as a guide for the Union soldiers resulted in local accusations of unpatriotic behavior.

33. Kinnie E. Smith, "A Sassy Little Rebel," in *Confederate Veteran* (September 1919), 333-336, identified A. C. Kennedy as the partisan leader of a Wood County ranger company known as the Black Hawk Rangers. Kennedy was arrested later in the war and incarcerated at Atheneum Prison in Wheeling. Smith related details of Kennedy's escape from Atheneum in her article.

34. Matheney, *Wood County*, 81.

35. J. R. Scullin, "Reminiscences of Early Parkersburg," in *Parkersburg Sentinel*, 1 September 1925.

36. Ibid. *The Wheeling Intelligencer*, 6 June 1861, reported only that a trial of secessionists had been held in Parkersburg and that loyal citizens had driven Judge Jackson out of town. Matheny, *Wood County*, 80-84, discussed the trial in detail. There are no transcripts of the trial in Wood County records.

37. *Marietta Intelligencer*, 29 May 1861.

38. *Official Records, Series I, Vol. 2*, 828.

CHAPTER 4

1. *Official Records, Series I, Vol. 2*, (Washington, D. C.: United States Government Printing Office, 1880-1897), 828.

2. Boyd B. Stutler, *Civil War in West Virginia* (Charleston: Education Foundation, 1963), 24-25.

3. David Poe, *Personal Reminiscences of the Civil War* (Buckhannon, WV: Upshur Republican, 1911), 6.

4. *Official Records, Series I, Vol. 2*, 70-1.

5. Fritz Haselberger, *Yanks From the South* (Baltimore: Past Glories Press, 1987), 83-84.

6. *Official Records, Series I, Vol. 2*, 70-1.

7. Ibid., 828.

8. Roy Bird Cook, *Lewis County in the Civil War* (Charleston: Jarrett Printing Co., 1924), 44, 123. Lively was paroled from prison, arrested a second time and paroled again, and finally joined the Confederate Army. After the war he returned to Weston and became a prominent leader of the West Virginia Democratic Party.

9. *Official Records, Series I, Vol. 2*, 915.

10. Ibid., *Vol. 2*, 930-1.

11. John M. Ashcraft, *31st Virginia Infantry* (Lynchburg: H. E. Howard Co., 1988), 15.

12. *Official Records, Series I, Vol. 2*, 236.

13. Ashcraft, *31st Virginia Infantry*, 15-17.

14. *Official Records, Series I, Vol. 2*, 236-7.

15. Ibid., 239.

16. Ashcraft, *31st Virginia Infantry*, 17.

17. Haselberger, *Yanks from the South*, 190-3. Haselberger's work, although undocumented, is the most thorough examination of the Rich Mountain Campaign presently available. The work is most valuable for dozens of anecdotes relating to the campaign collected from both Union and Confederate sources.

18. Ibid., 193.

19. Ibid., 194-5.

20. Ibid., 195. The courier's report was incorrect. Union troops did not seize the road until one o'clock on the afternoon of 12 July.

21. *Official Records, Series I, Vol. 2*, 285.

22. James Hall, *Diary of a Confederate Soldier*, ed. by Ruth Woods Dayton (Berryville, VA: Chesapeake Book Co., 1961), 16-18.

23. Ashcraft, *31st Virginia Infantry*, 18-19.

24. Stutler, *Civil War in West Virginia*, 94.

25. Jack Zinn, *R. E. Lee's Cheat Mountain Campaign* (Parsons, WV: McClain Printing Co., 1974), 152-154. Zinn proved that there actually were three thousand soldiers at Cheat Summit on 12 September 1861, not three hundred as later Confederate memoirs stated.

26. *Official Records, Series I, Vol. 5*, 187-91. No Confederates, including Lee, filed reports of the action on 12 September 1861. The only official report of the action at Cheat Summit on 12 September came from the Union commander of the fort, Col. Nathan Kimball, Fourteenth Indiana Infantry.

27. Douglas Southall Freeman, *R. E. Lee, Vol. I* (New York: Charles Scribner's, 1946), 554-578.

28. Jed Hotchkiss, *Confederate Military History, Vol. IV, Virginia* (Wilmington, NC: Broadfoot, 1987), 167.

29. Ashcraft, *31st Virginia Infantry*, 22.

30. A. T. McRae, "Map of the Battle Ground of Greenbrier River," reprinted in Stan Cohen, *West Virginia's Civil War Sites* (Charleston: Pictorial Histories Publishing Co., 1990), 83.

31. Ashcraft, *31st Virginia Infantry*, 21.

32. Ibid., 22.

33. *Official Records, Series I, Vol. 5*, 225.

34. Ibid., 226-7.

35. Poe, *Reminiscences*, 10.

36. *Official Records, Series I, Vol. 5*, 221, 223, 227-8.

37. Hall, *Diary*, 20-1.

38. Mark M. Boatner, *The Civil War Dictionary* (New York: David McKay, 1959), 430.

39. Ibid., 438.

40. Susan A. Riggs, *21st Virginia Infantry* (Lynchburg, VA: H. E. Howard, 1991), 5.

41. Ashcraft, *31st Virginia Infantry*, 24.

42. Stephen A. Morgan, Diary entry for 26 December 1861, quoted in "A Confederate Journal," ed. by George A. Moore, *West Virginia History 22* (July 1961), 215.

43. Stutler, *Civil War in West Virginia*, 147-151

44. "Loss of C.S.A Stores at Huntersville, Va," *Southern Historical Society Papers 17* (January-December 1889), 169.

45. "Communication from Col. Wm. L. Jackson to Gen. Ed. Johnson," *Southern Historical Society Papers 17* (January-December 1889), 170.

46. Ibid., 171.

47. Ibid., 172.

48. Ibid., 171.

49. Several members of the Thirty-first Virginia Infantry kept diaries during the war or wrote memoirs later. Among them were David Poe, James Hall, John Worsham, George Morgan, and Stephen Morgan. None of them made any comments critical of Jackson's leadership.

50. John Bowers, *Stonewall Jackson* (New York: William Morrow, 1989), 146.

51. Thomas J. Jackson to Alfred H. Jackson, 11 October 1861, quoted in Cook, *Lewis County*, 118.

52. Cook, *Lewis County*, 118.

53. Thomas J. Jackson to Jonathan M. Bennett, 28 February 1862, quoted in Rice, *Jonathan M. Bennett*, 263.

54. Rice, *Jonathan M. Bennett*, 129.

55. James I. Robertson, *Stonewall Jackson* (New York: Macmillan, 1997), 450.

56. Ibid., 338-49; Robert Tanner, *Stonewall in the Valley* (New York: Macmillan, 1976), 117-29. Ironically, the Union forces which put the famed Stonewall Brigade to flight were commanded by Col. Nathan Kimball, the same colonel whose Indiana regiment had been stopped in part by William Jackson's Thirty-first Virginia Infantry at the Battle of the Greenbrier, 3 October 1861. Kimball was promoted to Brigadier General as a consequence of his success at Kernstown.

57. Tanner, *Stonewall*, 153-4.

58. *Official Records, Series I, Vol. 12, Pt. 3*, 904.

59. Ibid., 906. The highest rank given to staff members in the Confederate Army was major. William Jackson retained his rank of colonel while serving on General Jackson's staff.

60. Jedekiah Hotchkiss, *Make Me A Map of the Valley: The Civil War Journals of Stonewall Jackson's Topographer*, Archie P. MacDonald, ed. (Dallas, TX: Southern Methodist University Press, 1973), 53.

61. *Official Records, Series I, Vol. 12, Pt. 1*, 716. The report of the Battle of Port Republic and other events of Jackson's Valley campaign were not written until April 1863. They were not submitted to the Confederate War Office until after Jackson's death in May 1863, when an aide found them in Jackson's trunk.

62. Robertson, *Stonewall Jackson*, 323-457. Robertson's study is the most recent of hundreds of historical examinations of Jackson's Valley Campaign.

63. Hotchkiss, *Make Me A Map*, 57.

64. Henry Kyd Douglas, *I Rode With Stonewall* (Chapel Hill: University of North Carolina, 1940), 97. Douglas did not mention that William L. Jackson accompanied Stonewall Jackson when he "disappeared" on the night of 17 June. Douglas did not mention William L. Jackson or Alfred H. Jackson by name in his entire memoir although he often mentioned Jackson's other aides by name.

65. Hotchkiss, *Make Me A Map*, 58.

66. Robertson, *Stonewall Jackson*, 479.

67. Douglas, *I Rode With Stonewall*, 100-05. Douglas did not mention the confusion over Jackson's transmission of orders to Whiting and Winder.

68. Robertson, *Stonewall Jackson*, 484.

69. Douglas Southall Freeman, *Lee's Lieutenants, Vol. 2* (New York: Charles Scribner's, 1943), 23-51.

70. *Official Records, Series I, Vol. 12, Pt. 2*, 185.

71. Cook, *Lewis County*, 119; Robertson, *Stonewall Jackson*, 535.

72. Douglas, *I Rode With Stonewall*, 126; Freeman, *Lee's Lieutenants, Vol. 2*, 32, 33n. Douglas graphically described the terrible wound suffered by Andrews and his remarkable medical treatment.

73. *Official Records, Series I, Vol. 12, Pt. 1*, 648.

74. Robertson, *Stonewall Jackson*, 675-6.

75. Morgan, "A Confederate Journal," 210.

76. Robertson, *Stonewall Jackson*, 447, 450.

77. Rice, *Jonathan M. Bennett*, 32.

78. Ibid., 34, 48-58.

79. Ibid., 78. In an ironic twist, Elisha McComas, the Kanawha County politician who won the nomination for lieutenant governor over Bennett, resigned the position in 1857. William Lowther Jackson was appointed by Governor Wise to replace him.

80. Ibid., 82-83, 113.

81. *Official Records, Series I, Vol. 51*, 620-22.

82. Rice, *Jonathan M. Bennett*, 131-4.

83. Randall Osborne and Jeffrey C. Weaver, *The Virginia State Rangers and State Line* (Lynchburg: H. E. Howard, 1994), 113.

84. *West Virginia Heritage Encyclopedia, Vol. 19*, 4195-6.

85. Matheny, *Civil War in Wood County*, 39; *Official Records, Series I, Vol. 51*, 71.

86. *Official Records, Series I, Vol. 5*, 1008-09.

87. Osborne and Weaver, *Virginia State Rangers*, 113.

88. *Official Records, Series I, Vol. 25, Pt. 2*, 631.

89. Ibid., *Series I, Vol. 51, Pt. 2*, 686.

90. Richard L. Armstrong, *Nineteenth and Twentieth Virginia Cavalry* (Lynchburg: H. E. Howard, 1994), 1.

91. Ibid., 5.

92. *Official Records, Series I, Vol. 12, Pt. 3*, 212-13.

93. Stutler, *Civil War in West Virginia*, 131-5, 173-7.

94. Armstrong, *19th and 20th Virginia Cavalry*, 3-4, 116.

95. In Braxton County, the surname "Chewning" was pronounced "Tuning." Consequently, many records referring to Jack Chewning identify him as "Jack Tuning."

96. John D. Sutton, *History of Braxton County and Central West Virginia* (Sutton, 1919), 190-1.

97. Armstrong., *Nineteenth and Twentieth Cavalry*, 108.

98. *Official Records, Series II, Vol. 4*, 43-46, 49, 53, 55, 601, 774, 776, 907-8.

99. Poe, *Reminiscences*, 3.

100. Jack L. Dickinson, *Tattered Uniforms and Bright Bayonets* (Huntington, WV: Marshall University Library Association, 1995), 16.

101. Matheny, *Civil War in Wood County*, 39. William L. Jackson attempted to persuade the Wood County Militia to report to Grafton in April 1861 when Governor John Letcher ordered the militia to mobilize. The Wood County men refused to honor the order because they had no desire to go to Grafton and fight for the Confederacy.

102. *Compiled Service Records, Record Group 109, Microcopy 324, Nineteenth Virginia Cavalry*, Rolls 159-162 (Washington: National Archives, n.d.). The Compiled Service Records included only soldiers for whom written records existed. Many soldiers who fought with the Nineteenth and Twentieth Virginia cavalries had no documentation of their service. The most accurate and complete abstract of the roster of the Nineteenth Virginia Cavalry was compiled by Richard L. Armstrong, *19th and 20th Virginia Cavalry*. Armstrong's compilation did include several misread names and confusion among men with similar names.

103. S. W. N. Feamster, interview with Mrs. W. D. Slaven, 1908, in *The Journal of the Greenbrier Historical Society 6* (1995), 23.

CHAPTER 5

1. *Official Records, Series I, Vol. 12, Pt. 2*, 756-768. With less than six hundred mounted men, Jenkins had ridden a circle around the heart of the proposed state of West Virginia. He captured three hundred prisoners, appropriated five thousands rifles from a federal arsenal, and relieved a federal paymaster of nearly six thousand dollars in gold at Ripley, Jackson County.

2. Communication from Col. Wm. L. Jackson to Gen.Ed. Johnson, 18 January 1862, *Southern Historical Society Papers 17* (Jan-Dec 1889), 169-72. In his battle reports and communications Jackson seldom identified the forces he fought. In the few instances where he named a Virginia or West Virginia regiment as his opponent, the name of the regiment always was prefaced by the term "bogus." Most often Jackson used the term "the enemy" when referring to his opponents.

3. Rice, *Jonathan M. Bennett*, 118-20; Robertson, *Stonewall Jackson*, 233.

4. *Official Records, Series I, Vol. 12*, 949-953.

5. *Ibid., Series I, Vol. 25, Pt. 2*, 652-3.

6. John A. McNeel, "The Imboden Raid and Its Effects," *Southern Historical Society Papers 34* (Jan-Dec 1906), 294.

7. Ibid., 301-2. McNeel recalled that the meeting at Col. McNeel's home occurred around the first of April. However, during the meeting Jackson stated that he had just arrived from Richmond to form companies for a new cavalry regiment. The first regiment of the Nineteenth Cavalry was mustered into Confederate service on 1 March 1863, and the tenth and last company was enlisted on 20 March. Since Jackson had not formed any companies yet for the Nineteenth Cavalry when the meeting occurred, it had to have been prior to the first of March, not April.

8. *Official Records, Series I, Vol. 25, Pt. 1*, 90-97.

9. McNeel, "Imboden Raid," 301. Although McNeel recalled Jackson saying that he was "forty-two years old," Jackson had just turned thirty-eight at the time of his visit to the McNeel home.

10. Armstrong, *Nineteenth and Twentieth Cavalry*, 10.

11. *Official Records, Series I, Vol. 25, Pt. 2*, 704-5.

12. Ibid., 712.
13. Ibid., Pt. 1, 99.
14. Ibid., Pt. 2, 705.
15. McNeel, "The Imboden Raid," 305.
16. *Official Records, Series I, Vol. 25, Pt. 2*, 98-105.
17. Ibid., 102, 104.
18. Ibid., 120.
19. Festus P. Summers, *Johnson Newlon Camden* (New York, G. P. Putnam, 1937), 108.
20. *Official Records, Series I, Vol. 25, Pt. 2*, 104.
21. Armstrong, *Nineteenth and Twentieth Cavalry*, 11.
22. *Official Records, Series I, Vol. 27*, 206.
23. Armstrong, *Nineteenth and Twentieth Cavalry*, 11.
24. Herman E. Matheny, *Major General Thomas Maley Harris* (Parsons, WV: McClain Printing Company, 1963), 62-3.
25. Armstrong, *Nineteenth and Twentieth Cavalry*, 11.
26. *Official Records, Series I, Vol. 27, Pt. 2*, 806-8.
27. Ibid., 808.
28. Ibid., 810-16.
29. Ibid., 809-12; Poe, *Reminiscences*, 23-24.
30. *Official Records, Series I, Vol. 27, Pt. 2*, 808-9.
31. Ibid., 806; Matheny, *Major General Thomas Maley Harris*, 64-65.
32. *Official Records, Series I, Vol. 27, Pt. 2*, 809.
33. Ibid.
34. Matheny, *Major General Thomas Maley Harris*, 65.
35. *Official Records, Series I, Vol. 27, Pt. 2*, 809.
36. J. L. Scott, *36th and 37th Battalion Virginia Cavalry* (Lynchburg: H. E. Howard, 1986), 53, 55.
37. Armstrong, *Nineteenth and Twentieth Cavalry*, 12.
38. Ibid., 13.
39. Stephen Cresswell, "A Civil War Diary from French Creek: Selections from the Diary of Sirene Bunten," *West Virginia History 48* (1989), 136.
40. Boatner, *Dictionary of the Civil War*, 35.
41. Ibid., 451.
42. Shelby Foote, *The Civil War: Fredericksburg to Meridian* (New York: Random House, 1963), 300.
43. *Official Records, Series I, Vol. 25, Pt. 2*, 246.
44. Ambler and Summers, *West Virginia*, 226-7.
45. *Official Records, Series I, Vol. 27, Pt. 2*, 806.
46. Ibid., 806.
47. Ibid., 809.
48. *Supplement to the Official Records of the Union and Confederate Armies, Vol. 70* (Wilmington, NC: Broadfoot, 1994), 120-121.
49. *Official Records., Series I, Vol. 29, Pt. 1*, 48.

50. Ibid., 48-9.

51. Ibid.

52. Ibid., 42, 48.

53. Ibid., 39-40. Stutler, *Civil War*, 242-243.

54. Ibid., 48-50.

55. Ibid., 49-50.

56. Ibid.

57. Ibid., 51.

58. Ibid., 57.

59. Ibid., 52.

60. Ibid., 37

61. Ibid., 34, 52. Armstrong, *Nineteenth and Twentieth Cavalry*, 28, stated that compiled service records for this August campaign did not show any men wounded but twenty-two captured. Averell claimed in his report that in his movement against Jackson on 23 August he captured six men and killed twelve. Available records do not support Averell's claim.

62. *Official Records, Series I, Vol. 29, Pt. 1*, 57.

63. Ibid., 626-7.

64. Ibid., 627-8.

65. Ibid., 629.

66. McNeel, *The Imboden Raid*, 303.

67. *Official Records, Series I, Vol. 29, Pt. 1*, 43.

68. Ibid., *Series I, Vol. 29, Pt. 2*, 692-3.

69. Ibid., *Series I, Vol. 30, Pt. 4*, 604.

70. Ibid., *Series I, Vol. 29, Pt. 1*, 52.

71. Ibid., 37.

72. Ibid., *Series I, Vol. 30, Pt. 4*, 604.

73. Armstrong, *Nineteenth and Twentieth Cavalry*, 206.

74. Betty Hornbeck, *Upshur Brothers of the Blue and Gray* (Parsons, WV: McClain, 1967), 132. Centerville, now known as Rock Cave, was the second largest town in Upshur County in 1863. Only Buckhannon, the county seat, was larger.

75. Ibid., 132-5.

76. Ibid., 136-7. Of the eighty-seven prisoners taken by Kessler, forty-three of them died in southern prisons. John Eagle's father, George Eagle, and Henry Eagle, his brother, were not present at the militia muster on 12 September. Henry Eagle was killed in 1864 by unionist bushwhackers, and George Eagle left Upshur County around that time and returned to Pendleton County.

77. Armstrong, *Nineteenth and Twentieth Cavalry*, 29-30.

78. Stutler, *Civil War*, 250-1, said that Jackson's plan was "to push on to Glenville, where he would strike a turnpike leading through Spencer to the Ohio River at Ravenswood, and perhaps on to the lower Great Kanawha Valley." Stutler cited no source for this plan.

79. Ibid., 248-9. The route followed by William Jackson's army to reach Falls Mill on the night of 12 October 1863 is a matter of conjecture. No official report by William Jackson of the Bulltown campaign has been found. The identities of local guides and the roads over which they guided Jackson's army are traditional stories in Webster County.

80. Ibid., 248.

81. Sutton, *History of Braxton County*, 172-4. Sutton's account of the Battle of Bulltown was based on a personal reminiscence of Elias Cunningham, an eyewitness and a son of Moses Cunningham on whose farm the battle was fought.

82. Ibid.

83. *Official Records, Series I, Vol. 29, Pt. 1*, 481. Captain Mattingly made the only official report of the Bulltown battle, and his report consisted of a dispatch sent to Colonel Nathan Wilkinson at Clarksburg asking for reinforcements, more ammunition, and a surgeon to take care of a wound Mattingly had suffered in the thigh. Mattingly stated that he had been attacked by one thousand rebels, had killed fifty in the initial charge, and that he was mortally wounded. All of these statements were false.

84. Ibid.

85. Sutton, *Braxton County*, 174.

86. Stutler, *Civil War*, 251.

87. *Official Records, Series I, Vol. 29, Pt. 1, 481*. Stutler, Civil War, 251, said that Lieutenant John Holt of the Eleventh Infantry also was wounded, and a few other men suffered slight wounds. No federal soldiers were killed in the Battle of Bulltown, and only Mattingly's wound required the care of a doctor.

88. Sutton, *Braxton County*, 174. The McElwains exhumed the gun in 1871 and took it to Sutton intending to discharge it as part of a wedding celebration in front of the court house. They overcharged the gun, and when they touched it off it exploded. No one was injured but several windows in nearby buildings were shattered.

89. Ibid., 331.

90. Armstrong, *Nineteenth and Twentieth Cavalry*, 32. The name of the creek Kelley erroneously designated as Jackson's route of retreat was "O'Brien's Fork."

91. Sutton, *Braxton County*, 173-4; Stutler, *Civil War*, 249; Armstrong, *Nineteenth and Twentieth Cavalry*, 31-2. Armstrong cited Daniel S. DeWees, a member of Company K, Nineteenth Virginia Cavalry, as one source of the rumor that officers at Bulltown, including Jackson, were drunk. However, DeWees' memoir, *Recollections of a Lifetime* (Grantsville, WV: Grantsville News, 1904) included no reference to the use of alcohol by anyone at the Bulltown battle.

92. *Official Records, Series I, Vol. 29, Pt. 1*, 536-7; Terry Lowry, *Last Sleep: The Battle of Droop Mountain* (Charleston, WV: Pictorial Histories, 1996), 94-158. Lowry's study is a comprehensive account of the Droop Mountain campaign.

93. Ibid., 540.

94. Poe, *Reminiscences*, 28.

95. *Official Records, Series I, Vol. 29, Pt. 1*, 537.

96. Ibid., 504-5.

97. Ibid., 538. In his post battle report, Jackson revised his first accurate estimate to claim erroneously that subsequent information indicated the federals had nearly seven thousand five hundred men.

98. Ibid., 528-9, 531.

99. Ibid., 505, 537.

100. Ibid., 538.

101. Ibid.

102. Ibid., 529-30.

103. Ibid., 506.

104. Ibid., 538.

105. Ibid., 506.

106. Ibid.

107. Ibid., 533.

108. Matheny, *General Thomas M. Harris*, 71-72.

109. *Official Records, Series I, Vol. 29, Pt. 1*, 533.

110. Ibid., 535.

111. Poe, *Reminiscences*, 29.

112. *Official Records, Series I, Vol. 29, Pt. 1*, 525-6.

113. Ibid., 526.

114. Ibid.

115. Ibid., 539.

116. Armstrong, *Nineteenth and Twentieth Cavalry*, 38.

117. *Official Records, Series I, Vol. 29, Pt. 1*, 549.

118. Ibid., 550.

119. Ibid., 500-1, 507.

120. Ibid., 933.

121. Ibid., 926.

122. Ibid., 950-1.

123. Ibid., 951.

124. Ibid., 925-31.

125. Ibid., 951.

126. Poe, *Reminiscences*, 30.

127. *Official Records, Series I, Vol. 29, Pt. 1*, 951.

128. Ibid., 951, 962-4.

129. Ibid., 929-30.

130. Ibid., 952.

131. Ibid.

132. Ibid.

133. Ibid., 953.

134. Ibid., 946, 953.

135. Poe, *Reminiscences*, 31-33.

136. *Official Records, Series I, Vol. 29, Pt. 1*, 953.

137. Ibid., 931.

138. Ibid., 925.

139. Ibid., 931.

140. Ibid., 965.

141. Ibid., 967.

142. Stutler, *Civil War*, 262. Stutler quoted an editorial from the Richmond Examiner which said in part: "General Lee was informed of the situation of affairs. Here comes the reign of major-generals and military science. Maj. Gen. Jubal A. Early came. Maj. Gen. Fitzhugh Lee came. Brig. Gen. Walker came. Brig. Gen Thomas came. Their staffs came. They all took a drink. Gen. Early took two."

143. *Official Records, Series I, Vol. 29, Pt. 1*, 945.

144. Ibid., 948-950.

145. Ibid., 946.

146. Armstrong, *Nineteenth and Twentieth Cavalry*, 46-7.

147. William T. Price, *Historical Sketches of Pocahontas County, West Virginia* (Marlinton, WV: Price Brothers, 1901), 605-606.

148. *Official Records, Series I, Vol. 33*, 446.

149. Ibid.

150. Ibid., 547.

151. Johnson probably enlisted in the Tenth West Virginia Infantry. Col. Thomas Harris on several occasions permitted captured rebel guerrillas to enlist in his regiment rather than go to prison. However, compiled rosters of the Tenth Infantry do not list Jasper Johnson as a member of the regiment.

152. Poe, *Reminiscences*, 36-37; Armstrong, *Nineteenth and Twentieth Cavalry*, 135.

153. *Official Records, Series I, Vol. 29, Pt. 1*, 954.

154. Armstrong, *Nineteenth and Twentieth Cavalry*, 50.

155. *Compiled Service Records, Record Group 109, Microcopy 324* (Washington: National Archives), Rolls 160, 162.

CHAPTER 6

1. *Official Records*, Series I, Vol. 33, 1085-6.

2. Ibid., 1239.

3. Ibid., 1243.

4. Ibid., 1302.

5. Poe, *Reminiscences*, 38.

6. *Official Records*, Series I, Vol. 37, Part 1, 65.

7. Jenkins died from a ruptured aorta soon after federal surgeons amputated his shattered arm.

8. *Official Records*, Vol. 37, Part 1, 47.

9. Ibid., 64-5.

10. Ibid., 30-36.

11. Ibid., 738.

12. Ibid., 48.

13. Ibid., 64.

14. Ibid., 740.

15. Milton W. Humphries, *A History of The Lynchburg Campaign* (Charlottesville: Mitchie Co., 1924), 28. Humphries, an artillery commander credited with inventing the technique of indirect firing, commented on the confrontation between French and Jackson's troops with Crook's forces at Gap Mountain with the statement, "Colonel W. L. Jackson, with a force which seems to have exceeded 2,000, got out of Crook's way." The thinly veiled criticism implied that Jackson should have been able to interfere with Crook's retreat, but that he simply moved aside and allowed Crook to escape. Humphries was not at Gap Mountain and knew nothing of the condition of Jackson's men.

16. *Official Records*, Series I, Vol. 37, Part 1, 748-751.

17. Ibid., 755.

18. Ibid., 120, 755. David Phillips, *Tiger John* (Leesburg, VA: Gauley Mount Press, 1993), 205-7.

19. Phillips, *Tiger John*, 212-15.

20. *Official Records*, Series I, Vol. 37, Part 1, 760.

21. Thomas Yoseloff, ed., *Battles and Leaders of the Civil War*, Vol. 4 (New York: Castle Books, 1956), 486.

22. Armstrong, *Nineteenth and Twentieth Cavalry*, 55.

23. *Official Records*, Series I, Vol. 37, Part 1, 100.

24. Phillips, *Tiger John*, 230-44.

25. *Official Records*, Series I, Vol. 37, Part 1, 766-8.

26. Armstrong, *Nineteenth and Twentieth Cavalry*, 56-7.

27. *Official Records*, Series I, Vol. 37, Part 2, 15.

28. Ibid.

29. Armstrong, *Nineteenth and Twentieth Cavalry*, 108, 170. Sprigg formed a company with Albert and Fred Chewning, brothers of Andrew Jackson Chewning. Nearly all of the company's members were from Braxton and Webster counties, and most of them were veterans of the Nineteenth Virginia Cavalry.

30. Charles C. Osborne, *The Life and Times of General Jubal A. Early* (Chapel Hill, NC: Algonquin Books, 1992), 286.

31. Armstrong, *Nineteenth and Twentieth Cavalry*, 57-8.

32. Poe, *Reminiscences*, 55-6.

33. Jubal A. Early, *A Memoir of the Last Year of the War for Independence in the Confederate States of America* (Toronto: Lovell & Gibson, 1866), 68; Freeman, *Lee's Lieutenants*, Vol. 3, 570. Freeman did not discuss Jackson's brigade role in bringing on the engagement with Averell on 19 July or the part Jackson played in preventing a demoralizing defeat for Ramseur's division.

34. Armstrong, *Nineteenth and Twentieth Cavalry*, 60. Potts' memoir was published in 1923 under the title *A Boy Scout of the Confederacy*.

35. *Official Records*, Series I, Vol. 43, Part 1, 753-4.

36. Phillips, *Tiger John*, 316; Freeman, *Lee's Lieutenants*, Vol. 3, 571-4. McCausland had clear orders from Early to burn Chambersburg if the city refused to pay the ransom demand.

37. *Official Records*, Series I, Vol. 43, 993.

38. Armstrong, *Nineteenth and Twentieth Cavalry*, 62-3.

39. Phillips, *Tiger John*, 181, 234-8.

40. *Official Records*, Series I, Vol. 33, 1086. Robert E. Lee in a letter to Samuel Cooper, Confederate Adjutant General, commented, "General Early in a recent letter states that his operations were impeded, and in a measure arrested by his inability to get service from General Imboden's men."

41. William C. Davis, ed., *The Confederate General*, Vol. 6 (Washington, D.C.: National Historical Society, 1991), 80-1.

42. Osborne, *Jubal*, 286.

43. *Official Records*, Series I, Vol. 43, Part 1, 925.

44. Armstrong, *Nineteenth and Twentieth Cavalry*, 63; Official Records, Series I, Vol. 43, Part 1, 574. Jedekiah Hotchkiss noted in his journal that Jackson was back in the saddle on 19 September at the Battle of Opequon Creek.

45. *Official Records*, Series I, Vol. 43, Part 1, 639.

46. Ibid., Series I, Vol. 43, Part 2, 96.

47. Robert J. Knotts, Jr., and Robert E. Stevens, comps. *Calhoun County in the Civil War,* (Parsons, WV: McClain Printing, 1982), 88.

48. *Official Records,* Series I, Vol. 43, Part 1, 554; Jeffry D. Wert, From Winchester to Cedar Creek: The Shenandoah Campaign of 1864 (Carlisle, PA: South Mountain Press, 1987), 42-3, 45.

49. Ibid.,, Series I, Vol. 43, Part 1, 47, 518.

50. Wert, *From Winchester to Cedar Creek,* 98-9.

51. *Official Records,* Series I, Vol. 43, Part 1, 552.

52. Jubal A. Early, *Autobiographical Sketch and Narrative of the War Between the States* (Philadelphia: J. B. Lippincott, 1912), 429-30.

53. Wert, *From Winchester to Cedar Creek,* 109-11; *Official Records,* Series I, Vol. 43, Part 1, 556.

54. *Official Records,* Series I, Vol. 43, Part 1, 611.

55. Ibid., 556; Freeman, *Lee's Lieutenants,* Vol. 3, 584.

56. *Official Records,* Series I, Vol. 43, Part 1, 499; Wert, *From Winchester to Cedar Creek,* 132-3.

57. Ulysses S. Grant, City Point, Va., to Philip H. Sheridan, Halltown, Va., 26 August 1864. In *Ulysses S. Grant: Memoirs and Selected Letters* (New York: Viking Press, 1990), 1067.

58. *Official Records,* Series I, Vol. 43, Part 1, 1166; Wert, *From Winchester to Cedar Creek,* 160. Lee was wounded at Winchester and returned to Richmond to convalesce. Lee's successor, Williams Wickham, was a member of the Confederate Congress. When Rosser arrived in Early's camp, Wickham asked Early to relieve him to enable him to take his seat in Congress. Early, unhappy with Wickham's performance, quickly obliged him.

59. *Official Records,* Series I, Vol. 43, Part 1, 698; Official Records, Series I, Vol. 43, Part 2, 329.

60. Ibid., Series I, Vol. 43, Part 1, 447.

61. Harry Gilmor, *Four Years in the Saddle* (New York: Harper and Brothers, 1866), 266-7.

62. *Official Records,* Series I, Vol. 43, Part 1, 612-3.

63. Ibid., 559.

64. Wert, *From Winchester to Cedar Creek,* 221-3.

65. Ibid., 215; *Official Records,* Series I, Vol. 43, Part 1, 613.

66. Armstrong, *Nineteenth and Twentieth Cavalry,* 69.

67. Ibid.

68. *Official Records,* Series I, Vol. 43, Part 1, 565.

69. Armstrong, *Nineteenth and Twentieth Cavalry,* 71.

70. *Official Records,* Series I, Vol. 43, Part I, 677; Phillips, *Tiger John,* 378-9; Armstrong, *Nineteenth and Twentieth Cavalry,* 73-4.

71. Early, *Autobiographical Sketch,* 459.

72. Armstrong, *Nineteenth and Twentieth Cavalry,* 75.

73. *Official Records,* Series I, Vol. 46, Part 2, 1111.

74. Armstrong, *Nineteenth and Twentieth Cavalry,* 75.

75. *Official Records,* Series I, Vol. 46, Part 2, 413.

76. Stutler, *Civil War,* 288-90.

77. William C. Dodrill, *Moccasin Tracks and Other Imprints* (Charleston, WV: Lovett Printing, 1915), 134; Armstrong, *Nineteenth and Twentieth Cavalry,* 108, 170.

78. *Official Records*, Series I, Vol. 46, Part 2, 573.

79. Ibid., 839.

80. Ibid., 1234-5.

81. Early, *Autobiographical Sketch*, 466.

82. Krick, *Lee's Colonels*, 125-6.

83. Wert, *From Winchester to Cedar Creek*, 250-1.

84. Early, *Autobiographical Sketch*, 462-3; Freeman, *Lee's Lieutenants*, Vol. 3, 635-6.

85. Early, *Autobiographical Sketch*, 462.

86. Hotchkiss, *Make Me A Map*, 260.

87. Early, *Autobiographical Sketch*, 466.

88. Freeman, *Lee's Lieutenants*, Vol. 3, 635.

89. Armstrong, *Nineteenth and Twentieth Cavalry*, 76.

90. Phillips, *Tiger John*, 381.

91. *Official Records*, Series I, Vol. 46, Part 1, 521-3.

92. Poe, *Reminiscences*, 80.

93. *Official Records*, Series I, Vol. 46, Part 1, 1310-14.

94. Ibid., 1323.

95. Ibid., 1322.

96. Poe, *Reminiscences*, 81.

97. *Official Records*, Series I, Vol. 46, Part 1, 521-3; MacDonald, *Make Me A Map*, 265-7.

98. *Official Records*, Series I, Vol. 49, Part 2, 400.

99. Ibid., Series I, Vol. 46, Part 3, 1109.

CHAPTER 7

1. George C. Rable, *The Confederate Republic* (Chapel Hill: University of North Carolina, 1994), 299-300; Thomas, The Confederate Nation, 304-5.

2. Freeman, *R. E. Lee*, Vol. 4, 202-3. Lee was never brought to trial, and the indictment against him was dismissed in 1869.

3. Michael J. Pauley, *Unreconstructed Rebel* (Charleston, WV: Pictorial Histories, 1993), 77; Phillips, *Tiger John*, 383.

4. Shelby Foote, *The Civil War: Red River to Appomattox* (New York: Random House, 1974), 1020-3.

5. Ezra Warner, *Generals in Gray* (Baton Rouge: Louisiana State University, 1981), 153-4; Mark Boatner, *The Civil War Dictionary* (New York: David McKay, 1959), 433; *West Virginia Heritage Encyclopedia*, Vol. 12 (Richwood, WV: Jim Comstock, 1976), 2478.

6. Robert White, "West Virginia," in *Confederate Military History*, Vol. 3 (1899; reprint, Wilmington, NC: Broadfoot, 1987), 131-3.

7. C. R. Williams, *Southern Sympathizers: Wood County Confederate Soldiers* (Parkersburg, WV: Inland River Books, n. d.), 20. Local historians in Wood County determined that Williams published Southern Sympathizers around 1930. Williams stated that Thomas Stinchcomb died at Mt. Pleasant, Texas, "in the forty-third year of his age," or 1887.

8. *Parkersburg Daily Times*, 22 September 1865.

9. Thomas F. Wildes, *Record of the One Hundred and Sixteenth Regiment Ohio Infantry Volunteers* (Sandusky, OH: C. F. Mack, 1884), 364.

10. *Official Records*, Series I, Vol. 37, Part 1, 291-3.

11. *Wheeling Intelligencer*, 26 July 1864.

12. *Marietta Daily Times*, 31 October 1865.

13. Ibid.

14. Warner, *Generals in Gray*, 154; Matheny, *Wood County*, 451. Matheny also wrote that Jackson had lived in Marietta, Ohio, for a short time before relocating to St. Marys.

15. *Parkersburg Daily Times*, 4 December 1865.

16. Rice, *Jonathan M. Bennett*, 160-1; Cook, *Lewis County in the Civil War*, 123.

17. *West Virginia Heritage Encyclopedia*, Vol. 3, 460.

18. "Lease from Wm. P. and J. C. Rathbone to J. N. Camden," 18 December 1860, *Wirt County, Virginia Deed Book 4*, p. 596.

19. Festus P. Summers, *Johnson N. Camden* (New York: G. P. Putnam, 1937), 86-7.

20. Ibid., 90.

21. *West Virginia Heritage Encyclopedia*, Vol. 3, 460.

22. Summers, *Johnson N. Camden*, 105-6.

23. *Official Records*, Series I, Vol. 2, 1401.

24. Ibid., 1400.

25. Summers, *Johnson N. Camden*, 106.

26. Ibid., 107.

27. *Official Records*, Series I, Vol. 25, Part 2, 120.

28. Summers, *Johnson N. Camden*, 116-8.

29. *Parkersburg Daily Times*, 4 December 1865.

30. Summers, *Johnson N. Camden*, 94.

31. Ibid., 118.

32. Krick, *Lee's Colonels*, 371.

33. Williams, *Southern Sympathizers*, 17-8.

34. Curry, *A House Divided*, 40.

35. Matheny, *Wood County*, 84.

36. Curry, *A House Divided*, 126-8.

37. Matheny, *Wood County*, 40-1, 266; *West Virginia Heritage Encyclopedia*, Vol. 12, 2474.

38. *Wheeling Intelligencer*, 4 February 1864.

39. *West Virginia Heritage Encyclopedia*, Vol. 12, 2474.

40. John G. Morgan, *West Virginia Governors* (Charleston, WV: Charleston Newspapers, 1980), 39.

41. *Parkersburg Daily Times*, 4 December 1865.

42. *Parkersburg Daily Times*, 15 December 1865.

43. *Parkersburg Daily State Journal*, 29 May 1883.

44. Warner, *Generals in Gray*, 154.

45. Sutton, *History of Braxton County*, 197-8.

46. *Official Records*, Series I, Vol. 29, Pt. 1, 946.

47. Ibid., Vol. 33, 1085-6.

48. John A. McNeel, "The Imboden Raid and Its Effects," 302.

49. *Official Records*, Series I, Vol. 46, Pt. 2, 1235.

50. Armstrong, *Nineteenth and Twentieth Cavalry*, 60.

51. J. N. Potts, "Who Fired the First Shot at New Market," *Confederate Veteran 17*, no. 9 (September 1909), 453.

52. M. S. Browne, Letter to the editor, *Confederate Veteran 17*, no. 12 (December 1909), 623.

53. Milton W. Humphries, "Corrects About Battle at Cloyd's Farm," *Confederate Veteran 18*, no. 1 (January 1910), 61.

54. McNeel, "The Imboden Raid," 295.

55. *Official Records*, Series I, Vol. 46, Pt. 3, 1109.

56. Stephen Cresswell, "A Civil War Diary from French Creek,"136.

57. *Official Records*, Series I, Vol. 27, Pt. 2, 816.

APPENDIX LETTERS

1. Jackson reported for duty at Huttonsville on 11 June. General Garnett arrived to take command on 14 June. Consequently, this letter was written between 14 June and the date of the second letter, 27 June.

2. During the Civil War, Huttonsville was one of two towns in Randolph County. The county seat, Beverly, was located about ten miles northeast of Huttonsville. The Parkersburg and Staunton Turnpike, the major highway in the central western Virginia mountains, and the Huttonsville-Warm Springs pike made the town a crossroads community.

3. Robert Selden Garnett, commander of all Confederate troops in northwestern Virginia until he was killed at Corrick's Ford, Randolph Co., 13 July 1861.

4. The Thirty-first Virginia Regiment of Infantry.

5. Robert Latimrer McCook (1827-1862) was one of the famous "Fighting McCooks" from Steubenville, Ohio. The family furnished seventeen officers and soldiers for the Union Army. Robert L. McCook was killed near Dechard, Tennessee, in 1862, while commanding the 9th Ohio Regiment.

6. George Jackson was the younger brother of William L. Jackson. He was a graduate of the United States Military Academy (1856) and was in the Federal Army at the outbreak of the secession crisis. He resigned his U.S.A. commission and volunteered his services as a cavalry officer to the State of Virginia.

7. William Lowther Jackson Corley, was born 27 July 1827. His family was prominent in agriculture and merchandising in rural Braxton County. He was a lieutenant in the 25th Virginia Infantry and was captured during the retreat from Gettysburg in July 1863. He was a POW for over a year and a half. Exchanged in October 1864 he spent the next six months in hospital recuperating from the effects of his captivity. After the war he returned to Braxton County and was active in local politics. He served a term as County Clerk of Braxton County.

8. Possibly a reference to the skirmish known as "Blackburn's Ford, a preliminary engagement of First Bull Run. The skirmish involved men of Tyler's brigade (USA) and Longstreet's brigade (CSA). Union casualties in the skirmish slightly exceeded those of the Confederates.

9. James G. Bastable, a pre-war store clerk from Weston, Lewis County.

10. Reference to the Battle of Wilson's Creek, Missouri, fought 10 August 1861.

11. John J. Jackson.

12. Arthur I. Boreman, Jackson's successor as judge in Wood County and the first governor of the state of West Virginia.

13. Perhaps William Beard, a wealthy farmer in Wood County in 1860 and a native of Pennsylvania.

14. Huntersville was the county seat of Pocahontas County and the only organized community in the county in 1861.

15. The Reorganized Government of Virginia, established by Union supporters at the time Virginia voted to secede from the Union. The capital was located at Wheeling, and Francis H. Pierpont from Fairmont was "governor" of Virginia. This government gave Virginia's approval for the state of West Virginia to be formed in 1863.

16. Robert Bruce Moorman, born 1830, was a pre-war resident of Lewisburg, Greenbrier County. He attended the Virginia Military Institute, the University of Virginia, and Williams College. After the war he was a druggist. He died at Stafford Spring, Mississippi, in 1895.

17. The Greenbrier Cavalry, organized in Lewisburg in the spring of 1861, was part of the Confederate force at Laurel Hill where it was commanded by George Jackson, William L. Jackson's brother. The Greenbrier Cavalry became Co. D, Fourteenth Virginia Cavalry, in 1862.

18. Albert Rust from Arkansas, Colonel, Third Arkansas Regiment of Infantry.

19. Samuel R. Anderson (1804-1883), from Tennessee, General of the Second Brigade, Army of the Northwest.

20. Daniel Smith Donelson (1801-1863), from Tennessee, General of the Third Brigade, Army of the Northwest.

21. Reference to the Battle of Carnifex Ferry, Nicholas County, and the skirmishes leading to the battle.

22. Henry Rootes Jackson, from Georgia.

23. James Bennett was an attorney from Weston, Lewis County. He was a brother of Jonathan M. Bennett and a cousin of William L. Jackson.

24. Aaron Peterson, colonel of Lewis County militia.

25. Benjamin Bassell was a wealthy farmer in Upshur County prior to the war. He was one of the few slave owners in Upshur County. His unfortunate wife's name was Elizabeth, according to the 1860 census.

26. Carnifex Ferry, Nicholas County.

27. Samuel H. Reynolds was a graduate of the United States Military Academy (1849). He was assigned to command the 31st Virginia Infantry on 17 September 1861, but he resigned on 28 November 1861. At his request he was assigned to an ordinance division in Tennessee with the rank of captain. He died in Columbia, Tennessee in 1867.

28. Captain James Sweeney, a pre-war friend of the Jacksons.

29. Charles Russell, a political colleague of William L. Jackson and an influential member of the Virginia Assembly in 1861.

30. Albert Gallatin Jenkins, a pre-war political rival of W. L. Jackson, had a large plantation near Guyandotte on the Ohio River before the war. He was fatally wounded at the Battle of Cloyd's Mountain, Virginia, 9 May 1864.

31. Isaac Hartman, a wealthy farmer who lived near Greenbank, Pocahontas County.

32. A reference to the Tennessee River campaign that resulted in the capture of forts Henry and Donelson in February, 1862.

33. Federal forces commanded by Ambrose Burnside and Louis Goldsborough opened their assault on the Carolina coast on 13 January. See letter 36.

34. Jonathan M. Bennett, William L. Jackson's cousin and close political colleague. Bennett was from Weston, Lewis County, and had been active in the Virginia Assembly during the critical years immeidately prior to secession. During the war he was appointed Auditor for the State of Virginia. After the war he returned to Weston and was influential in the early years of West Virginia state government.

35. William John Bland, a physician from Weston, Lewis County. Bland served as regimental surgeon for the Nineteenth Virginia Cavalry when Jackson formed the regiment in March 1863. He also was elected in 1863 and 1865 to represent Lewis County in the Virginia Assembly in Richmond. Presumably the only voters were Lewis County residents who were soldiers in William L. Jackson's regiments at the time.

36. Cumberland County, presumably. The Pocahontas Rescuers and Cavalry probably were militia.

37. William Pope Cooper was a lieutenant and captain with the Thirty-first Infantry and commanded the regiment when it surrendered at Appomattox. After the war he was a newspaper editor in Fairmont, West Virginia.

38. Robert P. Bradshaw, a native of Monterey, Highland County, Virginia, was captain of Co. B in the Thirty-first Virginia. He was killed in action at Port Republic.

39. Stephen A. Morgan was a graduate of the Fairmont (WV) Seminary and a Fairmont attorney before the war. He was elected to the General Assembly in November 1861. He returned to Fairmont after the war and died there in 1911.

40. Kenna Stephenson and James Stephenson were both sons of prominent Parkersburg resident James M. Stephenson. Kenna Stephenson was an attorney and James Stephenson was a medical student before the war.

41. James L. Lepps, was the Presbyterian minister in Parkersburg before the war. He was thirty-six years old at the time of the 1860 census.

42. Obadiah Jennings Wise, son of former Virginia governor and William L. Jackson political ally Henry Wise, was killed while leading a defense of Roanoke Island on 8 February 1862. Wise was captain of Co. A of the 46th Virginia Infantry. William L. Jackson was lieutenant governor of Virginia during Henry Wise's administration.

43. Possibly Thomas Bartlett who enlisted in the 20th Virginia Cavalry formed by W. L. Jackson in early summer, 1863. Bartlett later deserted.

44. Possibly James Parks, a Roman Catholic priest who lived in Wheeling but also attended Catholics in Parkersburg and Wood County.

45. Thomas Stinchcomb, Willilam L. Jackson's step-father, died in Parkersburg.

46. William P. Thompson, later Lt. Col. Of the 19th Virginia Cavalry, and Colonel of Jackson's Brigade at the end of the war.

47. Reference to the Battle of Shiloh, or Pittsburg Landing, Tennessee, 6-7 April 1862.

48. McClellan laid siege to Yorktown on 5 April 1862 to open his Peninsula Campaign. Confederate defenders evacuated the town without a battle on 3 May 1862.

BIBLIOGRAPHY

Newspapers

Clarksburg (Virginia) *Intelligencer*, 19 March 1825.

Marietta (Ohio) *Daily Times*, 31 October 1865.

Marietta (Ohio) *Intelligencer*, 24 April 1861 – 29 May 1861.

Parkersburg (West Virginia) *Daily Times*, 22 September 1865 – 15 December 1865.

Parkersburg (Virginia) *Gazette and Courier*, 18 November 1847 – 4 July 1857.

Parkersburg (West Virginia) *News*, 22 March 1939.

Parkersburg (West Virginia) *Sentinel*, 1 September 1925.

Weston (Virginia) *Herald*, 2 November 1857.

Wheeling (Virginia) *Intelligencer*, 21 April 1849, 4 January 1861 – 6 June 1861.

Wheeling (West Virginia) *Intelligencer*, 4 February 1864 – 26 July 1864.

Periodicals

Alexander, Ted. "McCausland's Raid and the Burning of Chambersburg." *Blue & Gray Magazine* (August 1994): 11-18, 64.

————. "Old Jube' Fools the Yankees." *Blue & Gray Magazine* (August 1994): 19-20.

"Communication from Col. Wm. L. Jackson to Gen. Ed. Johnson." *Southern Historical Society Papers* 17 (1889): 169-172.

Confederate Veteran 17 (December 1909): 623.

Cresswell, Stephen. "A Civil War Diary from French Creek." *West Virginia History* 58 (1989): 136.

Humphries, Milton W. "Corrects About the Battle at Cloyd's Farm." *Confederate Veteran* 19 (January 1910): 61.

McNeel, John A. "The Imboden Raid and its Effects." *Southern Historical Society Papers* 34 (January-December 1906): 294-312.

Morgan, Steven. "A Confederate Journal." Edited by George A. Moore. *West Virginia History* 22 (1953): 201-216.

Potts, J. N. "Who Fired the First Shot at New Market." *Confederate Veteran* 17 (September 1909): 453.

Southern Historical Society Papers 17 (January-December 1889): 169-172.

County, State, and National Records

Hampshire County, (West) Virginia: Deed Books.

Harrison County, (West) Virginia: Court Minute Books, Deed Books, Marriage Registers, Will Books.

Lewis County, (West) Virginia: Deed Books.

Pleasants County, (West) Virginia: Court Minute Books, Deed Books, Marriage Registers.

Ritchie County, (West) Virginia: Court Minute Books, Marriage Registers.

Wirt County, (West) Virginia: Deed Books.

Wood County, (West) Virginia: Court Minute Books, Deed Books, Marriage Registers.

United States Census Returns, Free Schedules:
    1820 Harrison County, Virginia
    1820 Wood County, Virginia
    1830 Harrison County, Virginia
    1840 Harrison County, Virginia
    1840 Lewis County, Virginia
    1840 Wood County, Virginia
    1850 Harrison County, Virginia
    1850 Pleasants County, Virginia
    1850 Ritchie County, Virginia
    1850 Wood County, Virginia
    1860 Wood County, Virginia

United States Census Returns, Slave Schedules:
    1850 Wood County
    1850 Ritchie County
    1860 Wood County

Primary Sources

Acts of the Assembly, 1843, 1850-51. Richmond: William F. Ritchie.

Arnold, Thomas Jackson. *Early Life and Letters of General Thomas J. Jackson*. Richmond: Dietz Press, 1957.

Cammack, John Henry. *Personal Recollections*. Huntington, WV: Paragon Printing, 1920.

Cometti, Elizabeth P., and Festus P. Summers, eds. *The Thirty-Fifth State: A Documentary History*. Parsons, WV: McClain Printing Co., 1966.

Compiled Service Records. Record Group 109, Microcopy 324, Nineteenth and Twentieth Virginia Cavalry, Rolls 159-162. Washington, D. C.: National Archives, n.d.

Cook, Roy Bird. *Collection of Correspondence*. West Virginia Regional History Collection, Accession #1561, Series II, Box 2, Volume I. West Virginia University, Morgantown, WV.

DeWees, Daniel. *Recollections of a Lifetime*. Grantsville, WV: Grantsville News, 1904.

Douglas, Henry Kyd. *I Rode With Stonewall*. Chapel Hill: University of North Carolina, 1940.

Early, Jubal A. *Autobiographical Sketch and Narrative of the War Between the States*. Philadelphia: J. B. Lippincott, 1912.

Early, Jubal A. *A Memoir of the Last Year of the War for Independence in the Confederate States of America*. Toronto: Lovell and Gibson, 1866.

Gilmor, Harry. *Four Years in the Saddle*. New York: Harper and Brothers, 1866.

Grant, Ulysses S. *Memoirs and Selected Letters*. 1885-86. Reprint. New York: Viking, 1990.

Hall, James. *Diary of a Confederate Soldier*. Edited by Ruth Woods Dayton. Berryville, VA: Chesapeake Book Co., 1961.

Hotchkiss, Jedekiah. *Make Me A Map of the Valley: The Civil War Journals of Stonewall Jackson's Mapmaker*. Edited by Archie A. MacDonald. Dallas, TX: Southern Methodist University Press, 1973.

Lewis, Virgil A. *Second Biennial Report: West Virginia Department of Archives and History*. Charleston: State of West Virginia, 1908.

Poe, David. *Personal Reminiscences of the Civil War*. Buckhannon, WV: Upshur Republican, 1911.

Sims, Edgar. *Making A State*. Charleston: State of West Virginia, 1956.

Sims, Edgar. *Sims Index to Land Grants in West Virginia*. Charleston: State of West Virginia, 1952.

Supplement to the Official Records of the Union and Confederate Armies. Wilmington, NC: Broadfoot, 1994.

The War of the Rebellion: A Compilation of the Official Records of the Union and Confederate Armies. 70 Vols. Washington: United States Government Printing Office, 1880-1901.

Worsham, John H. *One of Jackson's Foot Cavalry*. New York: Neale Publishing Co., 1912.

Secondary Sources

Ambler, Charles H., and Festus P. Summers. *West Virginia: The Mountain State*. Englewood Cliffs, NJ: Prentice-Hall, 1940.

Armstrong, Richard L. *Nineteenth and Twentieth Virginia Cavalry*. Lynchburg, VA: H. E. Howard, 1994.

Ashcraft, John M. *Thirty-first Virginia Infantry*. Lynchburg: H. E. Howard, 1988.

Battles and Leaders of the Civil War, 4 Vols. 1887-88. Reprint. Edited by Thomas Yoselhof. New York: A. S. Barnes, 1956.

Bean, W. G. *Stonewall's Man Sandie Pendleton*. Chapel Hill: University of North Carolina Press, 1959.

Black, Donald R. *History of Wood County, West Virginia*. Marietta, OH: Richardson Publishing Co., 1975.

Boatner, Mark M. *The Civil War Dictionary*. New York: David McKay, 1959.

Bolton, Charles Knowles. *Scotch Irish Pioneers in Ulster and America*. Baltimore: Genealogical Publishing Co., 1972.

Bond, Beverley W., Jr. *The Foundations of Ohio*. Columbus: Ohio State Archaeological and Historical Society, 1941.

Bowers, John. *Stonewall Jackson*. New York: William Morrow, 1989.

Brown, Stephen W. *Voice of the New West*. Macon, GA: Mercer University, 1985.

Cohen, Stan. *West Virginia's Civil War Sites*. Charleston: Pictorial Histories Publishing Co., 1990.

Cole, Scott C. *Thirty-fourth Virginia Cavalry*. Lynchburg: H. E. Howard, 1993.

Concise Dictionary of American Biography. New York: Charles Scribner's Sons, 1964.

Cook, Roy Bird. *The Family and Early Life of Stonewall Jackson*. Richmond: Old Dominion Press, 1924.

Cook, Roy Bird. *Lewis County in the Civil War*. Charleston: Jarrett Printing Co., 1924.

Curry, Richard Orr. *A House Divided*. Pittsburgh: University of Pittsburgh Press, 1964.

Dabney, Virginius. *Virginia: The New Dominion*. New York: Doubleday, 1971.

Davis, Dorothy. *John George Jackson*. Parsons, WV: McClain Printing Co., 1976.

Davis, William C. *The Confederate General*. 6 Vols. Washington, D.C.: National Historical Society, 1991.

Delauter, Roger U., Jr. *Eighteenth Virginia Cavalry*. Lynchburg: H. E. Howard, 1985.

——————— *Sixty-second Virginia Infantry*. Lynchburg: H. E. Howard, 1988.

Dickinson, Jack L. *Tattered Uniforms and Bright Bayonets*. Huntington, WV: Marshall University Library Associates, 1995.

Dodrill, William C. *Moccasin Tracks and Other Imprints*. Charleston, WV: Lovett Printing, 1915.

Driver, Robert J. *Fifty-eighth Virginia Infantry*. Lynchburg: H. E. Howard, 1990.

Foote, Shelby. *The Civil War*. 3 vols. New York: Random House, 1963.

Freeman, Douglas Southall. *Lee's Lieutenants*. 3 Vols. New York: Scribner's, 1942-44.

——————— *R. E. Lee*, 4 Vols. New York: Charles Scribner's, 1946.

Haselberger, Fritz. *Yanks From the South*. Baltimore: Past Glories, 1987.

Haymond, Henry. *History of Harrison County, West Virginia*. Morgantown, WV: Acme Publishing Co., 1910.

Hemphill, William Edwin, Marvin Wilson Schlegel, and Sadie Ethel Engelberg. *Cavalier Commonwealth*. New York: McGraw-Hill, 1963.

Heritage of Braxton County, West Virginia. Marceline, MO: Walsworth Publishing Co., 1995.

Hotchkiss, Jedekiah. *Virginia*. Vol. 4 of *Confederate Military History*. Edited by Clement A. Evans. 1899. Reprint. Wilmington, NC: Broadfoot, 1987.

Humphries, Milton W. *A History of the Lynchburg Campaign*. Charlottesville, VA: Mitchie Co., 1924.

In Memoriam, General John Jay Jackson. Washington: W. H. and O. H. Morrison, (1877).

Jackson, Nancy Ann and Linda Brake. *Col. Edward Jackson 1759-1828*. Franklin, NC: Genealogy Publishing Services, 1995.

Johnston, Ross B., comp. *West Virginians in the American Revolution*. Baltimore: The Genealogical Publishing Co., 1977.

Judy, E. L. *History of Grant and Hardy Counties, West Virginia*. Charleston: Charleston Printing Co., 1951.

Knotts, Robert J., Jr. and Robert E. Stevens, comps. *Calhoun County in the Civil War*. Parsons, WV: McClain Printing, 1982.

Krick, Robert K. *Lee's Colonels*. Dayton: Morningside, 1991.

Leyburn, James G. *The Scotch-Irish: A Social History*. Chapel Hill: University of North Carolina, 1962.

Lowry, Terry. *Last Sleep: The Battle of Droop Mountain*. Charleston, WV: Pictorial Histories, 1996.

Lowther, Minnie Kendall. *History of Ritchie County, West Virginia*. Wheeling: News Lithograph Co., 1911.

Matheny, Herman E. *Major General Thomas Maley Harris*. Parsons, WV: McClain Printing Co., 1963.

——————— *Wood County, West Virginia, In Civil War Times*. Parkersburg, WV: Trans-Allegheny Books, 1987.

Maxwell, Hu, and H. L. Swisher. *History of Hampshire County, West Virginia*. Morgantown: A. Brown Boughner, 1897.

Morgan, John G. *West Virginia Governors.* Charleston: Charleston Newspapers, 1981.

Osborne, Charles C. *The Life and Times of General Jubal A. Early.* Chapel Hill: Algonquin Books, 1992.

Osborne, Randall, and Jeffrey C. Weaver. *The Virginia State Rangers and Virginia State Line.* Lynchburg: H. E. Howard, 1994.

Pauley, Michael J. *Unreconstructed Rebel.* Charleston, WV: Pictorial Histories, 1993.

Pemberton, Robert L. *History of Pleasants County, West Virginia.* St. Mary's, WV: Oracle Press, 1929.

Phillips, David L. *Tiger John: The Rebel Who Burned Chambersburg.* Leesburg, VA: Gauley Mount Press, 1993.

Price, William T. *Historical Sketches of Pocahontas County, West Virginia.* Marlinton, WV: Price Brothers, 1901.

Rable, George C. *The Confederate Nation.* Chapel Hill, NC: University of North Carolina, 1994.

Rice, Harvey Mitchell. *Jonathan M. Bennett.* Durham: University of North Carolina Press, 1943.

Rice, Otis. *The Allegheny Frontier.* Lexington, KY: University of Kentucky Press, 1970.

————, *West Virginia.* Lexington, KY: University Press of Kentucky, 1985.

Riggs, Susan A. *Twenty-first Virginia Infantry.* Lynchburg: H. E. Howard, 1991.

Robertson, James I., Jr. *Stonewall Jackson: The Man, The Soldier, The Legend.* New York: Macmillan, 1997.

Scott, John L. *Thirty-sixth and Thirty-seventh Battalions Virginia Cavalry.* Lynchburg: H. E. Howard, 1986.

Siviter, Anna Pierpont. *Recollections of War and Peace 1861-65.* Edited by Charles H. Amber. New York: G. P. Putnam's Sons, 1938.

Stutler, Boyd B. *West Virginia in the Civil War.* Charleston: Education Foundation, 1963.

Sutton, John D. *History of Braxton County and Central West Virginia.* Sutton, WV: p. p., 1919.

Tanner, Robert. *Stonewall in the Valley.* New York: Macmillan, 1997.

Thomas, Emory M. *The Confederate Nation.* New York: Harper & Row, 1979.

Warner, Ezra. *Generals in Gray.* Baton Rouge: Louisiana State University, 1981.

Wert, Jeffrey D. *From Winchester to Cedar Creek: The Shenandoah Campaign of 1864.* Carlisle, PA: South Mountain Press, 1987.

West Virginia Heritage Encyclopedia. 25 Vols. Richwood, WV: Jim Comstock, 1976.

White, Robert. *West Virginia.* Vol. 3 of *Confederate Military History.* Edited by Clement A. Evans. 1899. Reprint. Wilmington, NC: Broadfoot, 1987.

Wildes, Thomas F. *Record of the One Hundred and Sixteenth Regiment Ohio Infantry Volunteers.* Sandusky, OH: C. F. Mack, 1884.

Williams, C. R. *Southern Sympathizers: Wood County Confederates.* Parkersburg, WV: Inland River Books, n.d.

Williams, John Alexander. *West Virginia: A History.* New York: W. W. Norton, 1976.

Withers, Alexander Scott. *Chronicles of Border Warfare.* Reuben G. Thwaites, ed. Cincinnati: Robert Clarke Co., 1895.

Zinn, Jack. *R. E. Lee's Cheat Mountain Campaign.* Parsons, WV: McClain Printing Co., 1974.

INDEX

ABOUT THE AUTHOR

Ronald V. Hardway is a native of Webster County, West Virginia. He was the Blake Scholar in Confederate History at Marshall University in 1998-1999. He lives in South Carolina. *Photo by Victoria M. Cowger.*